TAKING CHARGE
WHEN YOU'RE NOT
IN CONTROL

TAKING CHARGE

W H E N

YOU'RE NOT
IN CONTROL

PATRICIA WIKLUND, PH.D.

BALLANTINE BOOKS   NEW YORK

A Ballantine Book
Published by The Ballantine Publishing Group

www.randomhouse.com/BB/

Library of Congress Cataloging-in-Publication Data
Wiklund, Patricia.
Taking charge when you're not in control / Patricia Wiklund.
p.   cm.
Includes index.
ISBN 0-345-43334-3 (alk. paper)
1. Life change events—Psychological aspects.   I. Title
BF637.L53W53   2000
158—dc21   99-40494

Manufactured in the United States of America

Text design by Ann Gold

First Edition: February 2000

10   9   8   7   6   5   4   3   2   1

CONTENTS

TAKING CHARGE
WHEN YOU'RE NOT
IN CONTROL

INTRODUCTION

How often our lives change with one phone call.

I had given myself a long overdue sabbatical. A few months off from the bustle of writing a book, national television and radio appearances, all-day seminars, and coaching business clients. I carefully planned my time, my money, and my itinerary. I borrowed my sister's motor home and started the adventure of a lifetime: living by myself on the road.

By the end of the fourth month, I'd traveled from northern Virginia, up through New England, and then to Florida to spend the Thanksgiving holidays with friends.

It was all working out so gloriously. I was outlining this new book, taking time to think, research, visit new parts of the country and old friends I hadn't seen for a long time. Waiting for me in Florida were holiday packages from friends and family, including a small tree, so I could have a very merry Christmas on the road.

Then, with a Thanksgiving day call from my sister, all my plans, indeed my life, changed.

At eighty-four, my father was being operated on for gangrene in his foot. There was no one else to take care of him. Come home to California. Daddy needed me.

For six days, I drove, ate, and slept. I arrived in Sacramento the morning he was ready to be released from the hospital.

It seemed some cosmic joke. Here I was, writing a book about how to take charge when you aren't in control, and I got a chance to practice all those lessons again.

There was no question what was in control. I wasn't, nor was my father. His physical condition was controlling both of us.

As I planned a course of action with my brother and sisters, it seemed clear this would be a time-limited project. He was so frail we were all sure it wouldn't be more than a few weeks. But as one sister suggested, with consistent care, good food, and someone to nudge him to eat and take care of himself, he could have a flight into health. He did. We had over a year of ups and downs before he peacefully slipped away one night.

That year was the best gift my father ever gave me.

He gave me one more chance to deal with what I have come to call *Imposed Change*: life-changing events we can't predict, didn't cause, don't want, and can't avoid. These are the life changes that get visited upon us: events, people, situations we can't control, but that dramatically impact our lives, maybe even bring pain and/or disgrace.

Everyone gets Imposed Change. You do and so do I. We can't control it. We can't make it what we want it to be, instead of what it is. If we aren't careful, fussing and fuming, worrying and struggling with our Imposed Change can take over our lives. We can spend all of our energy, time, and money and still not make it different, make it go away, or convince ourselves it doesn't exist. No matter what *we* do, the situation, or person, doesn't change.

Your situation may be different from mine. You might see mine as silly, trivial, or easy to resolve. I might see yours the same way. However, *our own* control issues with Imposed Changes are significant and vitally important to us. We believe that if *we just work harder, longer, differently, or more diligently, we can make things change. We can be in control. No matter what anyone says.*

We have bought into the myth that it's possible to control anyone or anything in our lives.

It isn't possible. Control is a myth.

You can't change other people, and there are lots of situations, events, and experiences you can't control, either. Whether they are mildly inconvenient or make your life a living hell, you can't control Imposed Changes.

Not that most of us don't try. Then we get into convoluted, compromised, uncomfortable positions that are successful only in producing the predictable consequences of frustration, anger, and despair. We work so hard and end up feeling like failures.

So what can you do?

Take charge when you're not in control.

Taking charge means doing what you can do rather than waiting for the situation to change, the other person to act, or a white knight to come and rescue you. Doing what you can do means finding the options that are available and then making choices about those options.

I'm willing to bet the very first thought you had when you read those words was, "This woman doesn't know what I'm up against. It's easy for her to say. She may have had options, but I don't."

Every situation has options. The Austrian psychiatrist, Viktor Frankl, was imprisoned in a concentration camp during the Second World War. He said after his release that while his guards had more liberty than he—they could go home to their families every evening—he had more freedom. The Nazis could imprison his body, but they couldn't control his spirit. Even in this horrific situation Frankl found a way to exercise choice. He lived his options, instead of letting them control him.

Every situation presents options, although not all options will be pleasant, easy, or without price. But every situation has options. Even paying taxes. In my seminars we often talk about choices and the price of choice. Paying taxes is always high on the list of things we can't control. However, the participants soon realize they don't *have* to pay their taxes. There is an alternative—one that usually provides them with three square meals a day and a cot to sleep on. So most of them choose to pay. Going to jail isn't worth the option of not paying taxes. The price of the option is too high.

Our options involve one of two choices. Like Frankl, we can change how we think and feel about a situation. We can change our minds. Or like my students who paid their taxes, we can change our behavior.

We change our minds when we break out of the victim mentality and make choices about and changes in our lives.

When we define ourselves as victims, we stay stuck in the morass of what happened to us, what other people did to us, and how awful it all was. When we define ourselves as victims, we put ourselves at the mercy of other people, situations, and especially our own pasts. And then, as we keep reliving the event, we keep the hurt alive, preferring to pick off the scab rather than allow the healing to take place. When we make our sense of self-worth dependent on someone else changing, apologizing, or even acknowledging their part in our hurt, we allow them to continue to control our lives. Asking for their permission to change, or waiting until they're also ready to heal, just keeps us stuck in recovery.

We change our minds when we start seeing ourselves as entitled to living full and satisfying lives; as capable and competent enough to be in charge of our lives; as smart enough to understand what has happened, what choices and options we have; and as able to make good decisions about what we should and could do.

We change our minds as we embrace our lives as they now are, rather than what they were, could be, or should have been. We look clearly and honestly at what is and make the best of what it can be.

However, changing our minds isn't enough. To take charge, you have to take action. When we are in challenging circumstances, we are called upon to take action we didn't know we could take. We need to learn new information, new skills, and new habits. Then we have to do what needs to be done, even when we don't want to, don't feel like it, or even don't think we can.

Almost six weeks after my father died, I woke with a start one morning. I knew something was different, but wasn't sure what it was. Then I realized it was the first time I had slept through the night in over six months.

If someone had told me up front I would nurse my father for over a year, not sleep through the night for six months, stop my business, and totally devote my life to his care, I would have told them I couldn't do it. I was too old, too unskilled. I couldn't take more time away from work. I didn't have the money. I didn't think I could do it.

I could do it. I did do it. There was more of me than I knew.

That is the gift of Imposed Change. As we successfully pass through the despair and grief, the anger and shock to rebuild our lives, we become more of who we are. We grow and become stronger with the challenges we face. We learn more about ourselves, our lives, our relationships, and our potentialities. Our lives may never be the same, but they don't have to be ruined. It is up to us.

CHAPTER 1

THE CONTROL MYTH

On a morning like any other, Emily went to work in the clinic where she was a nurse. By that afternoon she was blind in one eye, her sight in the other eye and both her legs severely damaged by a bomb blast.

Heidi was asked to repeat a work assignment so routine she didn't even bother to use the safety equipment. Within moments, the car she was riding in was destroyed, her spinal cord fractured, her body paralyzed from the ears down.

While Carolyn watched a Christmas concert with a friend, her husband was killed, her son severely maimed by a gunman on their commuter train.

Lance went to the doctor and was told something that wasn't the best news you could get.

Bill's cherished son pulled off the freeway to change a flat tire. A stranger stopped to rob him, and the young man was killed in an instant.

David opened the newspaper one morning to recognize the rambling manifesto of America's most wanted serial killer as the writings of his brother.

We all have something we can't control. You do and so do I. And as much as we want to, we can't control it.

Much of what we can't control are imposed changes: life-changing events, situations, or significant people in your life—family, friends, or strangers—whose actions have affected your life. You can't change them. You may not even know them. Yet your life is different because of what they did.

We have bought into the myth that it's possible to control anyone or anything in our lives.

It isn't possible.

Control Is a Myth

Your control issue doesn't have to be as dramatic as Heidi's, Carolyn's, Lance's, Bill's, or David's to dramatically change your life. Even the seemingly routine situations of everyday life can have an impact.

Your out-of-control person may be a teen who's taking drugs, having unprotected sex . . . or just having sex. It may be a willful four-year-old who specializes in tantrums in public places. Your mother may call you ten times a day or criticize you in front of the whole family. A coworker may be driving you nuts. Or your out-of-control person may be a spouse or loved one who's abusing you or someone dear to you.

Even if out-of-control people aren't malicious, frightening, or dangerous, they can be very frustrating. Consider a spouse who always leaves a bigger mess after cleaning the kitchen than there was before, or a mate who always leaves the gas on empty after using the car, or a teen who is embarrassingly dirty, foul-mouthed, or slow. And the list can go on and on. Few of us escape having a person in our lives who's difficult to deal with and impossible to control directly.

Perhaps your out-of-control something is an event or situation you can't avoid or change. Your company may have been awarded a huge contract, and you've been removed from hands-on participation by being put in a supervisory capacity. Or your company may have lost a large contract, and now you're facing possible layoffs. Almost as bad, you might be one of the few still working after your teammates have gone. It could be that a new government policy has changed your financial situation or living options. A disease or infirmity has slowed you down. You go out to empty the garbage, slip on the ice, and break your leg in three places. Or you may have been one of the many pummeled by Mother Nature—coping with floods, fires, earthquakes, tornadoes, hurricanes, or volcanic eruptions.

In every life, there's something uncontrollable. And yet we doggedly keep trying to change things that can't be changed, with no result except to feel worse about the situation and worse about ourselves.

Labeling, Blaming, Shaming

And to make a bad situation even worse, the notion of control is getting a bad rap. It's become fashionable to be critical of controlling people, to feel ashamed or guilty when you activate your own control wants and needs, and to label control as an addiction, weakness, or sign of immaturity.

But labeling, blaming, and shaming don't help you deal with challenging people or situations. They don't help you figure out what you can do, what will help you feel better, or what will get you over the feelings of crisis so you can go on with your life. They don't help you take charge of situations you can't control. And they don't help when you're trying to deal with the control wants and needs of your family, friends, coworkers, or even strangers.

When your four-year-old pitches a hissy fit in the grocery store at five o'clock, you may feel ashamed, as if you're not a good parent. But feeling ashamed doesn't help. You still have an angry, willful, crying child who needs to be "controlled," so that you can pay for your dinner items and get both of you safely home.

You might label your coworker addicted to control when he locks the latest test results in his files while he is out of the office. He says it's just to keep them safe; you know he doesn't want anyone else to have them. However, labeling him as addicted to control doesn't get you access to the data you need to finish your work.

And when at a family gathering, your eighty-year-old mother once more teases and shames you for being overweight, it isn't enough to label her abusive and manipulative. You want her to stop, but you haven't been able to make her stop abusing you in over thirty years.

You feel guilty about screaming at God for sending the rains again—as you helplessly stand by while the creek rises, the road disappears, and your belongings are washed away—again.

Labeling, blaming, shaming, or feeling guilty doesn't help resolve control issues or the challenges that activate them. So why do we continue to do these things that don't help?

We want to know why this happened to us. We're sure we'll feel better if we can just know why. Even if we have to make up a reason for, or a story about, why something happens, we'll feel better. So we search out (or make up) a rationale for why things happen. We believe if we just know why, then we'll know what to do to fix things.

Therapists and self-help programs are great at making up reasons, telling stories about why people do the things they do. Your childhood was painful. Your family was dysfunctional. You wanted to get rid of your father and have a romantic relationship with your mother. You feel unworthy, have low self-esteem. You aren't empowered. You're in denial. The explaining story depends as much, if not more, on which approach the therapist or self-help group takes and what stories they prefer than on what is actually happening to you.

Another solution might be to read a self-help book. There are multitudes of them on the shelves of every bookstore. In them, the author gives a reason for why things happen, what it means, and how best to cope with it or get on with it. The same warnings apply to this book, as well as to any other. The validity of the explaining story varies depending on the author. You can only hope this time the story will be helpful.

Pat Hudson, a therapist friend, and author of *The Solution-Oriented Woman,* tells of meeting a shirttail relative at a family gathering. Realizing Pat was a therapist, the woman blurted out that she was codependent, her husband was addicted to their relationship, she had been in recovery for seven years, she went to group four times a week, and she read every new book she could find. Pat's response was to suggest there should be a new category of "dysfunction": women who read too much.

As much as it feels better to understand, the search for reasons and understanding can get in the way of taking charge with situations and people you can't control. In therapy sessions, I would sometimes see clients who wanted to process every mood, action, and interaction in their significant relationships.

Bertha complained her relationship was foundering because her partner wanted to go out and play instead of spending hours "getting to the root" of a misunderstanding. She was well on her way to spending the whole hour telling me about each and every word they had said, when I stood up and announced, "We're going out for ice cream." "Right now?" she asked. "Right now!" I said.

As we licked our double cones by the fountain and the flower beds outside the ice cream parlor, we talked about the glorious spring day, the delicious ice cream, and our plans for the weekend. She wanted to get to the bottom of the miscommunication with her partner—and estimated it would take most of Saturday. I prescribed a hike in the desert to see how many flowers were blooming, with no talk about the misunderstanding.

She didn't get it. She was confusing understanding problems with resolving problems. She wanted to focus on the worst part of their relationship; her partner wanted to build some good memories. I explained that when you spend all your time focusing on your problems, they can expand to fill all your time. You'll have precious little time to enjoy living.

Of course, there are going to be times when you must talk about and resolve differences and conflicts—but not all the time and not at the expense of enjoying time together. Shared fun nourishes and grows any relationship—even if it means ice cream in the middle of a therapy session.

Being in Control: What Does It Mean?

So what does *control* really mean? We've heard the word since we were kids.

Remember when your mom or dad said, "Control yourself!!!" Think for a moment of a specific time you heard those words, usually delivered at full volume and affixed to your given first name. "Patricia!! Control yourself!!!" Not Patty or Pat at that moment. Control doesn't allow for nicknames.

I usually knew when I was "out of control." It meant I wasn't acting in ways expected of a grown-up girl of eight or ten. I was talking when I should have been quiet, was giggling when I should have been serious, was touching myself inappropriately, or was even yawning or wriggling in church. The command to control myself meant "Stop doing what you're doing—and stop it right now!"

Or I might have been angry and fighting with a brother or sister, afraid, frustrated, uncertain, or even not knowing what I should be doing or feeling. At those moments, "Control yourself!" meant "Don't feel what you're feeling."

For adults, "Control yourself!" usually means don't *show* what you're feeling. Don't let people see you cry, get mad, be hurt. Keep a stiff upper lip. Avoid difficult topics. Don't upset others. Be nice, be bland, go along with things whether you like them or not. Keep the peace. Stay in control of yourself.

As adults we're also admonished to control our children. This request often comes from the older generation in our own families or even from our siblings. It usually means make your kids look right; sit down; not talk, laugh, or cry; and, for heaven's sake, stop squirming—especially at family gatherings.

We all have control issues and make decisions about how we express those needs and issues. It's just too difficult and too scary to consider the possibility of no control. Wanting control, or feeling we need control, lets us organize our world and make predictions about what can happen and what can't. We need a belief in the possibility of control so we can feel what we do matters, that we have an effect on our world. And when we reach our limits, we want someone else to take control, someone we can trust to be the boss and to make things happen the way that will be best for us.

Wanting Control: A Natural State

Let me make this very clear: You have no reason to be ashamed or apologetic because you want control. It's a natural state. Watch a newborn. They don't think they control the universe; they think they *are* the universe. They've moved from a comfy, warm, protected womb to bright lights, loud noises, and discomfort. All of a sudden all kinds of indignities are visited on them. They're wet, tired, messy, cold, bumped, and jostled! It's not life as they've come to know it for nine months. Fortunately for them, most infants have magical, willing servants dedicated to restoring their comfort. But even the best servants get tired, hungry, uncomfortable, and cranky. Soon the infant starts to realize the universe is bigger than he is, and thinks, "I may still be at the center of the universe, but that universe—or the other people in it—aren't as accommodating as I want." And so a control issue is born!

As children grow, become teens and then adults, control issues also continue to evolve and grow. The specific context and behaviors may change with age, but from our self-centered perspective, control remains the issue. Who's in control? How do you get what you want?

When and how must you conform to the directions and needs of others? How do you recognize and make good behavioral choices? How do you know when there is a choice? And most important, how can you be sure in situations when there isn't a choice?

Control Gives Meaning to the World

We need control in our lives. It gives us meaning, security, guidelines for what we want and for what we should do. Having control means there's an underlying structure to the world. It isn't random and chaotic.

Every civilization, even the most primitive people, has a belief in a spiritual being who is the ultimate cause and the ultimate control. The names are different: Higher Power, God, the Great Spirit, Yahweh. The stories vary in the details. But at its source, a deity provides meaning for a people. It gives the reasons for why things are the way they are.

Tami's class in comparative religions had her worried. Both the class and the professor had the reputation for being very tough. In this class, the students were not only expected to learn about every faith and belief throughout the world, but to understand them. Most of the grade would depend on how well they did on the final exam.

For the final, the students brought their sharpened pencils and blue books to class. The professor admonished them to do their best. Then he wrote the exam on the chalkboard. It was one question: "Why?"

Tami said she panicked. She watched some students outlining and then writing pages and pages of answers. Other students seemed to scrawl a word or two on the page and turn in their papers. Finally she wrote two words. Then she turned her paper in.

When the grades were posted, Tami said the students who had written pages and pages received a C in the course. Her two words earned her a B. A very few of the students had received As. Her two words: "Why not." The A students' word: "Because."

An unseen Supreme Being lends assurance that some greater power is in control, even if the spiritual mysteries can't be understood by mere mortals.

Meaning Allows Security

With meaning comes predictability. With predictability comes certainty. You can start to see cause and effect. "If I do this, then that will be the result." You can rely on past experience rather than starting from scratch every day.

Cause and effect lets you make changes in what is. You feel powerful because what you do makes a difference. You can make choices. You can start to feel as though you're in control.

Control Allows for Morality and Justice

Having choice and predictability connects your actions to your future. You can be held accountable for your choices and actions. You knew what results you'd get by doing—or not doing.

But watch out! Here's where it gets slippery. When good things happen, we assume we made good choices or did the right thing. We deserved what we got. We were good children and earned our reward.

But when uncomfortable, negative, or unpleasant things happen, it's tempting to look back to see what we did to hurt ourselves. We assume that good things flow from acting good, and that bad things occur because we were naughty and did something we shouldn't have.

Of course, from that perspective, it's just a short step to deciding that when someone suffers or experiences misfortune, they must have done something to deserve or cause it. So we blame victims for their trouble.

Blaming the victim gives the rest of us relief. We can refute the random nature of pain and crisis. We can assure ourselves that what happened to them will never happen to us. We didn't do, wouldn't do, what they did. We're safe. We get caught up in a *Just World* belief: victims get what they deserve and deserve what they get. We don't have to worry about random pain and misfortune.

Control Realities

The problem doesn't come from wanting control. We all want it, it is a natural feeling to expect it, and for the most part, our daily experiences reinforce our belief that we can get it.

The problem is that we can't always get the control we think we should have, want, and need. There are lots of things and people in our lives that are out of our control. No matter how hard we work or what we do, feel, think, or believe, we can't control everything in our lives. We can't control other people. Sometimes we can't even control ourselves. We don't cause everything that happens to us. And we aren't in charge of the universe. Even if we keep trying to act as though we do and we are.

You Can't Make People Change

It's impossible to make someone else be who we want him to be or do what we want him to do. In fact, sometimes we can't even get ourselves to change.

In a therapy session sometimes, a client would say they wanted me to change their partner's feelings. I'd jokingly grab their partner's arm or leg and change the position of their body. "Now," I'd ask, "how do you want me to change their feelings? Cut a hole in their head and jumble up what they think and feel?" We'd all laugh, but under the laughter was the deadly serious concept: you can't *make* someone change their feelings or thoughts. It is up to them.

Behavior is a little easier. Often we can encourage others to change their behavior. By managing how we act and respond to another, we can have an enormous influence on what they do. This is the big job of parenting. How we parent dramatically affects our children's actions. This is primarily because kids, especially little kids, want to please their parents. So they do what we want them to do, or what we show them we think is important and valuable. Even when the activity isn't a lot of fun.

As a school psychologist, I'd often be asked by parents to help get a child to do their homework. There are lots of ways to help kids make the change from a nonhomework kid to a homework kid. For the most part, we'd be successful because we helped the parents learn how to be the mother or father of a homework-compliant kid!

Periodically, we'd get a parent who would balk at being included in the homework project. They'd tell us they not only wanted their Jimmy to do his homework, but they also wanted him to *want* to do his homework. We'd always turn down that assignment. There's no way to get another person, be he child or adult, to want to do what someone else wants him to do just because somebody wants him to do it, especially something considered as universally unpleasant as homework. Get him to do it? We had ways to do that. *Want* to do it? No way.

The frustration in trying to effect change in another person is that the harder we try to get him or her to be what we want, the less successful we are and the more irritated he or she becomes. It's like the bumper sticker: "Don't try to teach a pig to sing. It won't work—and it annoys the pig."

While we work hard on getting others to change, lots of us work even harder at making changes in ourselves—and we can't always do it. Think about it: Are you still smoking? Eating food you know isn't healthy for you? Not exercising enough? Not studying thoroughly for an important exam? Not preparing for a crucial presentation? Still watching five hours of TV a night? We've all been there.

> *Trish and Susan started therapy with me on the same day. Trish was a writer, Susan an artist. Both were happily married, had good jobs, were about the same age, and had similar education. They were very much alike, except Trish had writer's block. Formerly a well-regarded, published author, now she couldn't put anything down on paper. Susan, on the other hand, was very obese. She just couldn't lose weight. No matter what diet, eating strategy, or exercise program she started, she was quickly back to her old habits and a new but even higher weight. Her struggle with her size, what she ate, and how she looked was painful and frustrating. Although she said she wanted to get back to the thin girl she was before she was married, she was ready to throw in the towel and live her life as a fat woman.*
>
> *Now here is the strange part. Trish was just as frustrated with her writing as Susan was with her weight. She struggled every day, spending hours in front of the computer, beating herself up because she couldn't write. However, she was very thin and fit. When I asked her how she stayed so trim, Trish dismissed it as being so easy anyone could do it. She didn't even think about it. It just wasn't an issue for her.*
>
> *When I asked Susan about the ease with which she painted,*

*she replied she never worried about being able to paint. She
never thought about not painting. She just did it.*

Both women experienced major successes in their lives. And both
saw themselves as major failures. They each called themselves unmotivated and out of control. They found it hard to understand and appreciate their successes. They could easily see their failures. And both let
their failures color their satisfaction with life.

As much as we tell ourselves we want to be different and want to
change—and even if we are successful making changes in other parts of
our lives—sometimes we can't make the specific changes we desire.
Martin Seligman, Ph.D., at the University of Pennsylvania, reviewed
years of psychological, behavioral, and physiological research on how
people change. He cataloged his findings in *What You Can Change . . .
and What You Can't*. It's sobering reading. While Seligman found people could change many issues and behaviors through therapy, self-help
programs, or medication, there were also many factors that were highly
resistant to change.

Losing weight was one of the resistant issues. Despite the billion-
dollar weight-control industry, dieting almost never works long term.
Seligman found the conventional wisdom about weight control and obe-
sity is almost entirely wrong. People who are overweight do not eat
more, exercise less, have less willpower, or possess an "obese personality." Almost everyone who goes on a strict diet regains weight after
they stop, no matter whether their "diet" is based on exercise, food, or
pills. An individual appears to have a "set weight," which is more
the result of physical factors—body chemistry, metabolism, build,
genetics—than an eating or exercise program. For Susan at fifty, expecting to get back to the weight she was at twenty sets herself up for failure.

Seligman also found little evidence of the effectiveness of alcohol
treatment programs. By age sixty-five, regardless of treatment attempts,
about one-third of the people with alcohol problems stop drinking
or are drinking socially. Another one-third are still trying to quit and
have episodic periods of success and remission. The final third are
either dead, very ill from disease, or in a decline directly related to their
drinking. The studies showed little evidence of an "addictive personality" in heavy drinkers, although some people did have a marked

susceptibility to alcohol that was more physiological than social or psychological. For these folks, abstinence was the only solution to their drinking problems.

This extensive review of the research showed that many of the popular self-help groups are no more effective in dealing with a defined issue than not getting help at all. It also proved that the two largest and most popular "change" industries—weight control and alcohol programs—have shown little effectiveness. Seligman isn't saying there haven't been people who have been helped by these programs, but not as many as they would like us to believe, and very few over the long haul.

We may have to face the possibility that it's just the way we are, that we can't/won't be able to change ourselves. Then we must take the next step and not let our inability to change a habit, attribute, or behavior pattern control our lives.

You Don't Cause Everything that Happens to You

There's no doubt we all get a ration of tough challenges. You've seen the bumper stickers: "Stuff Happens." We make trouble for ourselves when we start looking for why we suffer and how we cause our own grief and pain. It's a quick slide from asking "Why me?" to feeling bad about feeling bad. We can slide right into blaming ourselves for the injuries we experience.

It's typical to look for spiritual solace. Surely our suffering must be part of a larger plan.

From a Judeo-Christian perspective, the question becomes: How could God let this happen? We're faced with having to choose between a God who allows evil and suffering to occur, and a God who isn't as powerful as evil is.

Another school of thought believes our lives are predestined, that God has predetermined our life's path—and some people's paths just happen to include lots of suffering. Another idea is that our suffering is retribution for our sins and bad behavior. Somehow this current suffering is making up for poor performance in an earlier life.

One New Age spiritual perspective says that we've enabled, caused, or manifested this difficulty in our lives. We may not be consciously aware of why or how we made this happen, but as we can make good things happen, we can also make bad things occur.

Or we might take an Eastern approach and believe Buddha when he said life is ten thousand pleasures and ten thousand pains. Both are inevitable parts of any life, and the *why* is irrelevant. It's just the way life is.

Whatever your perspective, looking to your spiritual beliefs for comfort during major changes—especially negative changes—can bring on a spiritual crisis. For the devout New Ager, negative events bring on questioning and self-doubt. What unconscious or prelife decision brought this negative event into their lives? How could they have enabled, supported, or allowed this tragedy to take place? What was the matter with them that they manifested such a terrible occurrence?

From the devout Judeo-Christian conviction comes the plaintive wail of Job: How could God have forsaken me? You start looking for evidence of the sinful behavior that brought on this wrath of God. What could you have done to be punished so severely?

Dwelling on the *why* when things in your life are out of control almost always guarantees you'll feel worse. You'll not only have the specific event or situation to deal with, but a spiritual crisis, as well.

Whatever you tell yourself about what's happening and why it happens, there are still going to be situations and events in your life that are painful and unpleasant that you haven't created and can't control. These include all those laws of nature and the resulting phenomena: earthquakes, fires, floods, disease, and accidents. And they are especially frightening because they are unpredictable and unstoppable.

This doesn't mean there isn't anything you can do about these situations, including taking preventive or precautionary measures. It just means as prepared as you might be, you can't stop an earthquake. And, of course, it doesn't mean there is nothing you can do *after* such an event. No matter how traumatic, no matter what disabilities and losses occur, your life will still go on. It may be irreparably changed, but it's up to you to determine if it's going to be ruined.

You Aren't the Center of the Universe

This is the grow-up lesson. It's time to let go of those childish notions that the world is here to serve us and make our lives wonderful. We often act as if the world, especially our physical world, was put here for our convenience.

When I was living in Chicago many years ago, there was a proposal to put an additional airport out in Lake Michigan. They wanted to fill in a portion of the lake right off the shore of Chicago, and then build a causeway and tunnel out to the airport. Needless to say, there was lots of discussion and disagreement on the merits of the idea. Then a plane crashed at Midway, the small midtown airport. Several people, both on the plane and on the ground, were killed. One man was widely quoted in the uproar, saying the crash and the fatalities proved the new airport should be put in the lake where it belonged. *That's what the lake was for!*

While we may be amused by his self-centered approach to the situation, it isn't all that unusual. America especially has a long history of this type of patriarchy: the land belongs to mankind to do with what we will. And the price of our shortsightedness is evident in the played-out grasslands, forests, and mines, in the muddy landslides that result when the rains hit the bare hills, or the poisoned water supply when carelessly discarded tailings are left to drain into our wells. There is a price we have paid for being bad stewards and disregarding our natural resources. There's no free lunch. There's always a price to pay. Sometimes that price isn't evident for years—or even generations—but sooner or later we're faced with having to clean up a mess that was not of our making.

So How Do We Do It?

So where do we go from here? If trying to control the uncontrollable doesn't work, what else is there? What can we do?

Take charge when you're not in control.

Taking charge with Imposed Change means stop trying to control. Stop trying to force others to change, and start changing yourself. Stop letting the situation or people that impacted your life continue to run your life.

Take charge by changing two things: your mind and your behavior. To successfully take charge and flourish, you need to do both.

Here is the strange part: taking charge, making a change, even a little one, will have a big effect on how you see yourself and your life. You don't need to lose a hundred pounds, make your kid stop taking drugs, revive the contract your company lost, be rehired to the job you used to have, or grow all your hair back to start feeling better about yourself and your life.

You don't have to make huge changes to feel like you are in charge of your life, even when there are lots of things you can't control.

Change Your Behavior

The first step is to educate yourself. Find out all you can about what you are up against. Knowing more about your challenge means you will see more options. You can find out how other people handled their similar situations. You'll find resources you didn't know existed.

One of my worst fears was having to bathe my father. He was a big man, and I was afraid I couldn't prevent him from falling and hurting himself. I found out there are home health aides who specialize in bathing people who can't bathe themselves. With their help, my fears were dispelled.

Knowing more means you can make better decisions about what you can and should do. Accurate information allays fears, letting you feel more comfortable that you can take the right action.

The other essential behavior change is taking action. Often Imposed Change means major changes in who is in charge in your family. You might find yourself not just deciding what to do, but then having to do it. We may be called upon to do things that we have never done or never wanted to do. Yet we can't say no.

Our changes may thrust us into the public eye. So we learn to give speeches, appear on television, raise money, or take public action.

The one thing we can't do is go back or change things back to the way they used to be. When we're not in control, going back isn't an option. The changes are permanent.

Change Your Mind

If you don't want to be controlled by what has happened to you, you have to change your mind.

You have to change your mind about how you see yourself and your life. With Imposed Change, everything you believed about the way the world is and should be gets called into question. You can let the changes ruin your life or enhance your life. It's up to you.

Just because this happened to you doesn't mean you deserved it. Bad things happen to good people. This may be one of your bad things.

Start focusing on what you can do, not what you can't do. Our bodies and brains are miraculous instruments. We have more than we need. Even when part of us no longer works, there are still amazing things we can do with what we have left.

Let go of waiting for someone else to change, to admit they caused you harm, or to make amends before you can start healing. If you break your leg in an accident caused by someone else, you can't wait until after the case is closed to set your leg. You do healing for yourself on your time, not on the time of the person or situation that hurt you, and your life must go on as you deal with the things you can't control.

What about Feelings?

I can hear you now: I don't feel like taking charge. I hurt. I'm in pain. You don't know how bad it feels.

I do. It feels awful when tough things happen to you. It feels awful when bad things happen to me. We get depressed, dispirited, uncertain, and unhappy. Some of us cry a lot, eat too much, smoke too much, or drink too much. We sit around and moan and groan and can't stop talking about how we got "done wrong." You're not crazy. That's how people feel and act when bad things happen. If you didn't, I'd be really worried about you. You wouldn't be paying attention.

Fortunately our moods, even depression and anxiety, are included on the list of things we can change. And there are a variety of techniques we can use to change them. But first, we need to feel bad. We just don't have to continue feeling bad.

You need to grieve, to adjust to your new life pattern, but you don't have to feel awful forever. You aren't what happened to you—and that's why it's so important to shift your focus. Change your mind. Stop being *in recovery* and start getting *recovered*. Even though it sounds like we're playing word games, the subtle difference in the wording is very important.

Being in recovery means your focus is still external. You're defining your life by what *happened to* you, not who you *are*. You're still letting external events and people control you. You continue to look at what you can't change, rather than what you can. You're stuck in your past.

Being recovered means you can distance yourself from what has happened to you and stop letting it be the center of your life. Being recovered means moving on, regardless of what happens to those who have injured you. Being recovered means you're no longer waiting for someone else to atone for what they may have done.

Being recovered means you've taken charge of yourself and your life. You've broken out of the victim mentality and made choices about and changes in your life.

When we ourselves as victims, we stay stuck. We let our past define our present and our future.

One of the most powerful tools for shaping our lives is what we think about ourselves and say to ourselves. What we focus on increases. Every time we proclaim we are powerless, we reinforce the victim mentality and make healing and problem solving more difficult. Every time we label ourselves a victim, we focus on the fear, pain, and hurt we went through rather than the opportunity, hope, and joy that is ahead. Dwelling on the hurts doesn't help us heal. It keeps us hurting.

Protect Yourself

As you change, you can expect to get some grief. There will be people who won't like it that you're changing. After all, you've had an unspoken contract for a long time to dance the dance and play the game. When you stop performing your role in the drama, the other characters may get mad, whine, cajole, beg, grovel, or even use guilt to get you to go back to the way things were. They can't continue to play if you don't assume your part. So you'll have lots of invitations to stay in the same old stuff.

Breaking through and staying the course means you'll have to become okay with wanting what you want and not consider yourself bad, dysfunctional, or wrong for choosing your own course. It means you have to heal yourself, moving beyond recovery into recovered, detaching yourself from the past, and moving forward.

Taking charge also means you will have to decide what's best for you. Taking charge means figuring out what is possible even if it's unpopular or uncomfortable—and then doing it. It doesn't mean trying to do or thinking about doing it. It means taking action, even if that action is to actively and thoughtfully choose to continue doing just what you've been doing.

It may not be easy, it may not be fun, but the only way out is through. If you avoid learning the lesson today, you will for sure get another chance to learn that lesson tomorrow.

The magic is you make your own magic. The joy is that it is the most powerful kind of magic there is.

Exercises for Chapter 1

At the end of each chapter are exercises to help personalize what you've been reading, to apply the ideas and techniques to your own challenge. You might find it helpful to use a notebook to keep track of what you've been thinking, new insights you've uncovered, and ideas for action that will make the difference in your life. Be sure to date each entry. When you come back to reread what you've written, you can see if and how you have changed your mind or your behavior.

REPORT THE FACTS

Write the story of your control issue as if it were front-page news in your local paper. Write the story as if it were happening to someone else, referring to yourself by name and *she* rather than *I*.

Be sure you include all the facts: who, what, when, why, where, and, of course, how.

Put the story aside for a few days and then read it. What does this story say about the person? Who is she? What is important to her? How do you feel about her?

Pretend you are an expert consultant. What suggestions would you have for her to change her behavior? To change her mind?

CHAPTER 2

TAKING CHARGE:
THE DOABLE OPTION

Twenty years ago, stuntwoman Heidi von Beltz didn't strap herself into the safety harness when she repeated a simple stunt on the set of her current movie. The stunt wasn't all that dangerous; they'd just done one run-through with no problems. But this time, the car didn't respond to a turn and hit an oncoming van head-on. Heidi's spinal cord fractured and several neck vertebrae were severed as she hit the dashboard and windshield.

Doctors told her she had a C5-C6 spinal cord injury, which meant complete paralysis. She was lucky to be alive. They estimated her life span to be less than five years.

Heidi was unwilling to accept that prognosis. She knew she was still alive inside of her unmoving body. She rejected the doctors' suggestion to move to a permanent care facility and moved instead to a home furnished with a library and a high-tech gym. Now her own rehabilitation program includes eight hours a day of strenuous workouts, coupled with hours of reading philosophical and self-help books. She is able to sit, stand with braces, and is working on walking next.

Heidi and her doctors attribute her progress to both her strenuous program of physical therapy and her positive attitude. Believing anything is possible, she works hard to put her beliefs into action to reach her goals.

Heidi knows how to take charge when she's not in control. And she has worked hard to put her knowledge into action. She didn't wait, rely on the experts, or take the prognosis of those who should know as the truth for her life.

She did it herself.

In my seminars with people who have just been downsized, right-sized, or outplaced, I assure them we know what happens to people who are going through trauma and what it takes to help them get over it.

What works isn't what they think, though. Usually someone asks, "Just tell me what to do. If you tell me, I'll do it, I promise."

When our life is out of control, we want someone to tell us what to do. We want to know right now how to relieve our pain.

No matter how dark and dreadful, we want a solution. We want relief. So we ask the experts, or our friends, to tell us what to do, join a self-help group, look for a book, or go for therapy. We look for *the way* out. We want *the* answer on what to do, how to do it, and we want it now.

And we don't get the answer we want. No one can tell us the secret solution. If they do try to tell us, we don't get it. We do a lot of "yes, but that won't work" talk.

One of the hardest lessons for beginning therapists to learn is to not tell their clients what to do, but to let them discover it for themselves. The lesson is learned painfully by realizing every time you give direct advice to a client, not only will they not follow it, but they'll get angry at you.

Telling people what to do doesn't work. We learn better and get better results when we figure out our problems for ourselves. We need a *guide* to the way out, not the way out.

Other People's Experiences

The best guide is what's worked for other people. It's easier to see what other people do than what we do ourselves. We can see what they did right and what they did wrong. We can see what worked for them and what they should have done differently. And we can figure out what we would have done if it had happened to us.

We learn best from their stories. Stories give us a guide for action. We fill in the details to match our own experiences, wants, and needs.

The story is the process by which we make changes. We provide the content depending on the problems we face.

Personalizing the Process

Stories, fables, myths, and legends are the oldest and most popular self-help books. We remember the stories and then remember the lessons. The subtlety and complexity of stories are their greatest strength and their greatest challenge.

A story is a model for how things can work, sort of like a map. A map shows us where the mountains and roads are, where the pond is, and the best way to cross a river. It gives us the shapes, patterns, and possibilities of the land. But it is *not* the land. We can't really know the land until we go there. The map can only point out the way. It can't take us on the journey. We can't really know if the lesson in a story will help with our problems until we try it.

Stories point the way. They aren't the way. Stories are complex and subtle. They'll have many different meanings. Different people draw different lessons from the same story. You can even get a different lesson from the same story at different times.

We teach our children to be helpful to those in need with the Good Samaritan story from the Bible. Not until we're adults do we get the more subtle lesson of the story: the Samaritan was despised as a lowlife in his time. Yet he stopped to help someone who wouldn't have helped him. With this new awareness of the Samaritan, we get a richer, more challenging lesson than the one we heard as children.

If you ask someone what lesson they hear from a story, they'll tell you what works for them, what they need. And then they'll tell you that if you just do exactly what they did, you'll get the same results they got.

Paula was a very successful manager who was given harder and harder challenges by her management. A hard worker, she was renowned for her ability to deal with several tasks at the same time and for needing only five hours of sleep a night. She was a whirlwind of activity. Paula started therapy when she found out her husband was having an affair.

Her therapist was a specialist in stress reduction and encouraged Paula to start meditating twice a day. She hated it.

The more she didn't want to do it, the more he insisted she wouldn't be able to deal with her stress about her husband's in-fidelity until she could successfully meditate. Finally she in-sisted he tell her why he thought meditation was so essential.
"It was what turned my life around!" he proudly replied.

Paula's therapist was convinced that if it worked for him, it would work for everyone. He didn't stop to consider who she was, what her needs were, or even the issues that were bringing so much stress into her life. My suggestion to Paula when she asked if this was the way all therapy worked was to find a therapist who would help her address her marital problems, rather than trying to make her the same as him. While the therapist knew more about stress reduction than she did, Paula needed to be in charge of whether his interpretation of her story was right for her.

Taking Charge

Fortunately for us, there are lots of people who have been through the experiences, situations, and events that challenge us. We can look to other people's stories to help us know what to do. We just need to fig-ure out which will help us, which will fit with what we have been through, and which will help us not just survive but flourish.

The good news is there is always something we can do to take charge with people and situations we can't control. Even if we're se-verely injured like Heidi was. Taking charge helps us feel better and, for the most part, do better in that situation or with that person.

The bad news is that we have to do it for ourselves. You don't have to do it *by* yourself; there are lots of people you can call on along the way for support. But you have to do it *for* yourself. No one else can change you or your life for you. No one could do the physical therapy for Heidi. She had to do it herself. As Phyllis Sears, one of my favorite weight-control gurus, says, "No one can go on a diet for you. No matter how little they eat, you won't lose weight."

I've often had therapy clients come to me looking for the magic wand that I could wave over their heads to make things all different or, preferably, all better for them. They were soundly disappointed when I told them that, fairy godmothers notwithstanding, magic wands work only for the person holding the wand. They are strictly do-it-yourself tools.

Taking charge means changing your mind and changing your behavior. We can't keep doing the same things and expect we'll get different results.

As I was editing this section, moving paragraphs around, inserting words and phrases, I did something that hung up my computer. For the most part it is a wonderful machine and serves me well. But sometimes it has moments. As it sat here, screen frozen, I tried to make it respond. I must have pushed one button or another several times, and then repeated the whole sequence at least three times before I realized I needed to do something different if I wanted different results.

Aren't we amazing? So often we know what works and what doesn't, and it doesn't seem to matter. We don't use what we know—but stay on autopilot!

So what do we need to do to get off autopilot, to take charge of situations we can't control? Reconsider and change

- what we "know" about what has happened and the options we have: *we have to tell ourselves the truth of our experience.*
- what we think we deserve: *what kind of life we are entitled to live.*
- what we're capable of doing, what skills and abilities we have and need, and how much confidence we have in our competence: *how empowered we are to act in our best interests.*
- what we need to put behind us: *what we must let go of.*
- what we need to do, given the changes we have made in what we think and know: *what actions we need to take.*

Tell Yourself the Truth

Most of us don't choose to spend our lives spinning out of control. Something happens to us, usually when we aren't paying attention. Conditions change at work; you find out your spouse has been having an affair; your child has an accident; your parent gets sick; a hurricane heads for your neighborhood. Or we realize we're drifting, not getting what we thought we wanted; we've lost track of our lives, and nothing seems to be going okay. Whatever the cause, external or internal, the reaction is usually the same.

Initial Reactions

"Oh, no!" we say, and then enter an initial period of what is usually called denial. Denial has taken on a negative charge and is often stated as an accusation, as in "You are just in denial." This implies a willfulness on the part of the person experiencing denial. The accuser seems to imply that if the person in denial *really* wanted to, they could easily see what was going on and do something about it.

But when it's the initial response in a crisis, what's usually labeled denial is really the need to take some time to come to the full realization of what's just happened and what it means. It takes time for crises to sink in. It takes time to realize your life is dramatically different from what it was and from what you thought it would be.

> *When all the members of Angela's work team were called in and told their products had been canceled and they would be laid off, most of them cried out, "Oh, no!" One of the team even tried to convince the supervisor he was wrong. The employee was sure another product set was canceled, not theirs. He just knew it had to be a mistake.*

If the changes have been building up, it may take a long time to realize what's going on or the implications of what's going on. You may see the clues or experience an event and still not register the meaning of what's happening.

> *Tobi encouraged his wife to be more social with her coworkers. So when she wanted to sign up for a bowling league, he volunteered to stay with their kids so she could go. As the weeks went on, she came home later and later, and in more of a disheveled state. He continued to think she was just bowling late.*

Sometimes options aren't even evident. We don't realize we define our world to exclude them.

> *Mary Sue didn't start college until she was over thirty. She reported that in the small town where she grew up, no one, but especially girls, ever went to college. She never even thought*

about college for herself. It wasn't until she had married and moved to a large metropolitan area of another state that she realized she was smart enough, and interested enough, to want to further her education.

You have to realize you have a problem before you can deal with it: evaluate what is happening, figure out what it means, make choices and decisions, and start to take charge of your life. For most of us, acknowledging change takes time and purposeful action.

Making Judgments

As soon as you're conscious of change, you start evaluating and judging. That's what being conscious means: mulling over what's happening to make sense, figure out what's going on. The criteria we use for evaluating and judging are based on the rules we live by, the way we define our lives. They can come from previous experience: *I tried this before and that is what happened;* from what the experts say: *In our family, church, nationality we do things this way;* or by the worldview that we have adopted: *This is the way the world should be.*

Making judgments, especially judgments of other people, is currently not the politically correct thing to do. But we must make judgments if we are to take charge. We can't change without judging. We need to evaluate what's right for us and what isn't. We need to see how new options and information fit with what we already know and use. The crisis of Imposed Change happens because our new experiences don't fit what we've come to expect. What's happened isn't consistent with the way we thought our lives would be, or doesn't honor our spiritual ethics and commitments or possibly even the laws of our community.

This doesn't mean we should discount new information simply because it conflicts with what we already know. We may have to change what we think or the rules we've been using for our lives to accommodate what we now know.

Lucy said she would never be the same after she discovered her husband had been molesting children where he worked. She had never thought anyone she loved would do that, or that she would go to the police and cooperate in a criminal investigation and trial that would put him in jail for many years. She said she knew there were people like her ex-husband in the world, but she never thought it would affect her. She had always thought that this type of evil could not be a part of her middle-class, educated, professional life. Now she knew that who she was could not insulate her from this darker side of life.

Change changes you. But it doesn't have to ruin you. You'll be different, not necessarily worse.

Getting More Information

Change and crisis mean learning new things. We need information about what's happening, what's next, and how to help ourselves. We need to get the facts, evaluate different approaches and theories, and make choices about what to accept and reject. We have to sort out what's fact and what's wishful thinking, conventional wisdom, or just fallacy. We need to think clearly just at the time when everything that's happening isn't making much sense.

Darlene struggled to stand by her man when Stan was caught perjuring himself in a fraud investigation. While Stan had not been responsible for the fraud in his company, in an attempt to protect those he worked for, he lied to the grand jury. The responsible officers admitted what they did, and although it had cost their investors millions of dollars, they were let off. Stan was convicted and sentenced to five years in prison.

Darlene said later one of the most difficult things to deal with was friends and family who kept telling her what was happening couldn't happen. Stan couldn't be sent to prison when the men who had taken millions were set free. She said most people don't know how the justice system works until they're inside it.

Getting more information also means thinking about how you know what you know. How do you know what's true? How do you know if the experts you rely on are accurate, current, and honorable? How do you sort out which experts to believe and which to disbelieve?

When it comes to crisis, there is seldom one explanation or one choice for what to do next. Deciding how to decide is one of the biggest challenges we'll face.

Consider Yourself Entitled

Entitlement is directly connected with self-esteem, what we think we deserve, and who is in charge of our lives. It's really easy to assume you deserve this awful thing that's happened to you. Having a crisis assaults your self-esteem. It is typical to start questioning yourself, trying to figure out why you should be the one in pain.

But as much as you ask yourself, there is only one answer: You don't deserve it. Deserving has nothing to do with being out of control. You are not less entitled than anyone else. Entitlement is an inalienable right, and yet many of us have given it away. We let our families, the people next door, strangers shape our behavior, our wants and needs. What they couldn't take from us, we willingly give up by letting their standards shape our actions. In the process, we diminish ourselves and those we care about. Reowning yourself and your life restores your self-esteem and self-respect.

At a base level in the United States, we enjoy the inalienable rights to life, liberty, and the pursuit of happiness. Nothing says we are guaranteed to get them, just the right to have them. (Especially an issue with the *pursuit* of happiness.) And we can have difficulty with each of them.

We are entitled to life as we define it. Yet there are lots of opportunities for others to define who and what we should be, could be, or what they would like us to be. Parents are charged with this responsibility for guiding and molding their children's lives. But there comes the time when a person needs to make his or her own way, rather than accepting or allowing the definition of others to determine their life path. Short circuits can occur when people worry more about what the neighbors will think, not disappointing Aunt Mary, or conforming to unreasonable demands of what a good spouse should be.

Liberty, or freedom, is also elusive. We are determined to see limits rather than options. In both trivial and major issues we act as if we don't have freedom of choice, and in denying our freedom, we stop seeing what freedom we do enjoy. Or we focus on that part of our circumstances where there is no freedom and don't acknowledge the many things we can control, or where we can make a difference.

Entitlement is a state of mind, a reflection of what we think we deserve, what we should and could have. As such, it is both an indicator of sound self-esteem and a tool for increasing our self-esteem.

Consider Yourself Empowered

Most people see empowerment as something they get from someone else, rather than an attitude they have about themselves. Empowerment is a confidence issue: having the confidence in your own competence to live your freedom, not bowing in the face of the challenge.

When you feel empowered, you see yourself as capable of doing what needs to be done, being able to learn new skills and apply them. You know you can meet the challenges life offers and find a way to thrive.

Peggy worked as a teller at a local bank. She was always uncertain she knew enough to do her job properly. Then her supervisor wanted to promote her to head teller. Peggy was terrified. She was going to turn down the promotion because she didn't know how to be head teller.

Peggy didn't understand that her supervisor was promoting her, not because she knew how to do the job of head teller, but because he was sure she could learn how to do the job. Peggy had the competence. She just didn't have confidence in her own competence.

The confidence of empowerment is built on feedback and evaluation. Others notice what you've done or not done, and let you know if and how they approve or disapprove. You add your own evaluation, comparing your efforts against your own criteria and standards. You see the effects of your actions. And your confidence grows.

When Mary Sue started taking courses at the local community college, she wasn't sure she could pass the courses, much less get good enough grades to get a degree. She studied hard, but soon realized she didn't need to study all that much to understand her textbooks and her professors' lectures. As her excellent grades came in, she changed her goals. No longer was it enough to get a two-year degree. She now knew she wanted, and could earn, a four-year degree.

Empowerment comes from within. You acknowledge and assume your capabilities. You see yourself as having choices and the ability to act on your choices.

And act you will. Because, like Mary Sue, you'll develop confidence in your ability to make things happen. You'll resolve issues rather than avoid them. You'll take action. You'll focus on what's right rather than getting caught up in who's right. Getting credit won't be as important as solving problems.

People who are empowered are curiously immune to stings of external criticism and even the impact of their own failures or missteps. They take the accurate part of the criticism under consideration while distancing themselves from emotional and/or inaccurate attacks. Their own errors, missteps, and/or mistakes are seen as part of the learning process, rather than as attacks on their character or intellect.

Empowerment is an active, lifelong process, rather than a goal to be achieved. Even with a strong belief in your own self-efficacy, there are lots of challenges and opportunities. But in the end, considering yourself empowered means you have given yourself permission to be in charge of your own life.

Consider Letting Go

The meaning of the word *consider* shifts with letting go. With both Consider Yourself Entitled and Consider Yourself Empowered, *consider* means "assume you are; don't wait for someone to tell you or give you permission." Here *consider* means "think about," as in "consider the possibility." Same word, important distinction.

Consider letting go. Think about it, consider the possibility of letting go of the crises that have been defining your life.

What would letting go look like? Feel like? What would you lose? What would you gain?

I purposely use the words *letting go* rather than *forgive*, because your out-of-control person may have done unforgivable things, betrayed the commitments made to you, or purposely chosen to act in ways he knew would hurt you—unforgivable behavior.

If you are struggling with a large impersonal corporation, a government agency, or the forces of nature, whom do you forgive? Forgiving isn't the right concept for dealing with an earthquake. Even if you understand the government employee who was charged with carrying out the policy or procedure that propelled you into crisis, forgiving isn't quite right for the whole government, either. Hence letting go.

If your out-of-control situation has been a life-defining event, it will be hard to let go of it. At first glance, it's easy to see just the negatives: how you've been hurt, what you've lost, what's been destroyed. But there are usually positive consequences of crisis, even if some of them are a bit crooked.

There's often the opportunity to take the moral high ground, to position yourself with righteous indignation and judgment as you condemn the wrongdoer. Or you may have achieved a certain dose of public recognition or notoriety, support, or sympathy. Letting go means giving up these "positives," as well as the evident negatives.

Letting go means you are giving up the expectation that the other person will change, apologize, or even acknowledge what he did was hurtful to you, much less make it up to you. It means you no longer expect anything from him. You're going on without him. You no longer want or need him to make you whole.

Letting go means this incident or crisis is no longer the defining moment of your life. It was something that happened. It is not who you are. You are letting go of, giving up on, an identity that you had embraced or that was given to you. It means your life will change.

And that's the good news and the bad news.

Take Action

When we talk about making changes, we are usually talking about taking action. Action is visible; we know when it happens. In seminars, books, and lectures we are shown how to set goals, implement action plans, and do something, anything. Action does release pressure. Doing something, anything purposeful is a prescription suggested by therapist David Burns in his book *Feeling Good: The New Mood Therapy*. He found any purposeful action was especially powerful in lifting the spirits and motivating people with depression to begin to feel better.

But action can be just tension relieving, not goal achieving. Then you no longer have the discomfort to motivate you to keep changing. The underlying problem doesn't get fixed. Which means you just get to deal with another crisis.

Look for the Big Picture

Flourishing after Imposed Change is more likely when you focus on what you want, rather than on what you don't want. Look at the big picture, the overall vision of what you want your life to be. Focusing solely on what you don't want is like telling your child to stop jumping on the bed. In midleap they look at you with vacant eyes as if to say, so what should I do instead? Go beyond not doing what you have been doing. Think about what you want to happen, not what has been happening. Forward thinking will give clues on what to do next.

> *Julie wanted to change her drinking behavior. She knew she was drinking too much and had come to rely on Scotch as a way of relaxing and winding down in the evening after work. But it was starting to get in the way. She knew she wasn't an alcoholic, and didn't see herself as a problem drinker, but she was starting to see how her drinking was a problem for her. She had gotten into the habit of coming home every night after a busy day at a demanding job and drinking a hefty glass of Scotch while reading the evening paper. Then she'd have a second "relaxing" drink as she cooked dinner.*
>
> *By the time dinner was over, it was all she could do to help her younger child into bed and give a cursory glance at her older child's schoolwork before she collapsed into bed herself. She said later she wasn't sure whether it was the stress of the job, the alcohol, or the demands of the house and family that would do her in by nine o'clock every night.*
>
> *When she tried to think what she wanted instead, she said she wanted to relax when she came home, not hassle with cooking. We brainstormed alternatives. Her first choice was hiring a full-time cook. She saw herself meeting with the cook and going over menus and planning for a week's worth of wonderful meals.*
>
> *Although Julie discarded the idea of hiring a cook because of finances, it did give her a clue about what she could do. Instead of stopping at the grocery store on her way home every night, she started planning a week's menus. She did her grocery shopping and prep cooking one night a week. Several partially cooked*

dinners were always waiting in the fridge. She could finish dinner while she changed and went out and worked in her rose garden.

What Julie wanted from drinking was relaxation and the feeling of having someone do for her. When she changed her schedule, she felt more taken care of, drank when she chose to rather than from habit, and did a better job with the garden. She said she didn't miss the drinking, because it was more fun to be in the garden.

Julie's behavior-change program started with telling herself the truth about her drinking: It was not only not getting her what she wanted, but it was interfering with what she wanted for her life. The next step was making a clear determination of what she wanted instead. She looked for the big picture, what she wanted her life to be instead of what she had.

Challenges Should Not Be Overwhelming

Lots of the problems people have with taking action are caused by the ways they set their goals. To be most effective, goals need to be a challenge but not out of sight. Research by Mihaly Csikszentmihalyi at the University of Chicago has shown that moderately challenging objectives are motivating in and of themselves, while those that are too easy are discarded as boring and those that are too difficult are abandoned as being overwhelming.

We can sabotage ourselves unwittingly by choosing goals that are too easy or too difficult. We can challenge ourselves with unattainable objectives, or make the change so slight as to be trivial. Or we decide to change so many things at once that it's impossible to do any of them well, or we lose heart and quit when we realize we can't accomplish everything on the list.

Taking the First Step

The toughest part of taking back your life can be taking the first steps. Those first steps take on a symbolic meaning. They let you know you're on your way. You get it. You see how you are changing your life. You make your commitment to yourself visible as you take action.

Taking action is simple, but not easy. We can come up with an amazing variety of reasons why we can't/won't do what obviously needs to be done.

Betty suffers from analysis paralysis: She won't stop consider-ing alternatives, because she is sure there is a more perfect so-lution out there somewhere.

Elaine doesn't feel like it. She's so bummed out she spends most of her time escaping into historical/hysterical novels.

Ed did take action, once. He quit smoking for almost two weeks. But then he slipped and had a cigarette after a big set-to with his boss. Now he's right back to two packs a day.

Gene's not sure his family would like it if he took three weeks off to work at the low-cost housing program in town. He's afraid they'd be embarrassed for their friends to see him in his overalls and work shirt instead of his designer suits.

Eleanor sets so many hard goals that it is impossible for her to succeed. So she doesn't even try. Why bother when failure is inevitable? she asks.

Alma doesn't think it's fair she should have to do it all. Her ex-husband should help with the kids, but it's been years since he's offered.

These are the "good reasons" not to take action. The real reasons are more typically being afraid—fear of failure, of what friends and family would say, of success, of commitment—or being angry—life isn't fair, others don't share your values, what you want doesn't seem to count. So you don't do what you need to do or what you say you want to do. You stay stuck with your good reasons so you don't have to face the real reasons.

Other people hesitate because they don't feel like it yet. They're waiting until they feel motivated. In the meantime they sit. Motiva-tion is a funny thing. Often the best way to get motivated is to just do something, anything that will fit your purpose. David Burns, in *Feeling Good: The New Mood Therapy*, related stories of his depressed patients who would sit around waiting to feel better before taking action. They would end up feeling worse. David Reynolds, therapist and teacher of the Japanese Naikan and Morita therapies in the United States, explicitly demands doing what needs to be done. How you feel, whether you want to do it or not, is not the issue. Doing what needs to be done is.

Plan for Relapse

One of the biggest sabotages of change programs is not planning for reevaluation and reinvention of action plans. So the first sign of trouble or difficulty means failure. The accompanying self-talk usually sounds like "I don't know what I'm doing," "I shouldn't be trying to change," or "I just have weak will and shouldn't count on being able to change anything."

Whenever I coach clients on changing their behavior, I encourage them to plan for relapsing. Work at it. Choose a date when you'll fall apart. After they stare at me as though I've lost my mind, they usually laugh and see the point. We need to be prepared for the tough times that are sure to come.

> *A few years after I quit smoking, I took two summer classes at a local university. Between classes a group of us would sit in the cafeteria, talking and drinking coffee. For the first time in years, I had the urge to smoke. This feeling was such a surprise, it took me a while to figure out why I felt like bumming a cigarette from a classmate. Then I realized what was happening.*
>
> *I had been a heavy smoker in college. I would often sit in the cafeteria with friends and classmates smoking and drinking coffee.*
>
> *Here I was in the same environment. Even though the school and the people were different, the experience was so similar. All I was missing was the smoking! A very strong, determined conversation with myself about how that option was closed was enough to reinforce my choice. I reminded myself that* I am not a smoker. I do not smoke. *I did not ask for a cigarette.*

My "relapse" didn't occur, because I had planned for it. I knew what I was going to do. When my buttons got pushed, I put my plan into action. My plan wasn't all that elaborate: just a reminder that I promised myself I wasn't a smoker. Now here is the strange part. My successfully dealing with the temptation of relapse actually made my resolve stronger. I am not a smoker.

Planning for a relapse *does not* mean you should purposely choose to do the very thing that you have been trying to change. Do not smoke again, drink again, or call your previous significant other with plans for a romantic evening. Planning for a relapse means planning what you will do, can do, when you are challenged again. What will you say when you get the call suggesting a fancy dinner and a little romance when you know the relationship is over? What can you do when a friend or acquaintance asks you about your latest job difficulty? You will get the chance to put your contingency plans into action. You can't avoid the opportunity for relapses, but having plans in place makes dealing with them easier. And it makes it easier for you to say no to opportunities to slip into unwanted behavior patterns.

And what if you do relapse? What if you do the very thing you are trying to change? First, treat yourself kindly. We're so quick to blame, beat ourselves up, treat ourselves badly when we slip. The important thing is to recognize you're human, pull yourself together, and put into action the relapse contingency program you designed. The best thing you can do for yourself is to get back onto the horse that threw you— figure out what went wrong and then get back on track. One slip doesn't mean total failure. It just means you hadn't anticipated all the factors and issues you would need to deal with. Knowing about this issue means you can now take care of it.

Moving On

We all get challenges. Being challenged has little to do with the fairness of life, whether we deserve what we get, or get more than others. It isn't what happens to us that determines whether we are going to be crushed or uplifted, but what we do with what we get. And the tough part is, we have to figure out for ourselves what we can do, should do, and need to do to take charge and move beyond the crisis at hand.

In the next chapters we will look more closely at the options and opportunities that come when we are faced with a situation or person we can't control. And how others have taken charge, and what we can learn from them to take charge of our own challenges.

TYPICAL FEELINGS PEOPLE HAVE
WHEN "NOT IN CHARGE"

anger a feeling that one has been treated unjustly or injured by another person; usually shows itself in a desire to hit out at something or someone

anxiety a feeling of uneasiness, apprehension, or worry about what may happen

compulsivity an irresistible driving urge to perform a certain act, even though there is no real need or justification for performing it

depression a feeling of gloominess, dejection, sadness, or low spirits; may be due to discouragement, feelings of inadequacy

despair a feeling that there is no hope of success or happiness

frustration a feeling that one's efforts are to no avail in achieving a desired goal; feeling a strong need to achieve a certain goal while not being able to attain it

guilt a feeling that one has done a wrong or committed an offense; a feeling that one has acted against one's better judgment

hostility a feeling of enmity, ill will, unfriendliness, or antagonism toward someone

self-doubt a lack of belief in oneself; a lack of respect for or confidence in oneself; a feeling of inadequacy

self-pity feeling sorry for oneself; sorrow over one's suffering and misfortune

---

Exercises for Chapter 2

Use your notebook to answer the following questions.

EXPLORE YOUR CHALLENGE

Write a ten-word telegram about the incident or event you can't control. Draw a cartoon or sketch of the incident. What song or musical composition best represents the incident?

TELL YOURSELF THE TRUTH

What do you know, believe, and feel about the incident? What assumptions are you making? What judgments are you making? How has your life changed? Who else is affected? What have you lost? Gained? What do you anticipate for the future? How do you know all this?

CONSIDER YOURSELF ENTITLED

What do you consider you're entitled to regarding this incident? What is right for people like you in this kind of situation? Who says?

CONSIDER YOURSELF EMPOWERED

What can you do? What options do you have? Who says? Do other people in these kinds of situations have options you don't? How come?

CONSIDER LETTING GO

What have you lost? Gained? Whom do you blame? What do they think and feel about the incident? What do you want from them? How likely is it that you might get it? How will your life be different by letting go of the incident?

TAKE ACTION

So what can you do? What do you want instead of what you have? How would you look? Feel? Who else would you have in your life that you don't have now? Who will you need to move on from? What are the first steps you need to take? How will this get you what you want?

CHAPTER 3

IT'S NOT DYSFUNCTION, IT'S LIFE: DISCARDING A VICTIM MENTALITY

Carolyn McCarthy was attending a Christmas concert when Colin Ferguson opened fire on the commuter train her husband and son were riding on. Not until much later that evening did she learn her husband had been killed and her son gravely injured. A registered nurse, Carolyn now focused her attention on helping her son recover from his injuries, not on the man who had hurt him so badly.

Yet when Carolyn saw Ferguson complaining on television of the discomfort of being in jail, she lost her composure. As she was crying, she made up her mind that she would never let Colin Ferguson get to her again. Carolyn admitted he had made her a victim once, but he was not going to do it again. She wouldn't let him. She would take charge of her life, not give it up to him.

Carolyn went on to speak at the Democratic National Convention and then enter politics with an agenda of speaking out for gun control.

Time magazine called us a nation of whiners and blamers. We label our experiences, habits, or problems as dysfunctions, and then we define ourselves as the victims of our experiences. Dysfunctions have expanded to include the way we're brought up, accidents, trauma, or even illness. From this point of view, whatever happens to us scars us for life. We'll not be unaffected by these awful things that happened to us. Or so the dysfunction industry tells us.

As a therapist, I've found this whole trend disheartening. I've spent a good many years, many dollars, and a lot of my energy on learning how to help people get a fresh perspective on their lives, the experiences they've had, and then go on to live full, satisfying, and even joyful lives. And it works. Clients work through their problems, get a handle on them, and then go on with their lives.

Now here is a whole group of people telling me that not only I, but the whole field of mental health is wrong and that the best anyone can hope for is to be in perpetual recovery, never getting recovered from our "victimization."

My breaking point came when I heard a self-styled guru of the codependency/twelve-step persuasion in a television address. He told a story about a girl who grew up in what he described as an incredibly dysfunctional family. Her parents were both deaf. Since she could hear, she helped interpret for her parents when they needed to communicate with people who couldn't sign.

I was dumbfounded. He was labeling deafness and helping your parents dysfunctional!

I was so annoyed, I can't remember hearing the rest of the program. Here was a family pulling together, using their resources to help one another, to support and provide for one another. He labeled their caretaking dysfunction! I remember saying to myself, "That's not dysfunction; that's life."

This family was doing what we all hope our families would do for us when we hit tough times. We want our families to rally together and help one another.

The reality of life is that tough things happen. Some of these tough things are predictable. Others are unpredictable. Some we cause, some we don't. All of them have an impact on our lives.

Predictably, our children grow up and leave home. Our parents usually die before we do. In today's economy, most of us won't have the same job all of our lives.

Illnesses and accidents are usually unpredictable and may have tragic consequences. As well as you take care of yourself, you still may develop heart trouble, cancer, or a contagious disease. You can be in the wrong place at the wrong time and be seriously injured and/or disabled. You or a loved one may die unexpectedly. You may face the poignant tragedy of your children dying before you.

There are the unpredictable, and often devastating, geologic or atmospheric events: hurricanes, tornadoes, earthquakes, floods. For the most part, we're unable to predict exactly where these events will occur or what the consequences will be. And yet, we can know with some certainty that every year we will see each of them occur somewhere in the world.

Some of the tough things that happen to us are things that we literally cause. We're careless, don't pay attention, make bad choices or poor decisions. Others are imposed upon us. A loved one betrays us. A colleague breaks his word. A change in government policy costs us our business. Or, like Carolyn, a stranger hurts or kills someone we love. Imposed by others or through our own negligence, the consequences are the same. Whether we caused our problems or not, we still have to take care of ourselves when problems occur.

Labeling Doesn't Help

To label these tough times dysfunction not only doesn't help, it just makes difficult experiences even harder. Labeling our experiences dysfunctional implies that somehow we're dysfunctional: sick, bad, or crazy. There must be something the matter with us if we have trouble.

Labeling difficult events dysfunctional doesn't help us figure out how to resolve our problems. If we not only label what happened dysfunction but keep telling ourselves we are powerless over what's happened, then we're not only sick, bad, and crazy, but depressed and hopeless.

When we tell ourselves there is nothing we can do, we believe it even if it isn't true.

Labeling something dysfunctional and ourselves powerless also lets us off the hook for being accountable and responsible. It's as if we were saying, "What do you expect of 'little ole me' when something so terrible like this happens?" Since there's nothing *we* can do, surely you can't expect us to do something that will make a difference.

The reality is, we aren't hopeless and powerless, dysfunctional and helpless. We expect adults not only to take care of what happens, but work toward not having that same thing happen again. That's what adults do. They're responsible and accountable for what they do and for what they do about what happens to them. It may well be that we can't control what has happened, but we can certainly take charge and do something about what's happened.

Labeling ourselves dysfunctional supports blame and shame, not action and resolution. Continuing to focus on how bad things are, telling our sad story over and over—the suggested treatment for people who are dysfunctional—keeps us feeling bad rather than helping us to get on with our lives.

So let's look at how labeling and telling our sad story keeps us from feeling better and doing better.

Defining Our Expectations

None of us ever gets everything we want.

You've heard the myth, "You can have it all."

Well, you can't. There's not enough time, energy, or money to have everything you want, all of the time. Usually when we try to have it all, we end up doing a bad job of some of it.

We all have to make choices about where to focus and what to do. The frustration for many of us is that lots of our choices are mutually exclusive.

Many women have found that it's almost impossible to do an excellent job of raising their children and of pursuing their career at the same time. In fact, the latest research has shown that women who do have children and a career at the same time do not progress as quickly or reach as much success in either one of those areas as when they focus their efforts on one or the other. It just takes too much time and energy to be both a great mom and a great worker at the same time. Most of us just don't have that much energy.

Some of us may choose between the stability of staying in one town and one job with the attendant risk of boredom, or starting over in different towns or different careers with the risk of not being as successful or as supported as we'd like. And then, of course, there's always the choice between spending your money now or investing it for your retirement.

A common response to conflicting choices is to have serial points of focus. In their young adult years, many people choose to establish a family, then they'll shift emphasis to their careers as the children get older. Eventually, they may focus further afield and try new activities or adventures they wouldn't have been interested in while focusing on family and careers. Serial choosing provides a wide variety of life experiences by spacing them out over time. But even then, you can't have it all at the same time.

The lesson here is *life's not easy*. It's hard work. There are lots of situations or experiences we have that are unpleasant, that can bring us pain when we least expect it. And there's always a price to pay. By expecting it to be easy, we just get ourselves into trouble.

Life's also not fair. My mom used to say, the ticket to life said admit one. There's no guarantee of fair. Bad things do happen to good people. Living a good life is no guarantee that things will always go well. There are accidents. There are germs, malignancies, genetic disorders, and just plain ugliness. We may all be created equally under the law (and some people will even dispute this), but we are not all equally endowed. Some of us have special talents and gifts in arts, intellect, or athletics. Others are more limited. People are different. Some people seem to have gotten more than their fair share, while others of us seem to have been woefully neglected.

There's not always justice. We work hard and don't reap the rewards. Others take advantage of us, and there seems to be no recourse. We discover our good works are not always appreciated or don't even get results. We may have a legitimate dispute and find either through ignorance, procedural quirks, or a judge getting up on the wrong side of the bed our good case does not prevail. As one father of a young woman I was working with said after she had lost her court case, "We go to court looking for justice. What we get is a decision."

But whether we find good things or bad things happening to us, there seems to be an underlying human need to derive meaning, to look for the reasons, to ask why is this happening, and why is it happening to me?

People are incredibly vulnerable, especially during tough times. When we're in pain and don't know why, we're susceptible to anyone who promises crumbs of comfort, whether the offer is worthwhile or not in our own best interest. When we're hurting, we grab hold of the person or the way that promises us relief. Often, we don't even think through our choices or our decisions. Only later do we come to realize we've followed false prophets.

When you're hurting, it's easy to latch onto a support group you wouldn't otherwise consider joining. The allure is the promise of quick comfort. Seldom, if ever, is the cost of long-term alienation from family and friends considered.

In an anniversary retrospective of the Jonestown massacre, Jim Jones's son remembered with fondness the many fine people he knew in Guyana. He described how simple people and politicians, the poor and the powerful were swept up by the promises of his father's rhetoric. By the time they realized the promises wouldn't be fulfilled, the rhetoric had shifted to intimidation and fear tactics. By then it was too late. People were too afraid to speak out. They were caught.

No matter what path we take, there's always good news and always bad news. The very program that we think will help can also confuse and challenge us.

Elaine started going to a support group to "get in touch with the dysfunction in her family of origin." The group emphasized self-responsibility: we choose, promote, or allow everything that happens to us. Elaine became furious with herself. How could she have chosen to have parents so crazy and so abusive?

Elaine's friend Reena was very concerned with Elaine's anger and cautioned her to be very careful asking questions like that, because it could make her crazy. "There is no answer to that question," Reena told her friend. "And any answer you give yourself is a trap. It looks like a gift, but it's dangerous."

Reena tried to explain the dangers. "If you ask, 'Why would I choose to have such abusive parents?' the answer has to be, so you could learn an important lesson about abuse. And now that you've learned the lesson, you hate them and you never want to have anything to do with them. You've caught yourself in a terrible trap."

Reena went on to explain that if, in fact, she needed to learn an important lesson about abuse, then Elaine had perfect parents. So now, she should be grateful to them for providing the opportunity to learn the lessons she needed, rather than hating them for being abusive.

Elaine was confused. How could her friend tell her to be grateful to parents who were abusive? There was something the matter with this whole way of thinking, and she couldn't quite put her finger on it.

Elaine's problem was not just with her parents. No child deserves to be abused. And there is much that needs to be done to insure all children are free from this pain. But getting caught up in demanding that adults take the responsibility of "creating, allowing, or enabling" the abuse they experienced as children not only doesn't help them deal with their feelings about their past, but prevents them from moving on and healing.

Children don't create or allow their own abuse. To hold adults responsible for the abuse they experienced as children is abusive. It sorely discounts how little power children have, how little they can do to protect themselves when they have an abusing parent. To claim they were acting on a karmic or nonconscious level, and demand now they "take responsibility for their behavior" is a no-win setup.

Looking for Reasons

We need to be very careful in our search for meaning and reasons why our life has taken the turns it has, no matter what kind of explanations we use.

When we feel out of control, we want an explanation for why things aren't the way they should or could be. "Why?" is the question, even when there isn't an answer. The question may be "Why me?" "Why now?" "Why not someone else?" or some other variant of "Why?"

Usually we look to our spiritual beliefs, our personal beliefs on the nature of the world, or what we've been taught by our culture for the answers to our "Why?" questions.

Spiritual Reasoning

As we saw in chapter one, looking to our spiritual beliefs for the answers to "Why?" questions can be problematic.

I am not saying that you shouldn't find solace in your spirituality; just be careful. Looking for solace for your suffering is very different from determining why you have been singled out for pain and punishment.

Don't get caught up in feelings that you somehow deserve to be treated badly by others, no matter who that other is.

Personal Reasoning

Looking for personal answers brings the focus back on yourself. What is it about *me* that caused this crisis? The answers can take a biological or psychological slant. When we look at biologically based answers, we look at who we are as animals. We try to figure out what translates from lower animals and what doesn't. Or we focus on the chemical or cellular level, drawing connections between hormones and body secretions and behavior. An older friend tried very hard to convince me that feeling low (i.e., depression) could always be cured by taking a good physic (laxative). It was hard to argue with her when I knew her advice to take cranberry juice was excellent medicine for a kidney chill (bladder infection).

Psychologically, we look to previous experiences for effects on current behavior. We examine our childhood, family relationships, childhood friends, and early experiences to see the past roots of current issues.

While there are some similarities between animals and people, and we can always point to past events to explain current behavior, we need to be careful with the conclusions we draw. With animals, we tend to overgeneralize: we see animals acting a particular way and then assume that people behave the same way. Our conclusions can be too global, too general. Or as one humorist responded to a wag who tried to convince her that the natural order of women was to be subordinate to their mates because that's what happens with the lower primates in the wild, then we should expect men to climb trees and eat bananas.

With psychological issues, we do just the opposite. We get too specific, attributing current behavior to a specific incident or event. In our zeal to find a cause, we can overlook the general pattern of our experiences. An unusual experience tends to be remembered more than an everyday event. Or we'll label an experience or reaction pathological when it well could be an understandable reaction to an ongoing stressful situation or to an underlying family pattern.

Billy considered his parents cold and distant, always working rather than taking time for Billy or his brother. Not until he was settling his parents' meager estate did Billy realize they had taken on the responsibility of supporting Billy's aunt and uncle when the uncle had become disabled.

Billy attributed his parents' distance to their not caring. Now he realized they must have been very tired and worried about providing for both families.

Cultural Reasoning

Cultural reasons come from the media, our religious practices, educational training, and even what part of the country we have grown up in. Currently we're in a curious position of both blaming our culture and its cultural tools—such as the media, the nature of leadership and ethics, and how power is displayed and rewarded—for the "terrible shape the country is in" and accepting that we have been shaped by that same culture. It's like we're at war with our own culture. We know it has influenced us, and we're mad that it has.

In the United States today it is trendy to be addicted, codependent, or powerless in the face of dysfunctions. A multimillion-dollar industry has developed and is flourishing to support this view. Countless seminars, self-help programs, books, and conferences have sprung up all over the country. All of them encourage their adherents to see themselves as powerless, unable to resolve their own problems, and to let go and let God. Participants are described as "adult children," implying they are less than adult, not responsible for their lives. Tales of abuse and victimization are encouraged, while positive or even neutral experiences are defined as or used as evidence of denial.

Both Anne Wilson Schaef and John Bradshaw, gurus of the codependency movement, go so far as to label society itself as dysfunctional. All families are dysfunctional, they say, and there is no possibility of anyone not being codependent. From this perspective, we're all destined to be helpless, powerless to make a difference in our lives.

Unfortunately, some people use this excuse to justify irresponsible or immoral behavior, such as athletes like Wade Boggs, who claims to be helpless and sexually addicted as the excuse for his philandering. Politicians caught with their pants down (Senator Bob Packwood) or drugs in their hands (D.C. Mayor Marion Barry) use the claim of addiction and helplessness to excuse their unsavory and illegal behavior.

While the public figures draw the attention of the media, in countless communities and homes less public figures are using these same excuses to avoid taking responsibility for their past actions and/or to avoid taking charge of their current behavior. They can't help it; they are powerless against their addiction. It wasn't me, they say. It was the booze, sex, drugs, shopping that made me do it. And onlookers applaud. Not only does this excuse the behavior of others, but it lets us off the hook of responsibility for our secret sins, small or large.

The Role of Theory

We take our reasons for the way things are and make theories about why things happen. Some of our theories are valid, or testable; others are conjecture, made up out of whole cloth, or built on lies, obfuscation, and malice. True or not, the only value to our theories is in how they help us take action.

Our theories give us our model of how the world is organized. They let us feel a part of the group that shares our theories. And our theories distance us from people who think differently than we do. When we have our theory, our reasons, our worldview, we know who are our friends and who aren't, where we belong and where we don't. Our theories, our reasons, become our truths.

Our theories also point the way. They show us where we can go and where we should go. They help us focus our alternatives and options. They show us what we need to do to get what we want.

We can discover our story by looking at what we've done. Building a story is an iterative process: once we've taken one step, the next is evident. Then the second step will head us back to a variation of the first. Our daily behaviors and our theory about the way the world should be support one another.

The problem with both worldview and life story is that by midlife we discover they aren't what we thought they would be. What we do and think isn't as useful, as valuable, or as accurate as we once thought. Now we're really faced with a crisis: how to reconcile what we believe with our current experience.

We have three choices.

- We can ignore the inconsistencies and continue to do what we have always done and expect things to turn out differently from what they have been. This is the ostrich approach. Keep your head in the sand. Don't admit that what you've been doing won't work.
- We can change what we do, think, and/or believe to be consistent with the results gotten. (I can hear the criticism now: "Oh, no,

here comes more of that situational morality stuff. What's the matter with sticking with the old values, old ways of doing what we should be doing?" Keep reading; there is another alternative.)

- We can keep our core values and address our current reality. This is the master paradox of changing and staying the same.

This third alternative is the hardest, and yet the most rewarding. It is taking charge when we aren't in control. Taking charge lets us keep the stability of our purpose and character in a rapidly changing and confrontational world. It allows us to rethink what we're doing: Is what we are thinking and doing consistent with our current thoughts, feelings, concerns, and beliefs, or are we on autopilot, doing what we do because that's what we've always done?

> *As a young professional, I attended numerous training sessions on the then-new therapeutic model called transactional analysis. Excited about the applicability of what I was learning and how it could be useful in my clinical practice, I was sharing my excitement with a group of acquaintances. One of them reacted with scorn as he asked whether the theory would stand the test of time. Did I think I would be still believing this in twenty years, or would I be on to some other new and supposedly improved ideas? He caught me for a moment, then I laughed and said I hoped I would move on. He replied that my answer just proved to him that this was just a passing fad. I said no, if I didn't have any new ideas in twenty years, that would mean I had stopped growing, that I had stopped questioning and I was no longer intellectually curious.*

His life task was to find an end point. He was searching for Truth and Reality. Then he could be content that he'd have all the answers.

I see my life task as a process of uncovering meaning, purpose, and ideas. It is a journey, not a destination. Our core values were so different I realized we'd never agree on the role of new ideas.

The Dark Side of Life

We tend to avoid the dark side of life when we make up our stories, our theories of how life should be. If we're going to look at the full picture of life, we can't avoid looking at evil. I'm not talking about Satan, the popular conceptions of Lucifer struggling with God, or even a character such as Screwtape who was training his young ward to be a functionary of the devil.

I'm talking about the everyday, trivial, and banal evil each of us is capable of doing. When we treat other people as objects for our own pleasure and discount the humanity of others, when we act as if people are of no more value or use than the chair we are sitting on or the table we put our papers on, then we are talking of evil.

This banal evil gets played out in the streets as young people randomly kill one another for sport or to prove their own worth. It gets played out in private places where adults who should be caring for children hurt them instead. It gets played out in public as we jockey for the upper hand of self-righteousness and denounce others for the secret sins we ourselves have committed.

This evil is a spiritual, not a psychological or a social, disorder. It can be best exemplified by a quote that came out of the killing fields where an executioner dismissed a prisoner begging for his life by saying, "To destroy you is nothing."

This is the evil of people who do not hold the universal value for human life.

Any search for meaning about life and why things happen can't dismiss the existence of evil people. These are the people who feel no remorse as they use people as objects for their own pleasure. These are the people who take advantage, con, manipulate, and/or destroy others just for their own benefit. These are the people who blame those they have destroyed for their own destruction.

There is no escape from this type of evil. And no shame in being caught. If you have been caught by an evil person, don't blame yourself. It's a victimization you couldn't avoid. Like the wily old coyote who culls a lamb from the flock, they didn't give you a chance. Once targeted, there was no escape.

Language and Self-Talk

As kids we wanted to believe the retort "Sticks and stones can break our bones but names will never hurt us." Yet as we grow up, we realize that what we say does matter. It matters a whole lot.

Poets knew it. So did philosophers and the authors of Bible verses. Since time immemorial, the word has been out. Shakespeare said, "There is nothing either good or bad, but thinking makes it so."

It's not what happens to us but how we think about what happens to us that makes it good or bad. Therapists have been saying for years the meaning we give our life experiences is what counts, not just the experiences themselves.

Linguists show how our language systems are determined by the underlying assumptions we hold about the structure of our reality. This is why Eskimos have dozens of words for *snow*, while the rest of the country has only one.

While I was visiting my son in Japan, we were traveling by train into Tokyo. Mayumi, one of his Japanese friends, whispered to me that the two flashily dressed women who were speaking and laughing loudly weren't Japanese. I whispered back, "How do you know?" Mayumi replied, "They're speaking Chinese."

My Western ears couldn't tell the women weren't speaking Japanese. My Western eyes didn't know the differences between Chinese women and Japanese women. Mayumi was embarrassed to think I would assume Japanese would act so rudely on the train. She could hear the differences. She knew they were acting out of line. It was outside my experience. I didn't have the concepts to tell the difference.

Our speech and language both reflect and help perpetuate our deeply held cultural attitudes. Language is a powerful conceptual force. It not only transmits the biases and beliefs of a society, but it also can shape the way we think. What we tell ourselves shapes the way we think. How we think shapes what we say and what we do. What we say and do shapes our culture. And the cycle continues.

The question begs to be asked: If we change our language will we also start to change our beliefs and behaviors? Could the poets, the Bible, the philosophers, Shakespeare, all those therapists be correct? There is nothing either good or bad, but thinking makes it so?

Research conducted by Martin Seligman at the University of Pennsylvania and chronicled in his book *Learned Optimism* seems to prove the point.

Seligman looked at what makes the difference between people who are crushed by difficult experiences and those who can put their lives back together and go on to live full, satisfying lives. He looked at the differences between people who considered themselves victimized and those who didn't, even though they shared very similar horrible experiences.

What people told themselves about what happened made the difference. What people said to themselves and how they thought about the experience was much more important than the experience itself.

Seligman found three types of statements that made the difference between people he called optimists and those he called pessimists.

Optimists would see their troubles as isolated, temporary, and the result of happenstance or bad luck. Pessimists would see their troubles as pervasive, permanent, and personal, the result of their own shortcomings.

Their situations didn't differ, just what they said about those experiences. What they said to themselves, how they talked to themselves made all the difference in how their experiences affected them.

Seligman went on to continue his investigation of the impact of past experience on current behavior in his next book, *What You Can Change . . . and What You Can't*. He found little direct connection between specific childhood events and difficulties in adult years. This is not to say that people aren't affected by what's happened to them. They are. But like his work with learned optimism, he found that what people said about what happened to them, the meaning that they gave to those experiences, was a more potent factor in determining impact than the experience itself.

While many clinicians were unhappy with Seligman's findings of no direct link between childhood experiences and adult behavior, they were heartened by the unequivocal findings that what you say about what happened is more important than what happened.

It's this finding that leads us clearly to the position that no matter how awful something was, it's possible to recover and get past having your tough times ruin your life.

Seligman's research also points out how important it is to be careful about what you say about what you do. What you say does make a big difference in how you feel and what you do.

It may seem like I'm nitpicking to look so closely at our theories of life and at what we say when we talk to ourselves. I'm not. Both are really important as we look more closely at addictions theory. They both help us understand why addictions theory is not very helpful in classifying everyday life experiences as dysfunction, and why continually telling our sad story is not effective in moving beyond being hopeless and helpless.

Addictions Theory

As a theory to account for why people do what they do, addictions theory makes some sense when we're talking about physical and/or chemical dependency. There's no denying that some people very quickly come under the influence of their "identified drug of choice" and that their physiological responses make it difficult, if not impossible, for them to break their habits. In these situations, it's appropriate to talk about the problem as an addiction. Whether we want to go one step further and talk about it as an illness is still up for discussion in many circles.

The difficulty comes in taking addictions theory from physiological experiences (i.e., substance abuse) to behavior problems and bad habits. It's the problem we have with lots of theories. Theories are metaphors for what is happening. They aren't what's happening. Metaphors and theories aren't truth and reality. They're maps of reality.

Addictions theory started as a metaphor for understanding behavioral issues, but now we're taking the theory literally. We define bad habits, laziness, problems of ordinary life, and poor impulse controls as addictions. Extending the definition in this way not only trivializes addictions that are physiologically based, but also uses addiction as an excuse for bad behavior.

One of the most noxious of these is the concept of codependency. Codependency is a concept, a theory, a story, that was made up to explain why some people have difficulty in their relationships, especially in their relationships with people who are addicted. It's one more story we tell ourselves to explain what happens.

Now there's no denying that living with a drug addict or an alcoholic can make you absolutely crazy. (This is not a diagnosis! It's a description of how you feel when you live with an addict.)

To take the next step and label a person sick, bad, and crazy for being in a relationship with someone who's addicted is not only not helpful but becomes a part of the problem.

If we look carefully at the definitions of codependency, two things are immediately obvious.

First, the descriptions of behaviors labeled dysfunctional and co-dependent are the very characteristics that millions of women of middle age and older were taught to do to be considered good women. To take those attributes after the fact and label them dysfunction, to say you are powerless to solve your "problem," that you will never recover, that you are, in fact, sick, bad, or crazy for doing what you do, is the ultimate in blaming the victim.

First you were taught how to be good. Then you're told it's bad to be good. And then you're told there's nothing you can do about being bad. You'll always be recovering from being bad, but never get to being good again.

The treatment for being codependent is to publicly confess you're powerless over your problem—read *over yourself*. You must acknowledge there is nothing you can do. You have to rely on something outside of yourself to restore yourself to sanity. This means that you are not only sick, bad, and/or crazy, but that you can't help yourself.

The treatment perpetuates the problem. You never stop being bad. You'll just keep *trying* to stop. (Like getting on a plane with a pilot who's *trying* to fly to New York. No way!)

But since you can't help yourself, you'll never get better. You'll always have this disease: the disease of being bad for trying to be good. It becomes the ultimate in labeling rather than fixing, wallowing in the label rather than taking action to fix the problem.

When we label the whole society as dysfunctional, we're not adding any new information to the equation. It's not at all helpful to talk about how awful everything is all the time. It becomes one more exercise in whining and complaining, rather than seeing what can be done to make a difference.

Codependency is *not* something you *have*. It's something you *believe*. It's no more true or false than any of your other beliefs, or stories, about the way the world is or should be. During your lifetime you've heard, and believed, many different stories, reflecting many different views of the world. You listened to the story and were persuaded or drawn into believing it. Your belief was stronger than the "truth" you thought you knew. So you accepted even outrageous parts of the story that you knew couldn't *really* happen, because believing the story was so attractive.

Ask little children if Santa can really come down chimneys or fly in a sleigh through the air. Ask Linus, Charles Schulz's *Peanuts* character, if the Great Pumpkin brings candy at Halloween to believing children. They'll all assure you of the existence of the character, his magic ability to transcend the laws of physics and perform as the story promises.

We can understand why children want to believe in Santa, or even in the Great Pumpkin. The promise of treats is a great lure for kids.

The question is, why would anyone want to believe the story that they are codependent? What rewards are promised? What treats come from believing? How is your life better for believing?

Life: You're Responsible

The good news and the bad news is, if we stop labeling predictable and typical life events as dysfunction, then someone, somehow, has to take responsibility for them.

That's what being adult is all about. The reality is everybody has something, and we also have responsibilities to our community, our families, and ourselves to grow up, get a grip, and get on with it, even though we may not be getting what we consider to be our fair measure.

Only by holding ourselves both responsible and accountable for our actions can we function effectively as a society, as a family, and as an individual. Only then can we take charge even though we aren't in control.

Exercises for Chapter 3

Most of us have said at one time or another, "I can't help it. I'm just addicted to chocolate, television, eating, shopping, _____." (You fill in the blank.) Our grandparents would say people who were overeating, overwatching, or overspending lacked character or willpower. Use this exercise to get in touch with your behavior and character.

Choose your out-of-control behavior to work with in this exercise.

Think back to a time you overindulged. Reexperience how you felt in your emotions and how you felt in your body sensations. Recall what you said to yourself about yourself and about what you did.

Now shift. Consider having the same opportunity to overindulge and this time doing something different: eating a small dish of ice cream, not the whole carton; looking at the pretty things in a store and not buying anything.

Now what are you saying and feeling? What have you learned from this difference? Was it tough or not that bad? Were you surprised by what you felt and thought or by what you thought about how you felt and thought?

How does this exercise connect with how you need to change your mind? With how you need to change your behavior?

CHAPTER 4

IN RECOVERY OR RECOVERED? GETTING ON WITH YOUR LIFE

We can't recover unless we know what being healed or recovered means.

As medical terms, there are different meanings for healing and health. If I have had a cold and get better, there's little evidence I was ever sick.

After I've had the measles or the chicken pox, you can't tell I was ill. But my body knows. My immune system develops antibodies that protect me from getting the disease again. My immunity's invisible, but helps me.

When I was a kid, and again later as an adult, I cut my leg. Both cuts healed long ago, but you can still see the scars. The scars are the consequences of my accidents. The cut tissue isn't the same as it used to be. It looks different. It feels different.

The difference between the scars on my legs and the immunity that I got from the chicken pox is that the scars are only aesthetic: they change the way my leg looks, but they don't change what my leg can do. The chicken pox immunity can't be seen, but it protects me. I've been strengthened by that illness. My accidents had no long-term effects. I seldom think of them anymore. (Except to use them as examples . . .)

Most of you have scars like mine. You can tell where you were hurt, but it hasn't changed the way your body operates. You may have had chicken pox, too. And won't get it again. Our scars and immunities show us the different ways we heal and recover.

If I talk about healing as going back to the way I was before, I am talking about the type of recovery that comes from having a cold or a minor scrape or cut. I get sick or hurt, but pretty soon I can't tell—and no one else can tell—it ever happened.

But when I get the measles, chicken pox, or really hurt myself, there's no way I'll ever be the same. My body's changed either the way it works or the way it looks, or sometimes both. I'll always have the immunity built up from the illnesses. I'll always have the scars on my leg.

Having irreversible changes doesn't mean I'm not healthy. I'm as healthy as, some would say healthier than, I was before I was ill. My scars don't affect how I use my leg. I'm as fit as I was before my accidents. Even though I'm different from what I was, the difference doesn't limit me. I'm fully recovered.

When it comes to psychological crisis, we want the type of healing that's typical of common colds and minor scrapes. We want to go back to just like we were before.

It's not what we usually get. We usually get the type of healing and recovery as with the chicken pox or the more serious cuts I had on my legs. We'll never be the same. The effects last our lifetime. They can't be denied. But they don't need to define our lives or continue to be the center of our lives. Like my chicken pox, the experience can be invisible, but make me stronger. Or like the cuts, the evidence can be visible, but my ability to live my life is not affected.

Changing Habits and Behaviors

When it comes to taking charge of a behavior or habit, we can also make permanent changes. We can be healthier or more fit. I'm not suggesting changing habits or behaviors is easy, or is as easy for everyone. Some people find it much harder than others. Or sometimes we'll find one habit really hard and another much easier to change. Nonetheless, we can change even those activities that seem uncontrollable. Being recovered is possible.

One of the most common behaviors people have learned to control is smoking. Hundreds of thousands of people have stopped smoking in the last twenty years, most without formal behavior-change programs, therapy, self-help groups, or medication. And for the most part, former smokers report that they no longer think about smoking, want to smoke, or enjoy being around people who smoke. They're nonsmokers. They're finished with smoking.

I am one of those nonsmokers. While in college, and for a few years afterward, I smoked a lot. And then I quit one day. I haven't had a cigarette for more than thirty years. I no longer want to smoke, think about smoking, or enjoy being around smokers. I don't let people smoke in my house, I always sit in the nonsmoking sections of restaurants, and I don't even own an ashtray. Most of the time I don't even think about smoking or not smoking.

Recently in a seminar on behavior change, a participant confronted me and said, "Once a smoker, always a smoker." There was no such thing as a former smoker. Only a smoker who wasn't smoking today. I tried to tell her I would never smoke again. Her smirk and comment said it all: Just for today you are not smoking.

Later I reflected on my smoking and not smoking. Since I returned to take classes that summer at the university many years ago, I haven't even considered smoking again. That experience cemented my resolve. She was in recovery. I was done with it.

A colleague referred to one of her clients as having been in recovery for over twenty-five years. I was fascinated with the description she gave of his life. He defined himself as an alcoholic, went to several AA meetings a week, associated only with people who were in recovery, and had turned down several job opportunities and was feeling the economic pinch of his resultant limited income. For twenty-five years he put alcohol in charge of his life. He wasn't drinking, but drinking, or the fear of drinking, controlled him. Being "in recovery" had become his goal, rather than the process of achieving a goal. His goal was only one day long. He had lived day by day for twenty-five years. All I could think was, Wasn't it about time he recovered?

For the woman in the seminar, not smoking was a decision she made every day. For me, the decision was for a lifetime. No more cigarettes. Ever.

I want to have long-term goals, to take charge and craft my life for the long run, not live from day to day with the sword of Damocles, of smoking, hanging over my head. I don't want to define myself as a nonsmoker. I want smoking not to be an issue in my life.

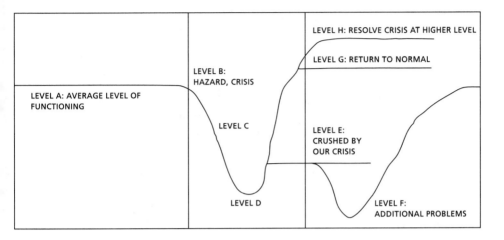

Figure 1. Recovered/recovery chart

Recovery and Recovered Models

All of us have a "normal" or typical level of energy, activity, and functioning (Level A, figure 1). We tend to hover around our typical level with ups and downs in response to the daily demands of our lives.

Then something happens, or we realize something has happened (Level B). Now we have a serious challenge.

Usually we respond to crisis by going into a tailspin. Our energy and attention for everyday activities is bled off into dealing with the crisis. We start exhibiting symptoms of anxiety, disorientation, depression, confusion (Level C).

With really big crises, within six to eight weeks we hit bottom. By this time, everything is awful. We hurt; we can't stand it anymore; we get sick and tired of dealing with the crisis or the pain of the crisis (Level D). This is the point where we start looking for help. We realize we can't get out of this all by ourselves. We want to stop hurting and we don't know how. We become receptive to help that might have been there all along. We want to stop the pain.

Getting past the crisis, "getting over it," can end up at different levels of functioning. It can take different routes. Some of us will never be the same. We can't get beyond the crisis. We may reach only Level E. At this level, it's obvious we've been crushed by what we've been through. We don't function at anywhere near the level we used to.

If we continue to be battered by difficult or uncontrollable events, we might even sink into a much lower level of functioning (Level F). We're no longer as effective as we once were. We can't do as much; we don't see the world in the same way. We lose hope and sight of what might have been. Even if we gradually get better, we seldom reach the level of ability and competency we once enjoyed. Our tough times have left us in dire straits. Our life isn't as bad as when we hit bottom, but it certainly isn't what it used to be.

A third alternative is returning to our previous level of "normal." We learn how to cope with our challenges, and we decide not to let them run our lives (Level G). We survive, not untouched, but certainly not crushed. It was a tough trip, but we made it.

The hardworking of us, like Heidi (chapter two) or Carolyn (chapter three), reach a higher level (Level H). We resolve our challenges at a higher level of functioning than we had before. We get it. We use our tough times to learn the lessons that make the difference in who we are and how we live our lives. We develop new insights, new behaviors, and new courage so we can go on to goals and objectives at a much higher level than before. We've raised the bar on our lives.

What makes the difference between reaching Level E and Level H? Not the types of hazards or tough times we're faced with. How we see ourselves and the way the world works for us is what makes the difference. Some of us settle for recovery (Level E). Others work hard and make the choices and sacrifices to reach recovered (Level G). And a few manage to transcend our challenges and reach a new, higher level than we would have had we not been challenged (Level H).

Why is it so important to differentiate between *recovery* and *recovered*? As we saw in chapter three, what we say to ourselves about what's happened to us is key in healing from trauma and difficult experiences. How we frame what happened leads us to what to do next. Subtle differences in how we talk to ourselves, which are often dismissed as "just semantics," can significantly affect what we think and what we do. The way we talk to and about ourselves becomes a self-fulfilling prophecy. We'll be who we say we are. How we define ourselves defines our accomplishments, our expectations, our world.

Mary Jane was assigned a complex copying and collating project. Her supervisor explained what to do and how to do it.

Mary Jane started the project as her supervisor said. But she saw another way to do it.

So Mary Jane approached her supervisor, apologized for being codependent, said she didn't want to cause a problem and that the supervisor was right to want it done another way, but she wanted to ask if it was okay for her to suggest a way that would be easier for her, with her limitations, to do it.

When the supervisor asked which way she wanted to do it, Mary Jane outlined a more efficient and effective way of proceeding. Her supervisor readily agreed to do it Mary Jane's way.

Mary Jane labeled herself codependent and then used the label as a reference point for anything and everything she did. Because she saw herself as incapable and inept, anything she could offer would be dysfunctional and inappropriate. She even felt it was necessary to ask permission for giving a suggestion to do her job differently. She assumed anything she suggested wouldn't be as good as what her supervisor would say. For Mary Jane, her way automatically meant a worse way.

She had caught herself in a downward spiral of self-doubt, deprecation, and discounting. Her negative view of herself influenced what she did in every area of her life. She put herself into the excuse-me-for-living category and seriously undermined her own self-esteem. She no longer saw her suggestions as contributions but as crutches for her dysfunction. She'd lost her ability to accurately judge herself.

In her attempt to feel better about herself, to move beyond understandable and appropriate limitations, Mary Jane sabotaged herself. She'd chosen a way to get better that actually made her worse. She undermined herself by how she defined herself, what she said about herself, and the possibility of her doing anything that would get beyond her problems.

Mary Jane's sabotage included

- buying into being powerless over her limitations;
- labeling them disease rather than ineffective habits; and
- believing there was no cure for her "condition," that it would always control her behavior.

This approach to recovery keeps you stuck in the same old stuff. You claim your powerlessness over and over again. You keep telling yourself you're out of control, addicted, diseased. There's nothing you can do. You aren't powerful enough to make the changes you need to make. In group sessions, you're encouraged to repeat what and how you did that was so bad, what was awful about what you did or what was done to you. Your self-image increases in helplessness, and you need to look outside of yourself for relief. Inaction is excused: what do you expect from someone who is diseased? At the same time, you're encouraged to be more childlike and powerless.

There couldn't be a better way to keep someone stuck in feeling bad and hopeless and never feeling better.

The Lure of Recovery Groups

The palliative effects of recovery groups are well documented. People who go to them report they "feel better." They invoke what psychologist Robert Barry, in his book *A Theory of Almost Everything*, calls the Rumpelstiltskin effect: By naming a condition, the patient starts to feel better. This is as true for physical conditions as it is for psychological issues. We're relieved when we know we aren't alone, that others share our pain. Even if we do nothing to cure the pain, just knowing brings relief. But relief isn't cure.

Recovery groups specialize in palliative relief. You feel better even if your "condition" doesn't get better. Part of the relief comes from the support other group members provide. For the first time, you're listened to, attended to, and agreed with. This support may stand in stark contrast to the annoyance, frustration, and lack of patience that family members may be showing at this stage of the drama. Finally you have someone who really understands how hard things are for you.

The process of the groups, encouraging members to tell their stories, sing their somebody-done-somebody-wrong songs, provides a rosy glow. Many members get energized and encouraged as they repeat their stories and reexperience the feelings of their past woes.

The problem is, palliative effects are habit forming. They feel good. So you want to feel them again and again. You get to feel better without really having to do the hard work of making your life better, or facing up to the responsibility of what you have done and need to do.

Or as my scuba-diving friend explains: It's like peeing in your wet suit. Many divers relieve themselves as they jump into cold water. It immediately warms up the water in their wet suits and makes the beginning of the dive more comfortable. The only problem is that it quickly cools off and you get to spend the dive in your own waste.

The Price of Being in Recovery

One price of being in perpetual recovery is yourself.

Like Mary Jane, when you define yourself as "in recovery," you undermine your efficacy. You no longer see yourself as a person who can make things happen. Instead you become a person to whom things happen: a subtle but important distinction. You're not only not in control, but you can't take charge of those things you can change.

The other price is your life. Your recovery becomes the center of your life; your work, family, faith, and friends take the backseat. And because there is no cure, only working the program one day at a time, there is no end to it. The expectation is that you will continually focus your energy on your recovery.

> SueEllen was respected as one of the most creative and effective science teachers in the junior high where she taught. No one was surprised when she was selected for a special exchange program with science teachers in France, England, and Spain. Everyone was surprised when she declined the trip. She couldn't be gone for three weeks from her recovery group.

If SueEllen had been in the first few months of withdrawing from hard drugs or living in a homeless shelter for chronic alcoholics, it would be more understandable that she wanted to concentrate her efforts on staying clean and sober rather than traveling abroad. But she was neither of these. Her group was for women who had poor relationships with their mothers. She had a responsible job, which she discharged with skill and grace. She worked a part-time entrepreneurial business. She was successfully living many parts of her life. But she was sure she would fall apart without the twice-a-week recovery group. Her successes in her life were overshadowed by her definition of herself as helpless.

The Effectiveness of Recovery

So does "recovery" work? Do participants really get better, or just feel better?

There's no hard evidence that they really get better.

There is no outcome research that has demonstrated the effectiveness of recovery groups. Outcome research looks at how people with similar difficulties do in different types of intervention programs. They usually include in their studies people who haven't been in any program. The comparisons between the outcomes people experience form the base for making judgments about which program is most effective.

For the most part, the claims of success or effectiveness with recovery programs have come from anecdotal evidence, a report of an individual participant who has found the process helpful. Unfortunately anecdotes, no matter how compelling, aren't sufficient evidence to demonstrate treatment effects. For every story of how helpful a program has been, it is possible to find a story of someone who hasn't been helped. Rigorous controlled outcome research is the only way to assess which treatment procedures are effective. It hasn't been done.

From a theoretical perspective, it is unlikely recovery groups would stand up to rigorous examination. The process and treatment procedures are the opposite of what we do know is effective for making changes.

People change when they take charge of their difficult situations, not avoid them. People who get better, and feel better, are those who take steps to resolve the difficulties they are having. Taking charge means telling yourself the truth about what has happened. It doesn't mean adopting a Pollyanna attitude of "everything is just fine," but facing the "what is" about the situation you find yourself in. Taking charge means doing the important internal work on yourself: seeing yourself as deserving of a satisfying, full life; seeing yourself as capable and powerful enough to make decisions, to make changes that will support your goals; not denying what has happened to you, but detaching from it so your past no longer runs your life. Taking charge means taking action, doing what needs to be done to get what you want from your life.

Taking charge isn't easy, it doesn't always feel good, and it certainly isn't always fun. But it makes a huge difference in your life. Taking charge is doing the hard work to move beyond palliative, feel-good relief to build a solid, empowered life.

Exercises for Chapter 4

What kind of healing is possible with your challenge?

Is this a "cold," which will pass with little consequence?

Is this more like the measles, which will have no visible consequences, but you'll be strengthened by the experience?

Is this more like the cuts on my leg? You can see the scars, but your ability to live your life hasn't been affected?

Where are you on the recovered/recovery chart (figure 1)?

Where would you like to end up? Where do you fear you'll get stuck?

What will make the difference between being stuck and getting to where you'd like to be?

CHAPTER 5

THINKING ABOUT THINKING

Stephen Hawking may have lost his voice, but he did not lose his mind. Best known for his work with the characteristics of black holes, Hawking discovered that these puzzling pieces of space emit radiation that can be detected by special instrumentation. His best-known books include *A Brief History of Time* and *Black Holes and Baby Universes and Other Essays*. He regularly lectures to scientists and students all over the world. All this from a man who hasn't spoken since 1985. Struck with amyotrophic lateral sclerosis while still a student at Oxford University, Hawking's body has slowly stilled while his mind has continued to race. Thinking has become his life.

We tend to spend more time attending to our feelings than we do to what we think. But how we think and what we think about are more important than our feelings. How we think and what we think about shapes our lives. Thinking has more impact on your life than your feelings do, because how we think shapes how we feel. Thinking determines our actions, our values, and our morals. Thinking is the very cornerstone of our lives.

But we don't think about thinking.

In fact, given the recent glut of books on the market that have *dummy* in the title, including one I saw recently called *Parenting for Dummies*, there seems to be a reverse chic at work. It's in to be stupid. Otherwise competent people claim to be unable to program their VCRs.

Managers who make million-dollar decisions pale at the thought of computers on their desks. Romance novels and series mysteries with their predictable plots and characters are the most popular of the popular literature. Songs and everyday speech are peppered with grammatical errors. Retail clerks can't make change without looking at the display on the cash register. We don't seem to be bothered by our lack of skills or inability to perform basic math and English.

At the same time, there's an explosion in the number of people who are searching for meaning and quality in their lives. Church and synagogue attendance is on the rise. Spiritual books and self-help books top bestseller lists. Taking early retirement and making lifestyle changes has become *the* activity of middle-age boomers.

But there is no *Finding Purpose and Meaning in Your Life for Dummies* manual.

You know the pattern. If we tell ourselves we're dummies, pretty soon we start to believe we aren't all that smart. We start to believe we're not smart enough to do what needs to be done. Not true.

You can think through what is happening to you. You are smart enough to do the work. You just have to decide that you *will* do it. It takes time and energy. But you can do it.

Making changes, making choices, taking charge of life's challenges is hard work. You have to think about what you're doing. And think about what you think about. If you don't, you'll always be out of control. Because someone else will be thinking for you and telling you what to do.

Our first step in taking charge when we're not in control is to take a look at what we know about the challenges we face and how we know what we know.

Kelly got a call from the local police to come down to the station and bail out her daughter, Gail. Gail had been arrested for possession and being under the influence of "controlled substances" (read drugs).

Pretend for a moment you were the parent that got that call from the police about your child. What do you know about kids who are on drugs? What kind of kids are they? What kind of parents have kids on drugs? Who's in control when kids are on drugs? What would you do with your daughter? Yourself? (Go ahead, make some notes in the margins.)

Your notes reflect what you think about kids on drugs, parents of kids on drugs, and what should be done when a family faces that challenge.

Control isn't an option with kids on drugs. We can't force our ideas or actions on the kids. They won't stand for it. They fight back, and usually the drugs end up winning. But that doesn't mean we can't take charge. Taking charge means changing either what we do, what we think about what we do, or both.

To make these changes, we have to think about what we think about kids on drugs. We have to decide what options we have and what we're going to do about *our* kids. If we don't think it through and make decisions about what we want to do, then other people will run our lives. If we want to take charge of what we're thinking, we have to think about what we're thinking. It doesn't just happen. We have to put in the effort. If we don't know what we think about what concerns us, it's impossible to change our thoughts and make those changes stick. I know it's hard work, and for lots of people it's not a whole lot of fun, or it's even frightening.

But we have to do it.

Thinking about what we think about has three parts:

- what we already know, what we have either made up or assumed is true;
- what we are aware of, how conscious we are of what is happening around us; and
- how we learn new things.

Assumptions

Assumptions are where we begin when we start thinking about something. They're the base of what we think the world is all about. Our assumptions are what we know before we think about what we know. We usually don't even think about our assumptions. We just have them.

It's popular in some circles to use the word *assume* as a pejorative, a negative. An author or seminar leader will write:

ASS U ME

And then they will boldly proclaim that the predictable consequence of making assumptions is to make fools of both of us.

The problem with this approach is that we cannot *not make assumptions*. Our brains don't work that way. When we encounter new information or ideas or people, we try to make it fit with what we already know. We make judgments and inferences about information, ideas, and people. We try to figure it (them) out. We want to attach meaning to our experiences. And the tool we most commonly use is what we already know and understand. So we make assumptions about new experiences. And for the most part, we do it automatically. We don't say to ourselves, "I'll make an assumption now." We just do it.

> *One of the assumptions Kelly made was that good kids get pulled into drugs by their bad friends. Certainly her daughter was raised better than to get involved with drugs. It had to be her friend Polly who introduced Gail to drugs. Kelly was astounded to find out Polly's mother thought the same way she did. Except Polly's mom was sure Gail was the lowlife who seduced her well-raised child into the horror of drugs.*

The difficulty is not in making assumptions, but in keeping our assumptions secret from ourselves. We don't believe we are acting from our assumptions. We assume what we assume is the way the world "really" is. Kelly was sure her assumption about bad friends pulling a child into drugs was accurate. She was also sure her assumption about her own child being sweet, good, and pure was accurate. She knew they were true. There wasn't a doubt in her mind that Gail was an innocent led astray.

I'm not saying don't make assumptions. You'll always make assumptions. Just make them visible. Check them out to assess their accuracy. Check out your automatic thoughts as you start thinking (and reading) about how you think.

Our assumptions will both open up possibilities and options and close off options and possibilities. Our assumptions shape the solutions we choose and the decisions we make.

Consciousness

How do you know? How do you know you know? How do you know who you are? These seemingly simple little questions have held the attention of philosophers, theologians, kings, and fools for all of recorded history. The short answer for all these questions is, no one agrees. The long answer involves looking at how we frame the question—and the answer.

Asking questions about how we know implies that we know we know—at least some things. All animals can take in sensory information. And lots of animals can make evaluative judgments about the information they are receiving. But the human animal alone has the ability to make up information, to dream, to fantasize, to tell stories, to lie. It is this ability to know about knowing that is consciousness.

Knowing is a mental activity. The brain/mind reacts chemically and electrically to organize the sensations it receives to discern meaning from experiences. As a physical organ, the brain has traditionally been the object of study of the physiologist, the physician, and the anatomist. The mind—the reasoning, perceiving, conscious apparatus—has been the object of study by psychologists and other behavioral scientists. Typically only psychiatrists considered both the physical brain and the mental mind.

Now both physiological and behavioral scientists have started to use the phrase *brain/mind*, or *brain/mind paradigm*, to capture more clearly the notion that the brain and the mind are so intricately and closely connected that it is impossible to consider the responses and activity of one without also considering the other. These scientists focus on the study of consciousness or the variety of conscious states.

Consciousness is that part of the mind that evaluates, analyzes, synthesizes, and makes useful the information we sense. Without consciousness, we'd have to rely on sensation, instinct, or habit to guide our actions. With consciousness comes the ability to consider, decide, choose, and predict the consequences of our actions.

Self-concept is a primary filter of consciousness. The *self* is a main component of consciousness. We tend to incorporate new information and experiences into our consciousness, into our self, that fit what we already know and believe about who we are. Then our new experiences reinforce our concepts of self. Likewise, we block or discount informa-

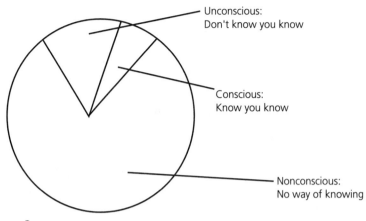

Unconscious:
Don't know you know

Conscious:
Know you know

Nonconscious:
No way of knowing

Figure 2.

tion or experiences that don't fit our self-concepts. Our *self* directs our attention. Our attention directs our consciousness.

But consciousness is only a portion of mental activity. We also seem to be able to solve problems, dream, "know," and understand without putting our attention to it. There are lots of theories to explain how we "think without being aware of thinking." One of the most commonly used theories includes both the unconscious and the nonconscious. These three—the conscious, unconscious, and nonconscious—make up the mind. As figure 2 suggests, consciousness is the smallest of the three. We're conscious of only a small part of what we know. The unconscious is larger, but the nonconscious is the largest of the three. Remember, we're talking about the mind here, not the brain. This is the knowing and thinking part of the brain/mind. You can't find a part of the brain, specific tissues, that corresponds to the conscious, unconscious, or nonconscious.

The conscious is what we're aware of. The unconscious and nonconscious both contain what we don't know. They are different in an important way. We don't know that we know what is in the unconscious, but we can have access to that information. With the nonconscious, we don't know that we don't know. It is very difficult, if not impossible, to access what is nonconscious. Nonetheless, our behaviors and feelings are influenced by both our unconscious and nonconscious beliefs.

The primary experience most of us have with our unconscious is through dreaming. While we are asleep, memories, concepts, and ideas are expressed in our dreams. Sigmund Freud characterized our dreams as a window to the unconscious.

The other window into the unconscious is through altered states of awareness. The most common of these is hypnosis or trancelike states. During a hypnotic trance, we can recall memories or experiences that we weren't aware of on a conscious level.

Some medications produce similar effects. Commonly called truth serums, they're the favorite tools villains use to extract information from captured good guys in spy movies. In real life they can be used to help psychotherapy patients access long-repressed or forgotten memories. Their effectiveness depends on the skill and the experience of the therapist, the cooperativeness of the patient, and the setting in which the medication is used.

Most people "know" what happens in hypnosis from watching stage hypnotists on television or in Las Vegas lounge shows; our knowledge of truth serums comes from mystery novels. In both of these settings the objective is to entertain, to play. The hypnotist makes outrageous suggestions and gives the subject permission to do things that they'd never consider when they were off the stage, like clucking like a chicken or taking off some of their clothes. In a therapeutic setting the objective is to ease the pain and suffering by illuminating what the subject has a hard time remembering about themselves and their experiences. The subject takes the lead, not the therapist.

Having said this, I know many of you who've just read this are still convinced therapists can make their patients believe anything while they are in a trance or medicated. If this is your response, think for a minute about how you know that what you know is true. What assumptions do you have about therapy? About hypnosis?

Even though we aren't aware of what's in our unconscious, our unconscious seems to influence our behavior. Traces of events and experiences register in our mind without our realizing it. We don't know we know.

Sometimes we'll repress the memory, unwittingly tuck it away into a dark, dusty corner of our minds. Repression occurs by automatic pilot. We don't decide to repress the experience. We just do. We forget it. Repression can be very thorough. If someone asks us, we may well say we don't remember the event or even remember the event took place. (Look to chapter six for a more thorough discussion of memory and forgetting.)

Suppression is more active than repression. We choose not to remember. We put it aside and don't think about it. Most of the time we suppress memories that are too painful or frightening. We don't want to remember. We work at forgetting. Sometimes the suppression is more trivial.

> *A friend talked me into going to the movie* Aliens. *She admired Sigourney Weaver and wanted to see the picture. I didn't know that much about the picture, so I went. Wrong thing for me to do. The type of terror and grisly images in that film usually gives me nightmares for weeks. I had to work on suppressing the images so I wouldn't have bad dreams. I didn't want to remember them. I wanted them out of my mind. I'll probably dream about them tonight. I may not be able to put the images out of my mind.*

Nonconscious is different from both the conscious and the unconscious. Not only do you not know, but you don't know that you don't know. Consider what happens when you are asleep and not dreaming. When you wake up, you know you must have been asleep. But while you were sleeping, you are without awareness. You were nonconscious. There's no way of knowing what you don't know.

Nonconsciousness can also occur when you are awake. The difficulty with nonconscious is that you don't know you are nonconscious and have no way of knowing you are. You don't consider yourself *nonconscious*; you are just who and what you are. Nonconsciousness is not denial. It's not knowing, and having no way of knowing.

Sometimes nonconsciousness is referred to as a blind spot, but it is more of a nonspot. People with the eye condition that results in physical blind spots, those who've lost a part of their visual field, are very aware of the "black hole" in front of them. They can see part of what is in front of them, but also see a dark hole. By moving their eyes or their heads, the spot without vision seems to move around, also. But we aren't aware of our psychological blind spots. They don't move as we change our perspective. They're totally nonconscious. We don't know we have psychological blind spots.

The most common experience of being nonconscious while awake is an unexamined worldview. Worldview is the organized explanation we all develop to explain why the world is the way it is. Most of the time we don't even know that we are coming from our own worldview. What we think, feel, and perceive is just the way our world, the whole world, is.

> *Shortly after Desert Storm, we had the opportunity to host a group of young marines in our home. Over beer and barbecued steaks, the young men started telling stories of how it was "over there." For the most part, these young men, still in their late teens and early twenties, had never left home before joining the service. Saudi Arabia was as different from home as anywhere on earth could get. When I asked what surprised them the most, they told of how they were caught off guard by the customs and mores of the people they were visiting.*
>
> *Except for one young man. Finally he asked, "You have a son, right?" When I assured him I was a mom, he asked if he could tell me something that was really gross. He was just bursting to talk about something that was bothering him. He took a big swig of his beer and whispered, "We had to watch our prisoners all the time, no matter what they were doing. We had to."*
>
> *"What did they do that surprised you most?" I asked.*
>
> *"They go to the bathroom funny. They kneel, even when they're urinating!"*

Talk about a mom issue! Talk about a nonconscious perspective. Other than behind the trees on the playground, or in the privacy of a physician's office, most of us never talk about elimination, or the varieties of elimination practices around the world. This young man and his buddies (this was too good a conversation to keep private) were astounded as the two moms in the group explained and described the varieties of bathrooms, toilets, and toileting practices people use. It had never occurred to these young men that not everyone in the world eliminated like their mothers had taught them to do. After all, that was the right way. Their moms told them it was.

It was a clear case of nonconsciousness. And as with most confrontations about how we nonconsciously order our thoughts and the world, when we find something that doesn't fit, we're jolted into awareness.

Like a fish that doesn't know it is wet, we don't realize we're order-ing the world to fit us. If a fish doesn't have a concept of dryness, how can it call its world wet? The fish's world is just what it is. And for each of us, our world is just the way the world is.

All three states of consciousness affect what we do and believe and how effectively we deal with others. For the most part, we aren't aware of how they do. When we bring what we know into awareness, make our memories, ideas, and the structures that guide our thoughts, be-liefs, and values conscious, we can use them to purposely guide our actions.

But awareness is only the first step. The next step is understanding, deriving the meaning from our memories, ideas, and why we are the way we are, and remembering and expressing the feelings associated with early memories and experiences, both traumatic and nurturing. Some recovery groups encourage members to unearth early traumatic memories and then to express them, to reexperience the feelings asso-ciated with the memories.

If the work stops here, uncovering trauma results in additional pain and problems rather than healing. Just feeling hurt doesn't help. We need to get beyond being stuck in the pain of our pasts. Being stuck just reinforces a victim mentality. This doesn't mean denying or discounting what has happened to you. What it does mean is going be-yond the pain of what has happened to integrate your past into who and what you are in the present. The aim is to achieve a detachment from the early experience so it can be a part of your past rather than driving your present feelings, actions, and decisions.

Bringing our unconscious and nonconscious into awareness and then integrating them into our current reality, beliefs, values, knowl-edge, and emotions allows us to recast the impact of previous experi-ences on our current life activities.

Going beyond Awareness to Knowing

Knowing becomes the primary tool for initiating and securing change.

But most of us don't think a lot about what we know or how we know it. We don't think about thinking. By the time we're adults, the patterns of learning and thinking we use are habits. We may have been taught "critical-thinking skills" in school or taken a seminar on the job.

Or we may have just figured out how to learn on our own. Or we may have decided our thinking and learning days are over. We finished school—be it high school, technical school, college, or grad school. And we don't have to be a learner again.

Until we want to change. Because change is not possible without thinking, thinking about thinking, and learning new skills, information, and perspectives.

Making changes challenges us to become philosophers. We need to reexamine what we know and how we know it: epistemology. Change challenges us to rethink how we reason and make decisions: logic. And change challenges us to review who we are and how we have invented ourselves: ontology.

These are ancient topics. They frame the exercises that allow us to bring meaning into our lives.

Especially when we are challenged by events and people we can't control.

Epistemology

Epistemology is the study of knowing what you know and how you know it. It starts to address questions like, What's true? How do you discover or apprehend that which you say you know? What tools and techniques do you use to get information? What is your standard of truth? How do you develop those standards? Are they moral or legal standards? How do you know? It can be confusing or fun, depending on how you look at it.

Knowing is both purposeful and unintentional. What we know comes from a combination of what we notice; what we're taught in school, by our parents, and by religious and civic organizations; what we learn on our own; what we remember; and of course, how we think and feel about all of the above.

What we notice is determined in large part by what we already know, what we want to know, what we think is important or intriguing, and what we focus on.

For a quick exercise in noticing, look up from this book for a few moments and carefully scan your surroundings. Look for all the things you see that are red. Do this now. . . . Have you done it? Did you follow the directions? Now make a list in the margin of all the things you saw that were blue.

If you're like most people, your list is fairly short. When you focus on seeing red things, you miss the blue things. Even if the items are numerous, distinctive, or important, we can miss them if we're focusing intently on something else.

We notice things that are important to us, that fit with what we want, have, or think the world should be. Recently I got a new car that is a silver-gray four-door sedan. I didn't choose it for the color, or even the model. I wanted a four-door sedan that got good gas mileage and had a good stereo. When I went to my local car dealership, this was the one on the lot. Now here is the strange part. I hadn't noticed too many gray four-door sedans before I bought the car. Now I see them everywhere. I filter the cars I see through a gray, four-door sedan filter.

What we know and what we're looking for filters what we see, how we see it, and how we learn.

Worldview

Our worldviews are one of our most important focusing filters. We can miss a lot, even if we are looking right at it, when our worldviews are filtering what we see and understand. Just like the fish who is always wet, we are always looking at our lives with our own filters.

Worldview also filters what we're taught and what we learn. The lessons offered in school, the lessons our parents, churches, mosques, governments, and youth organizations provide are designed to instill a worldview consistent with the culture we live in. This is what made the toileting habits of their prisoners such a source of wonder and surprise for the young soldiers. What they saw didn't fit with what they knew the world should be.

For the most part, our parents' lessons reflect their views of what good parenting is about. They aren't purposely giving us a worldview. They want to do right by their children.

While in graduate school in Chicago, I became friends with William, a fellow student whose five-year-old son was a proficient reader. William and his wife were teachers; each was working on an advanced degree. They had lots of books, both for themselves and for their son, in their home library. William told me how they thought they were doing a much better job of parenting than their neighbors who also had a five-year-old.

The neighbor boy had no interest in reading or books, was aggressive and loud on the playground, and didn't easily share his toys with the other children. My friend said they were smugly proud of their own parenting until the day they took their son skating at a neighborhood ice pond. As he struggled to hold up his son, William watched the other boy and his father put on a virtuoso display of skating. Then he recognized the other father as a player on Chicago's professional ice hockey team.

Each family taught their child what was important. They didn't decide what was best for their kids. They knew what was best.

As we learn early on what people like us value, believe, do, and don't do, we also learn that our way is the best way, the way things should be. And then we feel threatened, afraid, or dismissive of people who do things differently.

What makes our worldview so potent is both that it is pervasive—it impacts every facet of our belief structures and behavior, shaping how and what we learn, how we feel about ourselves, and what we remember and forget—and that it is for the most part nonconscious—we aren't aware ours is a learned view, or that others have different but equally valid views.

Any introductory anthropology text provides examples of different worldviews, most of which, to our Western eyes, are seen as charming, amusing, or outrageous. We read of Southern Hemisphere aboriginals who step off the end of a moving truck, not understanding that they are going as fast as the truck, and who are surprised when they hurt themselves. Or others, having always lived in the dense forest, who marvel that the world can shrink and get smaller when they first see the parallax of open land.

Or if we are fortunate, we will read of the Nacirema, a fascinating Northern Hemisphere people who have a highly evolved culture centering on home shrines and personal religious rites. Almost every dwelling has at least one shrine (the more prosperous members have more than one) that is characterized by ritual cleansing basins, special lights, and reflective glass. Each member of the group spends time alone in the shrine at least twice a day, with private ritual cleansing, self-examination, and careful grooming rites. Children are taught at a very early age how to perform their own rituals. At special times, the most intimate family members may share rituals, but it is very unusual. Certainly those young marines, like young people all over the United States, were taught those rituals.

Like the people who think the world shrinks, or those who worship at home shrines daily, your worldview structures how you live your life. While you share some ideas, values, and beliefs with your larger cultural group, you will also personalize your worldview. It shapes how you know what you know. And how you decide what is true and what isn't. Every day your worldview impacts your life as you make trivial and major judgments about new information, available choices, and the right thing to do. What music you listen to, the friends you have, people who you have conflicts with are all shaped by your worldview.

Phenomenological or Absolute?

We shape our worldviews phenomenologically or absolutely. The phenomenological approach is "scientific." We gather data and empirical evidence to find out what's true. You investigate a situation much as an objective scientist would and then draw your conclusions.

The absolute approach relies on "concepts and absolutes." Whatever evidence you gather, whatever data you collect is so imperfect and changeable as to be marginally useful. You need to rely on abstract absolutes that are implied by evidence, but are really of a much higher value.

For example, every circle, no matter how well drawn or conceived, is not as perfect as the idea of a circle. So we can never really know "circle," only the poor approximation of circle that we see or draw.

The abstract ideas we should depend on are derived from reason and careful analysis, not necessarily from experience. And when evidence conflicts with the abstraction, it's the abstraction that is accepted, not the evidence.

As you can see, these two approaches represent dramatically different ways of "knowing." Understanding the difference between them directly affects how we organize our everyday lives.

Do we rely on evidence we personally gather to know what is true, or do we rely on experts to tell us what is true? Neither way is perfect, nor even one better than the other. Both pose serious issues to work through.

We'll look at two problems that reflect the difficulties each approach to "truth" has. Assessing the truth of conventional wisdom highlights the issues with a phenomenological approach. The problem of the planets' paths will show the challenges with taking an absolute perspective.

Conventional Wisdom

Conventional wisdom, or what the "person on the street" knows or believes to be true, is often neither true nor wise.

One error of thinking occurs when a small sample of behavior, or a personal experience, is taken as the norm and then a generalization is drawn. So a person thinks what has happened to him is what always happens. Or more commonly, they'll hear about what happened to "poor old Joe" and generalize to every situation of this type. In these examples, conventional wisdom reflects a logical error of inference.

Typically conventional wisdom acts to support the power status quo or what would be best for the mainstream worldview. It's not unusual to hear conventional wisdom phrased to support the position of those in charge, with little regard for checking out what is really true.

One curious piece of conventional wisdom I dealt with when writing *Sleeping with a Stranger* was the belief that women claimed their husbands were molesters so they could get custody of the children during custody and divorce proceedings. Yet when we looked at the research, it was evident that accusations of molesting are seldom made, and the vast majority of the few claims made are found to be true. The fear of unfounded charges and the negativity of the charges themselves supported the conventional wisdom: charges are often made, and whenever they are made, there is no basis. The evidence cited in support of this conventional wisdom is based on anecdote, and those making the argument do not seem to be interested in reviewing studies that are available or other evidence that can refute the view.

While there is no similar conventional wisdom suggesting mothers are accused of molesting so dads can get custody, there is a belief that the mother always knows about the abuse and supports, encourages, or allows it. It seems to be more widely believed by women and former victims of abuse than by the abusers. Typically the abusers themselves and their victims will admit they worked hard at keeping the abuse secret. Nonetheless, most victims express far more anger toward their mothers, claiming their mothers really did know, than they do toward their abusing fathers. Preliminary reports seem to point to the victims wanting their mothers to know. They seem to prefer believing an adult knew but didn't act to protect them, than the possibility of her not knowing, which means there was no possibility of protection.

The issue with other women is different. Here the conventional wisdom—she had to know—acts as protection for them. They need the spouses of abusers to know, because then they don't have to worry about what's happening in their own homes that they don't know about. Yet independent studies demonstrate most women do not know when one of their children is being molested by a family member or friend.

Here again, research disproves conventional wisdom.

Conventional wisdom also supports less noxious but as outrageously false phenomena such as the alligators in the sewers of New York City and the attacks on solitary couples in lovers' lanes. And of course, my favorite from junior high: Everyone knows, I was told, that the meat loaf they serve in the school cafeteria is really canned dog food. Didn't you hear this at your school, too?

Paths of the Planets

The classic "problem of planets" points up the problem of relying on experts for the answers. The question about the nature of the planets had dogged philosophers and astronomers since ancient times.

Aristotle used the movement of the stars, the paths they took through the heavens, to support his position that the earth was the obvious center of the universe. It's easy to see the stars revolving around the earth. Today we use time-lapse photography to confirm the regular movement of the stars across the sky.

Except there was this problem with the planets. They didn't move correctly. They wandered around. They didn't have the regular paths that the stars did. The question arose: How could they wander independently of the earth if the earth was the center of the universe?

The problem became a theological as well as a philosophical issue. The early Christian Church took the position that the earth was the center of the universe and all the heavenly bodies revolved around it. Belief in this principle became an article of faith. You had to hold the belief to be a member of the Church. They reasoned God had designed the universe for man. The earth was the center of the universe. If you were a good Christian, you believed.

Except there was that problem of the planets.

Over the years many astronomers jumped through mathematical and theoretical hoops to explain how the planets really were revolving around the earth, even though it didn't look like they were. When observers suggested other explanations, they were given the choice of standing down from their explanations or being excommunicated and branded as heretics.

Most of them, like Galileo, recanted. The pressure was too great. They turned away from their observations and acknowledged the "truth" of the ancient experts and their faith. They discounted what they "saw" in favor of what they "knew." As we'll see, this is a more common occurrence than most of us realize.

Charles Darwin faced the same problem when he proposed his theory of evolution in *The Origin of Species*. Even his wife was concerned over the salvation of his soul for proposing the heretical notion of evolution. Many of the noted scientists of his day disavowed his theories, prompting one supporter to remind him that, for the most part, critics die rather than be convinced. It is only with the next generation that new theories and knowledge are embraced and accepted.

Most experts are loath to change their minds, their theories, or their public positions. Not only is there need for an internal consistency, but the threat of criticism from outsiders makes changing your mind very difficult.

One constituent reproached the late Senator Everett Dirksen when he changed his vote on a key issue, saying she was disappointed because she thought he was a man of principle. He assured her he was, and went on to say one of his principles was to remain flexible. Most of us don't have Dirksen's fortitude in the face of criticism.

Learning

What we know is built on what we have learned. Learning implies schools and classrooms, but educators and employers are starting to understand that the vast majority of what people know is learned outside of, or after they are finished with, their formal schooling. But for every dollar spent on schooling children, less than one cent is spent on adult education. And when money is spent on adult education, the adults with the most skills and education are getting the most new education. For most adults, learning more and keeping up has become the responsibility of the individual, not the state or the employer. And what a responsibility it has become.

The biggest question is what to learn, what to pay attention to.

Technology can bring us more data than we will ever be able to digest, understand, and use. In some fields it is impossible to keep up with the new information that is available. In others the technology itself is helping workers know what they need to know.

General Motors builds into each new car a computer chip that will run diagnostics on the operating systems and then teach the mechanics how to repair parts and systems.

Artificial intelligence systems are attempting to capture the stored knowledge and experience of employees who are retiring so that new workers can learn from old masters who are no longer available.

Computer-aided instruction can produce 30 percent more learning in 40 percent less time at 30 percent less cost than conventional classroom instruction.

We need a variety of tools, methods, and techniques to both learn and teach the skills that are needed in today's world. We also need to take advantage of the wide varieties of natural talents and abilities that people can use to make significant contributions. For too long we've relied on tapping only the verbal/linguistic or logical/mathematical skills. The wide range of physical/kinesthetic, musical/rhythmic, and visual/spatial skills are addressed only as adjuncts to the more important "academic" subjects.

But just as hardware and software alone account for only a small portion of the potential gains in productivity from automation, content-oriented skills and talents account for only a portion of the potential for gains in productivity through better interpersonal and intrapersonal management.

Changes in organizational management and human resources account for 80 percent of productivity gains. People, and how they work, are still the most important factors in productivity equations.

So sociotechnical systems address how humans use tools rather than being used by them. Human-factors engineering designs technology to be user friendly. High-performance work teams flatten hierarchies and concentrate on collaboration across professional expertise to decrease development and production time. All these interpersonal processes support the new order of getting more done with less.

All workers are challenged to contribute, empowered to bring their expertise and knowledge tools to the project. To do this effectively means tapping into intrapersonal skill development: to know how to think clearly, how to learn new concepts and skills, and how to use more of what you know to get more of what you want in the tasks you are charged with accomplishing on the job.

Unfortunately most of us are lazy thinkers when it comes to learning, reasoning, solving problems, and making decisions. We rely on what we already know, have a hard time analyzing new information or processes, look first at solutions we have already used when faced with new problems, and discount data or information that doesn't fit with our past experiences.

As we learn new skills and strategies, we capsulize them, not transferring them from the training room to our work site. Or we don't use what we learn at home at work, or what we learn at work at home.

Most of the nurses at the first session of an assertiveness class were surprised to see Lenore. A very competent floor supervisory nurse, she had the reputation of being able to make medical residents cry when she pointed out their skills or knowledge were lacking. None of the other participants saw her as in need of assertiveness skills. As each student told why she was in the class, however, Lenore told of how she could not make her teenage sons allow her to sit in her own easy chair in front of the television. If she got up out of the chair to use the bathroom or make snacks, one of the boys would claim the chair and not get up. She would have to sit on the floor for the rest of the evening.

At work, Lenore could easily use her assertiveness skills. At home, she acted as if she didn't know how to be assertive. She wasn't able to transfer her skills from one setting to another. The skills were the same, but she didn't recognize the need for these skills or didn't think they were appropriate to use at home.

Interpersonal skills and intrapersonal skills are process skills. What we know works at home will work at work. The skills we use to get a child to clean up his room are the same skills we use to motivate volunteers at our service clubs, our employees in stretching to meet a deadline, and our bosses to negotiate a raise. The skills we use at work getting grown men to pay attention and learn what to do will work on teenage sons at home. Lenore was astounded to realize she already knew what we were teaching in the class. She just didn't know she could use those techniques with her kids.

How we think and what we think about shapes not only our world, but our beliefs about ourselves. Not knowing about the challenges we face prevents us from effectively choosing how to deal with them. If we don't know, we can't change either our minds or our behaviors. By understanding how we think the way we do, we can see what and how we need to think about to make changes that will help us take charge of situations, events, and others when we aren't in control.

Exercises for Chapter 5

WHAT DO YOU KNOW AND HOW DO YOU KNOW IT?

What do you know about the challenges you are facing?

Who else is facing this same challenge? Are they approaching it in the same way or differently than you are?

What do they know that you don't?

CHECK OUT THE CONVENTIONAL WISDOM

What is the conventional wisdom about your challenge?

How does this fit your personal experience?

CHECK OUT YOUR ASSUMPTIONS

What are your assumptions about people who face your challenge?

How are your assumptions affecting how you feel about yourself? About the others who are involved?

CHECK OUT YOUR WORLDVIEW

What have you learned from your parents about the way the world should be?

How have your work/career choices been influenced by the work your parents did?

What do you think about other cultures, races, ethnic groups?

What do you think about the challenges you face?

What have you taught your children about the way the world should be?

Is it the same or different from what your parents taught you?

How did you decide what you would teach your children?

Is this the way your children think, believe, or act now? How come?

CHAPTER 6

TRUST YOUR MEMORIES . . . BUT CHECK THEM OUT!

I overheard a couple of women talking about a quilt displayed at an exhibit. One had asked the other the name of the design. Her friend replied that it was fifty-forty or something like that. Without realizing I was speaking, I said out loud, "Fifty-four forty or fight." They both looked at me, and we all three started laughing. I had to tell them that it was a fragment of something that was probably laid down during my fifth-grade history class. They both agreed I was right, and then we all agreed we had no idea what the phrase "Fifty-four forty or fight" meant.

It was a trivial experience, but one that shows how we remember, forget, and sometimes remember again everyday events.

How we remember and retrieve our memories is both complex and mysterious. Remembering can be filled with detours, side trips, false starts, and intense feelings and can change in real time. And this is just for regular everyday memories. Memory of trauma is a whole different story. There are significant differences in how we remember and forget everyday experiences and how we remember and forget traumatic events. Neither kind of memory is as straightforward as we sometimes treat them.

But with both "normal" events and trauma events, there are lots of things we remember, and know, without realizing we know them. We don't know we know. Then an event or experience will trigger a memory. It seems to pop out of nowhere. That's what happened to me at the quilt show.

How did I "know" "Fifty-four forty or fight"? At the time I had no idea of what it referred to. Not knowing really bugged me. I had to figure it out.

While I was still at the quilt show, I started reconstructing what the slogan could or should be about from other "facts" I could remember. American history just "felt right." So it must be right. Sounded like a longitude or latitude. I reminded myself that I always confuse them. So I didn't bother trying to figure out which it was. (Longitude and latitude are one of my ongoing confusions. I can never remember which is which. So I don't try. I can always look at a map and figure out what place it must be, I tell myself. In this case, if I had bothered to learn which was which it would have been a big help in figuring out what the slogan meant.)

I knew the slogan wasn't recent. The quilt was included in the part of the show that had historical patterns. I figured it had to be sometime during the 1800s, when quilt patterns were often named for current political or cultural happenings. From what I knew about quilt patterns, I reasoned "Fifty-four forty or fight" must have referred to something from the last century, not this one.

Before I started home, I had American history, probably sometime in the 1800s, and had to do with a place.

Now I started guessing what it must be from what I could remember about American history. (American history was not my best or favorite subject.) I decided it had to have something to do with a battle, or a war, or one of those ongoing skirmishes that were common in the 1800s. A battle cry. That's it! It was a battle cry! I was grasping for some kind of label or context that would bring meaning to the phrase. *I was as ready to accept an inaccurate meaning as an accurate one.* My desire to find meaning was stronger than the need for accuracy. And it gave me a next step to check out, a next path to take in my research. All I needed was an event to connect to the place.

The next steps I took are really embarrassing to admit. I started rambling around in my research. So I tried a couple of books of quotations. No luck. Then I tried a chronicle of American wars. No luck there either. Then I looked in an old book on American history. Sure enough, there it was. One reference on one page.

As I read through the paragraphs, it was as if I was getting this information for the first time. I still have no memory of ever knowing about the incident, the concept, or even spending that much time on this part of American history. I am sure I must have, no question here. Even though I didn't particularly like history, I did study so I could get good grades. I just have no conscious memory of studying this event. And I am still not sure of the place. The map didn't extend far enough north to include the longitude (or is it latitude?) fifty-four forty.

If I had just looked in my good, big dictionary, I could have quickly found what and where "Fifty-four forty or fight" referred to. It was not the rallying cry of a battle, but a political slogan during the determination of the border between the United States and Great Britain in the area of what is now the state of Washington. Even as I write this, I can't remember ever studying it in school, just reading it in the old history book I found on the shelf.

Memory and Forgetting

Remembering a century-old political slogan is not a significant memory exercise. But the process of remembering it, and reconstructing it, shows how we remember typical, everyday events in our long-term memory.

We don't remember most of what we learned in school, nor most of what we've done. We forget most of our lessons—unless, of course, we are now history teachers, or our favorite pastime is historical reenactments. And we forget most of what we have done.

Memory isn't automatic. Forgetting is. We forget without even trying. We don't choose to forget, but choose to remember. We have to work at remembering effectively and accurately.

Short-Term Memory

We have three types of memory, depending on the time involved and the effort we put into remembering. Short-term memory, covering a few minutes or a few days, fades very fast. We recite a phone number over and over as we walk from one room to the next so we won't forget it when we are dialing. And sometimes we do forget it. Especially if we are distracted along the way. We cram for tomorrow's test, then forget most of what we've "learned" by the final exam at the end of the year.

We remember the details of a work project while we are busy with it. But then we forget as we go on to the next project. Short-term memory is short. If we don't work at remembering, we quickly forget.

Intermediate Memory

Intermediate memory lasts for a few days, or even a few weeks. We review the events and experiences we have and then make conscious and unconscious decisions about remembering. I surely had remembered "Fifty-four forty or fight" for the test, maybe even for the final. And then it faded. Even subjects that we study hard in school, that we consciously and intentionally decide to learn and remember, will fade when they are not used consistently. Think about the computer classes you have taken, or hobbies, work procedures, or any new topic or skill you've learned recently. If you don't use what you learn, it quickly fades from memory.

Long-Term Memory

Very few of our experiences make it to long-term memory, especially specific, normal, everyday events. Normality is hard to remember. We more easily remember events and experiences that are unusual or not typical of our daily lives.

Most adults over fifty can remember the day President John Kennedy was shot. It was such an unusual and unexpected event that it was seared into our memories. Many of us remember where we were and what we were doing. I can still see the position of the furniture in my dorm room that day. I know where the radio was and what I was doing— putting clean sheets on my bed. I remember these things not because the room was distinctive or changing the bed was unusual, but because that's where I was when I heard the report on the radio that he'd been shot.

When we want to remember a normal day or typical pattern or behavior, we usually reconstruct, or guess what we think happened. Our reconstructions are biased by what we already "know to be true," and the thoughts, feelings, and beliefs we have about that knowledge and about ourselves. We piece together what we "know" always happened, or what we tell ourselves must have happened. We discard or discount what doesn't fit about the situation we're remembering. Then we swear our reconstruction is the absolute truth.

Reconstruction from Faulty Facts

Trying to remember the source for the quilt pattern was challenged by two major lazy-thinking habits I have. My bad habits prevented me from remembering at all and/or distorted the memories I did have.

My first bad habit was *not knowing*, or caring to know, the difference between longitude and latitude. If I'd kept these two straight, I'd have known that the location described by these numbers was nowhere near the Civil War.

When I decided "Fifty-four forty or fight" referred to an 1800s battle cry, I was sure it had to be connected to the Civil War. Here's where my *lazy thinking* about history kicked in. Not being much of a history student, I anchor a century with one big event, often a war. For me, U.S. history goes directly from the Pilgrims to the Revolutionary War to the Civil War to WWII—with little happening in between. As much of a bear as I am that we all should know the "basic facts," I have to admit that I don't do what I think people should do. Sure enough, it gets us in trouble when we don't know.

Once I had decided on "battle cry of the Civil War," I knew which direction to head with my research. My next steps were determined by what *I "knew was right," even though what I knew was all wrong.*

The other error I made was *not looking to the most general research tool first.* I should have looked in a dictionary, almanac, atlas, or encyclopedia. Any of them would have given me the answer very quickly. Instead I started browsing through the books I found on the shelf. All of which makes a good case for having basic reference books in our home libraries.

Errors of faulty facts come from not having the basic learning tools: how to read, write, spell, compute. Or they can come from not having the basic facts we were all supposed to learn in school: vocabulary, history, geography, science. When we don't know the basics, we're stopped by our ignorance. We more easily remember concepts that are familiar to us. When we know more, we remember more easily and more accurately.

Reconstructions Shaped by Feelings

Memory also depends on feelings and the emotional meanings of our experiences. We notice the events or items about which we feel strongly or that have meaning for us. We quickly forget events that aren't important or don't fit what we already believe to be true about who we are.

> *When I was a young adult, my mom invited me to lunch one day. She was obviously uncomfortable about something; her nervous laughter told me she planned some big agenda. Finally after ordering and receiving our food, she started to apologize for kicking my brother when he was two and I was fifteen.*
>
> *I had no idea of what she was talking about and told her so.*
>
> *She explained that one afternoon I came into the kitchen while she was cooking pasta. My brother was playing with the pots and pans on the floor near the stove. Not wanting to risk spilling the boiling water on him, she pushed him out of the way with her foot. In my adolescent righteousness, I scooped him up, berated her for abusing my precious baby brother, and took him to my bedroom and wouldn't bring him out.*

I had/have no memory of the event. Her memories of the incident had haunted her for years. We had totally different memories of the same incident.

While I didn't remember grabbing my brother and taking him off, I can reconstruct what probably happened. I do remember her cooking dinner—especially making pasta. With eight kids, we ate lots of pasta. That was a common event.

I can "see" my brother playing with pans on the floor. Again, it was something he loved to do and did often. I can even imagine her using her foot to scoot him out of harm's way. That part of the story I have no trouble with.

It's the rest of the story that's a blank. When I was in high school, I was "such a good kid." I studied hard, wasn't very social, baby-sat for my younger brothers and sisters, and helped around the house. Even the idea of mouthing off, being "bad," was so outside my view of myself, I didn't remember the incident. Such a good girl like me doing such an outrageous thing? No way. I have no memory of what I have no doubt really happened. It's not unusual to forget those incidents that don't conform to our views of ourselves. They're too uncomfortable to remember.

Story-Based Memory

Incidents make their way into our long-term memories through the stories we tell ourselves and others about what's happened to us. Our stories capture the gist, or theme, of the incident. Each time we tell the story, we fill in and expand on the details, both from the event itself and from the details we already remember about these same kinds of experiences. Both the gist and the details are essential parts of our stories.

We build our stories on gist and details because we remember details in a series of bits, or small chunks of memory. The details may be parts of lots of different individual events. We use these bits to build a variety of patterns. This lets us learn a new skill or problem-solving approach.

When I was a little girl, I'd follow my father around the house, handing him tools while he did small maintenance jobs. He'd let me use a screwdriver, a hammer, and even the saw if I was really careful. I never did a whole job, but I did learn how to use the tools and watched him as he approached each new chore. As an adult, I realized my dad had taught me how to be "handy." I could take his approach to household chores and my knowledge of tools and fix things I had never fixed before. I didn't know the whole job, but I knew enough of the parts to figure out how to do what needed to be done.

Remembering in bits, or parts, lets us transfer learning. We remember a bit of information in one context and then use it in another. It also means we can remember doing something, and not remember where or when we did it.

Remembering in bits also allows for the reconstruction of events that we don't remember. I don't remember the particular day my mom was talking about, but I do have lots of bits of memory about what the house looked like, what she looked like cooking pasta, and how my brother played. I also remember the bit about how important my baby brother was to me and how I would do anything for him. So I can even include how I would mouth off to my mom to protect my brother, although I don't specifically remember doing it. Knowing what happened in general lets me reconstruct a specific event. By remembering bits that happened in one context, I can transfer them to another that I don't remember.

While the bits of memory appear in our long-term memories as the details, remembering a specific event or situation is more dependent upon capturing the gist or the theme of our experience. We capture the gist by telling others, or ourselves, about the event, by talking about the event. Our initial telling captures the gist of the event for the next telling. If we don't tell the story soon enough or often enough after an event, the story doesn't come together. We remember where we were and how we felt when Kennedy died because we talked a lot about it when it happened and have told the story so many times since then.

If we don't tell the story, we don't file the event in our long-term memory. Each time we tell the story, we include details of the event from our previous tellings of the story, what we know should have happened, usually happens, or could have happened. We end up remembering not the event itself, but what we tell ourselves about the event. The event is long since forgotten. The story of the event lives on in our memory.

In his wonderfully colorful book about memory, *The Connoisseur's Guide to the Mind,* Roger Schank describes an elaborate gourmet dinner he planned for a group of friends. Schank could remember each morsel, each course, and the subtle blend of individual herbs and spices that made each dish a masterpiece. He was astounded that not only could his friends not remember the wonderful food a short time later, but some had even forgotten it was a special dinner.

For Schank, the dinner was a major event in his hobby of gourmet dining. For his friends, the event was either a time for being with people they enjoyed, a time for eating weird food, or a nonevent.

Our memories are personal. They form the structure and the drama of our lives, our personal histories. We see things first and foremost from our own points of view. We each take the role of lead player in the drama of our memories. Our memories are autobiographical. They focus on what's important to us.

Our stories fit what we think of ourselves and the other players in our lives. They reflect our philosophies of life. Our stories represent who we would like to think that we are, not necessarily what we "really are." We protect our identity and integrity in our own stories. We remember what will be enhancing, what we want to remember about ourselves, and don't remember what is not enhancing or appealing. So I didn't remember being mouthy. It just wasn't like me!

We shape our memories to support who we want to be, who we think we are, and to protect us from ourselves. And this is just with everyday "normal" events. It is not uncommon for two people to have totally different memories of the same event, or like my mom and me, for one person to remember and another not. Even if the event is remarkable.

> *Anna was delighted to see a former boyfriend at her twentieth high school reunion. She had kept her friends laughing for years with the stories she would tell about what the two of them had done when they were dating. Everyone's favorite story was about the time they were on a country road, late one night, necking in the backseat of his car. Because it was a warm summer night, the car windows were open. Suddenly a very large cow stuck her head into the backseat, scaring the two teens by mooing loudly.*
>
> *When Anna and her teenage heartthrob, now a staid middle-aged man, danced at their reunion, she mentioned the cow incident. He didn't remember it. Shocked, Anna started talking of different incidents she had remembered well. Later she said to me, "It was so disheartening. It was like he and I had a completely different relationship. It was so important to me, but he didn't even remember. I wonder if he was the same guy I dated!"*

We don't intentionally or maliciously distort our memories, but distortion nonetheless creeps in. Often details, the color of a car, the look on a person's face, details of a room are clearly remembered, while the central theme or gist of the event can shift as the story is retold. The more we tell of our experiences, the more likely we are to remember the story about the event rather than the event itself.

Memory of Trauma

In some ways memory of trauma is very similar to memory of everyday events, and in other ways it is very different. Some of the similarities and differences are easily recognized, while others are more subtle and need to be carefully examined and understood.

Getting clear on memory for trauma is critical when you are trying to take charge of situations you haven't been able to control. Only by understanding what has happened, and making decisions about what you are going to do about it, can you stop letting the past control your present and your future. Understanding and appreciating your memories of your past is essential for taking charge of your life.

The differences between our memories of traumatic events and our memories of normal events happen because

- we experience trauma differently from the way we experience everyday events;
- we remember trauma differently from the way we remember typical experiences;
- we tell our trauma stories differently than we tell stories of everyday experience, or we don't tell trauma stories at all; and
- the distortions that creep into trauma stories are different from the distortions that creep into daily life stories.

There's lots of disagreement on how and even if people can remember and/or forget trauma. Some people even doubt anyone can really forget traumas they experience, and then remember them at a later time. Others believe people can "remember" traumas that they didn't actually experience. To answer all these questions, we need to look at how memory of trauma is different from and similar to memory of everyday events.

The Experience of Trauma

It's hard to research memory of trauma, because we can't abuse or injure people just to find out how they'll react. So we must study people after the fact. In these studies, the researchers interview and evaluate people after horrific, frightening, or life-threatening experiences. They look both at those people who have been crushed by what has happened to them and at those who've been able to overcome their challenges. Unfortunately there's been ample opportunity to find people who have had such experiences.

Trauma research subjects have included war veterans, civilians caught in war zones, victims of natural disasters—floods, hurricanes, fires, and earthquakes—as well as people who have been the targets of "crimes against the person." Individual crimes—rape, assault, and abuse—as well as collective crimes—the Holocaust in Europe during World War II, the Armenian massacres by the Turks, or Pol Pot's reign of terror—have been included in memory-of-trauma studies. This research has investigated what has happened with adults, with children, and with the children of traumatized people. There is also a growing literature of studies on people who have been purported to be the perpetrators of trauma.

Two themes are evident from all this research: the terror of the experience and the reluctance of victims, perpetrators, and witnesses to know or deal with what's happened.

Both of these factors affect how we remember trauma and the accuracy of our memories.

The Altered State of Trauma

Trauma is not a normal state. The terror of the experience produces extreme alterations in the victim's arousal, attention, and perceptions. Scientists call this an alteration of consciousness. When we're being traumatized, we don't experience our world as we usually do. And that altered consciousness affects our memories of trauma.

Typically a victim's attention is narrowed and perceptions are altered. Remarkably, many people report no pain during trauma, even when they are gravely injured. Victims of car accidents or war wounds often report not feeling pain they knew should accompany their wounds. It's not unusual for people to report they felt as if their body "belonged to someone else." They knew it was theirs, but they had no sensation of what they knew was happening. They were depersonalizing, removing themselves from their bodies and the pain. We don't experience trauma the same way we experience everyday events.

As our perceptions alter, peripheral details, context, and time sense fall away. Time moves slowly, as if in a slow-motion video or movie. The whole experience appears unreal, as if in a dream or a fantasy. Awareness of place falls away, and even significant details are not noticed.

A victim of trauma enters a dissociative state. A common side effect of this dissociation is having no conscious memories of the event. We experience an amnesia for the event. Afterward, we'll acknowledge we've been injured, but we can't seem to remember how our injuries happened.

Memory of trauma is inconsistent. Even with similar experiences, very different effects can result. The late Dr. Joseph Wepman, renowned expert in determining the consequences of effects of physical injury on mental functioning, remarked that two similar injuries would often result in very different consequences. What would look like a minor trauma could have significant consequences, while a more significant injury could have an inconsequential impact.

It's impossible to predict which events, thoughts, feelings, or perceptions a person will remember, which will be distressing, and which will be dismissed as of no import.

This dissociative state during trauma is similar to what we experience during a hypnotic trance or the altered state of consciousness produced by "truth serums," some street drugs, or even during seizures.

During a dissociative state, memory is laid down very differently from when we're in a state of normal consciousness. Feelings, emotions, and body sensations may be deeply engraved into our memories, while the specific details of context, time, and verbal information are remembered poorly or not at all.

Being in a dissociative state during trauma also affects how we remember what happened. Because specific details of time and place and even specific words don't register during trauma, normal memory recall doesn't work with memories of trauma. Because the feeling state is so different, there is no connection to everyday, normal events. It's impossible to use the information bits remembered from normal, everyday experience to reconstruct memories of trauma.

For victims, recovering memories of abuse and trauma is unpredictable. They remember both too much and too little. Memories of the trauma may come flooding back, intruding on the victim's consciousness when they are not wanted. Or they may not be available when they are wanted. Try as they might, some victims of known trauma cannot remember what has happened to them. Big parts or even the whole memory of an event or series of events may be lost. Or they can remember parts but not all of an experience. Victims of assault may be unable to identify their assailants, even when they had "clearly seen them." They may have seen them, but it didn't register.

Many people report that during their normal waking states they're unable to remember the trauma they know they experienced. But specific sounds, smells, or events can trigger a feeling similar to that experienced during the original trauma. Then the whole experience comes flooding back.

> *Gary, a Vietnam combat veteran, couldn't remember what he did in the war. Within days after returning home his memories faded completely. He often said he'd remember if he could, but he just couldn't.*
>
> *When the Mediterranean fruit fly infestation became a grave concern to economists and agriculturists, helicopter spraying was started in his neighborhood. The sound of the helicopters directly overhead triggered a flashback reaction for Gary.*
>
> *The day the helicopters first sprayed his neighborhood, Gary's wife lost him. She said he'd gone to do some errands, and the car had come home but he didn't. She couldn't find him. She called friends, looked all over for him, and finally called the police. The search dogs found him in the storage area of his garage. He was curled into a ball, covered with canvas, mumbling incoherently about the enemy.*
>
> *After a short stay in the local veterans hospital, where he participated in therapy with other Vietnam vets, Gary found his memories were returning. The sound of the helicopters had been the trigger that broke through his years of not remembering.*

Numerous trauma-memory programs have benefited from the research done on post-traumatic stress disorder and how to trigger and then resolve flashback experiences in combat veterans. This same research has also helped explain how victims of trauma can sometimes remember in body sensations and actions even though they couldn't put words to their memories.

Current altered states of consciousness can also trigger long-forgotten memories of trauma. A person may not remember the trauma while they are awake but have nightmares that reflect their forgotten experiences. Sometimes drugs or alcohol may alter a person's consciousness enough to allow access to memories of traumatic events.

There is some evidence that perpetrators as well as victims experience dissociative states during the trauma incident. Their memories of the event can be as inaccessible to normal memory-recovery strategies as their victims' memories.

Although many people saw him do it, and millions more saw the news footage, Sirhan Sirhan reported no conscious memories of killing Robert Kennedy. But when he was in a trance, Sirhan not only remembered the events but seemed to relive the feelings and arousal he experienced during the shooting.

Being in a dissociative state while they were being abusive may be a factor in the pattern of abusers "denying" their behavior. They really don't remember doing it. And sometimes the trauma is so thoroughly forgotten, there never is a conscious memory or even a conscious denial that the event ever took place. It's as though it never happened.

A study of children who were traumatized before they could speak found that the children could not talk about what had happened to them, but expressed their memories in behavioral symptoms. There was no doubt the children had been traumatized; they were all hospitalized for their injuries and court-referred for abuse. They "remembered" physically, not verbally.

The Stories of Trauma

With memories of normal life events, telling the story moves the event into long-term memory. Victims, perpetrators, and witnesses often don't tell the stories, even to themselves, about what happened. They don't want to talk about it. They don't want to tell the story. They don't want to know about what's happened, and they don't question what's going on. When people do realize they've been traumatized or are forced to deal with their trauma, they quickly push aside their memories. The horrors they have experienced are unspeakable.

And because they're unspeakable, they're not spoken of. The stories aren't told.

Perpetrators keep their secrets. They won't volunteer their story of what happened. When they're caught, they'll tell the officials whatever they think the officers want to know, not necessarily what really happened.

Onlookers keep the secret, or insist what's happened was in the past and need not concern anyone now. So the crimes, or the horror, remain unresolved.

Even victims don't tell, or won't tell. They keep the story of their trauma to themselves, or from themselves. Either from shame or fear, they keep quiet.

By not telling the story, everyone forgets.

Growing up in California, Lori was twelve when she experienced her first earthquake. Although unhurt, she was terrified. Her mother insisted it was no big deal. She should just stop thinking about it. So she tried hard to forget.

When she was forty and living in New England where there aren't supposed to be any earthquakes, Lori heard a funny noise one day. The next thing she knew, she was up off the couch, grabbing the door frame and right back reexperiencing the first earthquake she had felt as a child. It took several months of work, both on her own and with a supportive counselor, to put the earlier earthquake into perspective. She said she knew her mother just wanted her to feel better, but it didn't work. She needed comforting and care, not discounting and denying that her terror was legitimate.

Lori was told to forget, to not remember. For whatever reason, her mother didn't want her to remember the earthquake. In investigations of mass trauma, like the Holocaust or a reign of terror, it's not uncommon for witnesses to tell the victims to be quiet, or for those who were involved in the terror to decide to keep quiet. They never tell anyone about their part in the atrocities and, if asked, avoid or deny talking about what they did or what they knew about.

Judith Herman, a trauma researcher from Harvard, tells about one young man who knew his father lived in Germany during World War II. The young man was sure his father wasn't involved in any anti-Jewish activities. He knew his father just ran a supply train. When asked directly what he'd done during the war, the father replied that he just ran a supply train. Sometime later the father admitted it had been a transport train. On repeated questioning, the father related several incidents that clearly indicted him in the horror of the genocide.

The youth was stunned as he told about what he'd learned of his father's war activities. During the follow-up to the study, a year later,

the young man not only said his father was never involved in the Holocaust, but couldn't believe his father would ever say he was. He also
couldn't believe the recording that was made of his previous interview,
even though he could recognize his own voice. Within a year, the
young man had totally forgotten his conversations with his father and
his conversations with the study team.

Like my not wanting to remember mouthing off to my mother, an
activity I thought was out of character for me, this young man didn't
want to remember such awful information about his father.

Both Gary and Lori forgot, also, but their bodies remembered.
Even though they couldn't put the words onto their memories, their
bodies knew what had happened. We can seem to forget what happened. But for many of us who "forget," a part of us remembers. You
can ask us what happened, even point to objective evidence, and we
still can't tell you what we remember. Then the memories can be triggered and will come flooding back.

> *Mary Beth was at a family gathering when she suddenly re-*
> *membered an incident from her childhood. She had idolized*
> *her big brother and loved to hang around him and his best*
> *friend from down the road. Her best friend was the younger*
> *sister of her brother's friend. Late one summer afternoon,*
> *when the two girls were ten and the boys sixteen, the two boys*
> *decided to punish the girls for hanging around.*
>
> *In moments, the boys came after the two little girls, held*
> *them down, and forced them to have sex. The boys laughed at*
> *the girls' cries and went off for a swim. The two girls never told*
> *anyone what happened. And they never talked about it with*
> *each other.*
>
> *Mary Beth said she had forgotten all about it until she saw*
> *her brother teasing her daughter, threatening to "get her" if*
> *she didn't go away and leave him alone. Seeing her daughter in*
> *danger triggered her memories of the assault.*

When Mary Beth came for counseling, she was frustrated, angry,
and hurt. It took her a long time before she decided what she wanted
to do. She was going to another family gathering and knew she would
see him. She felt she couldn't avoid him. And she wanted him to know

he had hurt her. She decided to talk to her brother about what he and his friend did, and ask him why he did it.

We role-played, brainstormed, and prepared for the conversation. We talked a lot about memories, how they are different for different people with the same event. She thought about what she would do if he got mad at her, if he denied it had ever happened, if he discounted her hurt. Finally the day for the visit arrived. Mary Beth reported she was ready, but not looking forward to the conversation. Whatever he said, she would know what had happened for her that day.

Later she said it was a real eye-opening experience. Her brother couldn't really remember the incident. She was in incredible pain about it, and he couldn't remember doing it! He didn't deny he had done it. He said all of his friends had sex with the younger girls in the neighborhood. The girls would scream and carry on, but they all knew the little kids really liked it.

It took a while for Mary Beth to come to terms with her feelings for her brother. She now knew he wasn't the idol she had thought he was as a little kid, but she hadn't realized how insensitive and self-centered he was. She realized no matter what she said or did now, he wouldn't change his mind. It was no big thing for him, even if it was for her. She was convinced that because he didn't see it as a problem, he wouldn't see any need to change how he felt about the experience. To him, it wasn't abuse; it was fun.

She also decided her daughter would never visit her brother's house alone. She said her daughter wasn't safe around her brother. He didn't care about the girl, only himself.

As we'll see when we get to letting go, sometimes, like Mary Beth, you take charge with a person you can't control by letting go of what you wanted or believed them to be. You see them for who and what they are. Then you can protect yourself from letting them hurt you again. You give up the wishful thinking they'll go back and make the past all better. They won't. And you'll continue hurting while you wait for them to be someone they aren't.

False Memories of Trauma

In the last few years, "false-memory syndrome" has become a popular description of people who've remembered earlier abuse, particularly sexual abuse. False-memory syndrome holds that the memories aren't memories of real events, but have been implanted in the victims by therapists. While the term has been used extensively in the popular media, there is no accepted diagnosis of false-memory syndrome found in any of the professional literature. It seems to be a popular defense by people who have been accused of being the abusers. They don't believe people will forget early abuse and then remember it at a later time. They often say the memories are false, because they are distorted, imprecise, or recently remembered.

But all memory is distorted to some degree. This is obvious whenever eyewitness accounts are collected. Seldom if ever is there absolute agreement on all the details of any event. We remember what we want to remember or what's important to us. Our memories of an incident may differ remarkably from the memories of others who shared the experience.

But there is no evidence that traumatic memories are more or less distorted than any other memories. The distortions evident in trauma memories may be different from the distortions in nontrauma memories. Trauma-memory distortions are typically distortions of context, peripheral detail, or time sequencing. But they are more accurate for gist and central theme.

Neither is there any evidence that people who report histories of trauma are any more suggestible, or more prone to lie, fantasize, or confabulate, than the general population. Yet when people do remember a traumatic event, they're often disbelieved. Even loved ones question the accuracy of their memories.

When Sondra remembered how a family "friend" abused her while he was supposed to be taking care of her, she confided in her fiancé, explaining what she was remembering and feeling. Byron responded with disbelief. She had to be making it up. Things like that didn't happen to people like her.

Sondra was startled by his response. Several weeks earlier they had seen a little girl riding a blue bicycle. Long-forgotten memories of the fun she had had with her blue bicycle came flooding back. When she shared those memories with Byron, he hadn't questioned the accuracy of her long-forgotten joyful memories. But he did question the accuracy of her painful memories and even the existence of the experiences.

Sondra's question to Byron: "How come you didn't question that I forgot all about the bike and then remembered it, but you can't believe I forgot about the abuse and now remember it? Why would you say I obviously remembered the bike and obviously made up the trauma?"

Conventional wisdom holds that we don't forget trauma. And when we say we do, we are just making up stories to be malicious and hurtful. But like so many other instances of conventional wisdom, this one is not supported by the research. Once again, what we "know to be true" is what we want to be true.

"Evidence" of False Memories

While most of the evidence for the existence of false memory is based on anecdotes, there are a few studies that are often quoted to support the idea that it's possible to implant memories, at least in a laboratory setting. While there are serious methodological issues with these studies, such as very low numbers of subjects and inconsistent results, the primary issues involve the validity of the design and assumptions of the studies themselves.

Methodological issues can compromise the outcomes of any kind of study, not just psychological research. Usually researchers design studies that address the issues they are curious about. They'll take a sample population, a number of people from the group of people they want to investigate, rather than trying to study all of them. They conduct the "experiment" to see how the sample of people behaves. Then they make generalizations about how all people in the target group will behave in similar circumstances. The validity of a study can be compromised by using very small sample sizes or by not carefully matching what happens in the study with what actually happens in real life.

When a sample is too small, making a generalization back to the larger group is problematic. It's extremely difficult to be certain the sample accurately reflects the group as a whole.

For example, say we expect five hundred people at a conference later this week, and we need to tell the chef what to prepare for dinner. But we forgot to ask the people who are coming what they want for dinner. So we grab the three closest people and tell them they can choose beef, fish, or vegetarian. Two say beef. One says fish. On the basis of this data, we tell the chef to prepare two-thirds steaks, one-third fish or vegetables.

Dinner comes and everyone is restless, and most of the steaks go back uneaten. Oops! We didn't know most of the group were animal-rights activists and wouldn't wear leather shoes, much less eat one of our furry or scaly friends. The three we happened to ask didn't share the animal-rights beliefs of the majority of the people expected at dinner. They weren't representative of the whole group. Our low sample size didn't give us an accurate picture of the whole group. If we had asked a dozen of our dinner guests, we'd have gotten more accurate information.

When any study uses five to ten subjects and then makes generalizations to the large populations, there's too much room for error. There are just too few people to be confident about predicting what people in general will do.

Since we can't traumatize children and then wait to see what they remember or don't remember years later, any study we design won't be just the same as real trauma. Even if we make the situation uncomfortable, the dissociative state that is an important part of trauma won't be there. We can't abuse people so severely that they dissociate just to find out what they'll do. So we have to look really carefully at the studies that are used to make sure what they're doing reflects what happens with trauma. We also have to make sure these studies will be similar to the experience people have with therapists who are supposed to coerce their patients into believing shameful horrific experiences actually have occurred.

In the studies that are most often used to support planting false memories, relatives repeatedly tell children they were lost in a shopping mall when the children were much younger. The children are then asked if they remember being lost. A child's report of remembering being lost is accepted as evidence of a false memory being implanted.

This procedure is reminiscent of a game we used to play as kids. All the big kids in the neighborhood tried to convince the younger ones that Santa Claus really did not exist, or that the bogey man really did, or that they were really adopted from a distant foreign land. The little ones would usually believe us, especially if we threatened to rub their faces in the mud puddles.

In a more serious vein, social scientists have known for years that it's possible to convince lots of people any number of things have occurred or exist. We can get them to question themselves while accepting the "truth" offered by someone with more power or status. These studies have more to do with compliance and group pressure than with false memory.

It's questionable that studies with small numbers of older relatives pressuring small numbers of children to believe they were lost in a mall can be used as evidence of what happens in memories of abuse and atrocities. It speaks to group pressure. Not memory.

It's also hard to believe that the scare of being lost in a shopping mall, a familiar setting for most children, can come close to the terror and trauma of being physically or sexually abused. The emotional experience that accompanies the trauma, that is a crucial part of the trauma, is not present in either the laboratory studies or the supposed earlier trauma. It would be like equating the memories a child would have of slipping off a rock to get a face full of water while swimming with family and friends with the memories of a child who gets caught in rapids or ocean waves and is held under by the force of the water until he can't breathe. Both are memories of swimming experiences. Quite different memories.

Kids who get lost in malls don't experience the dissociation, the alterations of time, space, and feelings of real trauma, nor do they fear admitting what has happened because their abuser has threatened to harm them or their family if they tell. Being lost in a mall often becomes part of a family's folklore. Physical and sexual abuse are unspeakable. Those stories are never told.

To use these studies as evidence that therapists can and do implant memories of abuse into their patients also rests on assumptions about what happens during therapy that are difficult to believe. The therapist would have to have a power over the patient that most therapists can only dimly imagine.

The patient would have to cooperate in the memory implanting over a long period of time and agree to accept a past that was more horrific and noxious than any that could have occurred. The patient would have to agree to have a past that would insure causing unimaginable pain to their family and themselves. And they would have to be willing to open themselves to public shame and humiliation as the tarnished victim.

The therapist would have to decide to knowingly inflict a painful past and the prospect for a troubled present and future on a patient they had agreed to help. The therapist would also be agreeing to the possibility of legal suits and malpractice issues, and to see themselves as having untold power over their patient.

All of these issues, and more, would have to be agreed and acted upon by both therapist and patient over a long period of time.

Implanting-Memories Experiments

The most significant assumption of all is that this type of memory *can* be implanted. The only public information about implanting false memories comes from the brainwashing projects the KGB and CIA conducted during the Cold War. While we are quick to accuse the Soviets of running such outrageous projects, we seldom acknowledge that the United States was doing essentially the same thing.

These projects were started in reaction to the brainwashing successes of the North Koreans during the Korean War. Recently declassified CIA documents describe memory-implanting projects, conducted over long periods of time, using a variety of mind-altering drugs and verbal programming techniques.

A glimpse of the methods that were used was seen in the film *The Manchurian Candidate*. Although the film was fiction and based on a novel like many techno-thrillers we see today, the technology and procedures used are the same as are being used in real life. In the film, Laurence Harvey's character was "programmed" to assassinate the president. The film was fiction; it wasn't true. It portrayed what people feared could happen or what some people wanted to have happen. The Soviets did not actually try to program someone to kill the president. In the film, the programming was successful. In real life, neither the CIA nor the KGB was successful. The projects in both countries were failures.

Neither the KGB nor the CIA was able to implant false memories in adults.

This raises the serious question: If the KGB and the CIA couldn't implant false memories with the best, most sophisticated, well-thought-out, carefully executed, determined-to-succeed, well-researched techniques done by talented, professionally trained operatives, what leads anyone to believe that any therapist, with their limited resources, time, money, and inclination, could be successful, even if they wanted to?

Or as a therapist colleague said recently, "If I could implant false memories, don't you think my patients would want, and I would prefer, implanting memories of a positive happy childhood, rather than a traumatic awful one?"

Summary

Our memories are our own personal histories. They make up the colorful tapestries that are our lives. We "know" who we are, where we came from, and our places in the world by what we remember. But we have to be careful!

- All memory, of both everyday events and trauma, is distorted.
- Our memories are the stories we tell ourselves about what happened, not necessarily what happened. Our memories are autobiographical.
- Memory of everyday events is more distorted in gist and central themes, less distorted in details, time, and context.
- Memory of trauma is more distorted in details, time, and context, less distorted in gist and central themes.
- There is considerable research supporting the forgetting of trauma.
- The research used to support the ability to implant false memories has serious methodological and design flaws.
- Even in well-designed, long-term experiments, neither the CIA nor the KGB could implant false memories.

Exercises for Chapter 6

EARLY MEMORIES

What's the earliest memory you have of a childhood event? How often have you "told the story" of this event?

How has your story changed with the retellings?

DIFFERENTIAL REMEMBERING

Compare memories with a sibling or friend about what you did in high school. How are your memories similar or different for the same event?

MEMORIES OF TRAUMA

Almost all of us have events or incidents that can be classified as traumatic. The most common are accidents or injuries. What is the story you tell about your trauma?

What can you remember of the event?

How sure are you of the gist of the story? Of the details?

CHAPTER 7

BEING YOUR OWN EXPERT

A s a young man, Nelson Rockefeller had great difficulty learning to read. He never did become a proficient reader. He didn't let his inability to read well stop him, however. After he served as governor of New York, Congress approved his appointment as vice president of the United States. He joins the list of other notables as diverse as Albert Einstein, Jules Verne, Tom Cruise, and Magic Johnson, as well as Whoopi Goldberg, Agatha Christie, and Luci Baines Johnson. If we look back in history, this same list includes Galileo, Mozart, the Wright brothers, Beethoven, Thomas Edison, and Auguste Rodin. The common thread on this list is not that they all had trouble reading. But they did/do all exhibit signs of being learning disabled, or having attention deficit disorder. They didn't let their limitations or struggles define them. They moved beyond what many others have labeled a dysfunction or disability to live lives that have touched us all.

These people were able to move beyond what's stopped many others. Why were they able to do it, and not some of us? Why was change easy for some, and not easy for others? Why was it easy at one time, and not at others?

When I faced my own crisis, I watched the pattern of my behavior. I carefully examined and monitored what made a difference and when. It was not classical research with control groups and statistical tests. I can do that; I had to do it to get my degree. This research was more intuitive and in some ways goes further.

When I was in graduate school at the University of Chicago, I took a class in psychological testing from Joseph Wepman. Dr. Wepman was known, both at the university and in the field, as an excellent diagnostician, especially in differential diagnosis: determining if the difficulties a person was experiencing were organic, the result of physical brain trauma or disease, or if they were psychological, the result of or reactions to life experience. Dr. Wepman was quite the curmudgeon, and frankly, as a young graduate student, I was afraid of him. But he had a way of bringing reality and common sense to the fore. He said psychological testing is what we put between ourselves and the patient until we learned to trust our ability to know the other person. We would need to rely on experts only until we realized we were the experts.

Psychotherapist and author Sheldon Kopp reiterates this theme in his book *If You Meet the Buddha on the Road, Kill Him*. He says when you trust another more than yourself, when you believe the other knows better than you who you are, when you let them decide what you need and/or want or what's good for you, you have given yourself over to the other person and diminished yourself.

What I learned from both these teachers was that we can know, better than anyone else, who we are and what works for us. We have to work at it, though. Self-knowledge doesn't come easily, quickly, or cheaply. And we'll have lots of opportunities to learn the lesson and be tested on our belief in ourselves.

> *A fellow graduate student brought the lesson home to me. I've long ago forgotten his name, but I still remember his face, his words, and my response. We were both in residence at a training for therapists. As the training sessions progressed, anything and everything became grist for the diagnostic/ intervention mill.*
>
> *One night, while we were sitting on the terrace after dinner, someone suggested an evening hike to the top of the hill through the redwood forest. When I said to count me out, that I didn't want to stress my recently injured foot on the uneven trail in the dark, he quickly broke in, telling me my foot wasn't really injured. He claimed I was just using the injury as an excuse to avoid the fearfulness of the night forest.*
>
> *I was confused at what he said, and it must have shown on*

my face, because his next statement was "There you go with that confusion racket. You always get confused when you don't want to face the fact someone has called you on a number you run." (In English he meant I'd act confused to avoid facing an unpleasant truth.)

What made this exchange such a lesson for me was my reaction to his remarks. At first I was stopped cold. He had such an excellent reputation, and he was further along in school than I, older, more experienced. I started to defer to him. And then I caught myself.

While I was growing up in northern California, redwood forests, day and night, had been my summer playgrounds. I hadn't been afraid in a redwood forest for over twenty-five years. And the support bandages had been removed from my foot the day before I came to the training. I'm proud to report I didn't yell and curse him for his unsolicited, inaccurate, condescending comments. But I did forcefully, clearly, and thoroughly warn him to stop making pronouncements with such certainty when he knew little of the facts and less of my background and character.

At my protests, he turned to another person in the circle, muttering, "See, I knew it wasn't her foot."

No matter what I said to my colleague that evening on the terrace, he was sure he knew better than I who I was, what I should do, and why I did what I did. It wasn't easy to confront him, and it was frustrating to see that my confrontation was ineffective. We had a slang expression for what he was doing—mind raping. He was attempting to disempower me by defining who I was and what I was doing. He wanted to assert his control over me.

I learned an important lesson that evening, and it was well worth the price. I learned no one would ever be able to know me as well as I knew myself—and I was in charge of my life, no matter what any self-styled expert said.

When we let someone else think for us, when we adopt without thinking their view of the world and our place in it, we diminish ourselves.

By having confidence in our own ability to think through issues that are challenging us, to solve our own problems, and to make decisions for ourselves, we take charge even when we can't control the situations we're faced with.

This is not to say we shouldn't use the expertise and the support of others. Experts can be very helpful as we are sorting through data and making decisions. They can be good resources for us. We don't need to give them power over us.

"I'm Not Smart Enough"

Lots of people think they aren't smart enough to think for themselves.

One of the most savvy businesswomen I know is an immigrant who has the equivalent of a technical school diploma. She came to this country in her early twenties and started her business career practicing her craft. Although she doesn't have a formal education, she is very astute. Her business and practical people skills are excellent. She can pick up subtle nuances of what people think and do. She has an avid curiosity and is relentless in asking questions and thinking carefully to understand new concepts and ideas. She's educated herself, not just in her craft, but in what it takes to run a business and work with people. She's long since left the craft of her business and is now a sought-after business entrepreneur and consultant. She claims her success came from hard work, not her intelligence. She "knows" she isn't smart. Her teacher told her she wasn't long ago. She still believes her teacher was right.

My friend demonstrates a different type of knowledge than those of us who are formally educated demonstrate. The type of skills and talents she has are not the type that are reflected on the IQ tests or classroom tests we all have taken. Like Rockefeller, she hasn't let what her teacher said about her stop her from succeeding.

Is she less intelligent than the scholar who's scored high on an IQ test and then accomplished little with his life? With little ambition, he'd rather keep his head in the clouds surrounding his ivory tower. He does little more than drift from one low-paying, dead-end job to the next.

Or consider another person who's so very smart that she finished college in record time. But she's so obnoxious she keeps getting fired.

She's more interested in tilting at windmills and so inept socially that others don't want to do business with her.

What's an IQ?

Standard IQ tests were originally designed in France to predict which children would do well in school. So the tests included items that were similar to the topics and problems schoolchildren would be expected to do. Even now, IQ tests don't necessarily address the challenges and information we need in our everyday world. As hard as teachers try, it's still difficult to help kids transfer information, skills, and strategy from the classroom to their lives, and back again. Kids who can do very well on their math tests can have all sorts of problems counting the change from their purchases. Others will easily keep track of the payments and balances due for their paper routes while failing their math tests.

When I was a school psychologist, I worked with a team of evaluators for the Bureau of Indian Affairs. We were responsible for identifying Navajo children who were handicapped and needed special assistance to succeed in school. One of the instruments we used in our evaluations was a standard IQ test. Because many of the smaller children were not proficient in English, we often needed translators. Some questions and answers that made sense in an Anglo environment simply couldn't translate into sensible questions in Navajo.

One question asked, "What should you do if you see smoke coming out of your neighbor's house?" The "right" answer was to call the fire department. Most of these children lived in isolated areas, where everyone heated their homes with coal and wood. Smoke was always coming out of a neighbor's house. Smoke just meant people were at home. Another question asked, "How many pennies are in a nickel?" The Navajo word for *nickel* is *five-cent piece*. So the question in translation became "How many pennies are in a five-cent piece?" Most of the children couldn't figure out why we'd be so silly to ask such a question.

Needless to say, lots of the children didn't do that well on our paper-and-pencil tests. Especially the youngest of them. Many of those children had lived in hogans, helping their families tend their herds of sheep, and had little, if any, experience with books, paper, or pencils before they came to boarding school. I was amazed at the difference between their skills and those of my own son who was about their age at the time.

Then I came to realize these children had skills my son would never learn. Even the youngest of the Navajo children were often on their own, for days at a time, with the full responsibility for their herd. Even though they couldn't do the math problems in the schoolroom, they could and did count their sheep and never lost a one. I am sure my son, even though he knew all his numbers and could read at a higher grade level, would have never survived on the high desert, by himself for days at a time, with just his sheep and a dog to help.

Our intelligence, or IQ, is only one factor in our effectiveness.

Intellectualizing

Intellectualizing is a favorite tool for those who want to obfuscate. They can hide behind large words, subtle concepts, or unusual references for common activities. Then they can discuss ideas or propose activities, and no one will know what they're talking about. Much of what they talk about isn't all that hard to understand, if they'd just use clear and/or everyday language and concepts. Or if they'd use examples that others could quickly understand.

For example, physicists talk about Einstein's theory of gravity, the space-time continuum, which can be proved by discovering irrefutable evidence of frame dragging. Most of us have little if any idea of what the theory is all about, what frame dragging is, or why we should care. More important, most people reading the sentences never get to the word *continuum*. You start to read the words *Einstein's theory*, or *space-time*, and then shut down. You may be able to recite Einstein's famous equation, $E = mc^2$. But you aren't sure what it means and don't think you could learn about it from someone else, much less figure it out on your own. It was one more science lesson (science is too hard, we tell ourselves) to daydream through.

Then the day came in late 1997, when scientists found evidence that confirmed Einstein's theory. This was big news. Science reporters were challenged not only to report what happened, but to explain it in such a way that the story could be understood by the lay public, people who would automatically click off when they heard gravity and Einstein.

K. C. Cole, in an article syndicated by the *Los Angeles Times*, used a wonderful word picture of an elephant sitting on a twisted bedsheet to help her readers understand such complex concepts as space-time, frame warping, and the pull of gravity on space.

While few of us have elephants dropping in to sit on our beds, we can certainly visualize what would happen if one did. Cole's example links the space-time continuum with the sheet, the elephant with black holes, and the twisted sheet with the effects of "frame dragging" space-time around a black hole.

When we use good examples, even confusing or sophisticated concepts can be more easily understood. Would you be willing to consider that some of the things you don't understand just haven't been well explained, rather than you're not smart enough to understand them?

Jargon

Jargon is a pain when you're the new person in an established group. Most groups at work, in community clubs, and in social situations use acronyms, initials, slang, and in-group words as communication shortcuts. When you haven't been with a group, are hesitant to look like you don't know, or if there is no one to ask, jargon keeps you in the out group. I was working with one engineering group for weeks before I realized that what I thought was cold seaweed was actually chilled CMOS, a type of computer part or process.

In one professional women's group I belonged to, we had an agreement that anyone could ask anything, no matter how trivial. One day, one of the other women and I were talking about an acquaintance who was not easy to work with. One of us made the comment she was OTL. At this, another group member spoke up, challenged us therapists on our jargon, and asked just what type of diagnosis we had given the other woman. We had to explain *out to lunch* is not an accepted psychiatric diagnosis.

Misleading Words and Concepts

When a speaker doesn't specify which meaning is intended of a word that has multiple similar meanings, it's understandable that you get confused. This isn't because you aren't smart enough, but because they aren't clear enough.

One of the most common examples of this kind of confusion is the word *average*. *Average* has three different meanings. Which meaning is used isn't always all that clear. If you think they mean one when it's actually another, misunderstanding is predictable.

Most of us remember *average* from school. A teacher would add up all the grades the class members received on a test, and then divide by the number of students in the class to get the average. (This type of average is also called the mean.) In most classes there were one or two really smart kids who would be the D.A.R. (Darned Average Raisers). The two high grades could easily increase the class average.

The median average isn't as affected by extreme scores. This average is the midpoint. Half the students scored above, half below the midpoint. The problem here is if most students had similar scores. Then a few points could make a significant difference in letter grades.

The mode considers the average the most frequent score. If your teacher gives the average a C, and most of the kids score really high, then this may not be so good for your letter grade.

Same word, three ways of determining average. Which one the teacher uses makes a big difference in your grade. Check out acronyms, ask for glossaries of terms that are specific to a project, and challenge the academics to explain what they are saying in everyday terms. Often you'll find you're not the only one who doesn't know, and lots of people can't give clear examples of what they're talking about.

Check out Your Experts

This is not to say don't use experts. Just be careful. We all have a tendency to use or hire people with whom we agree and to ignore or discount those "experts" or points of view that don't agree with our view of the world. We tend to see "our experts" as telling the truth or having the right idea, and the others we dismiss as biased.

There is no unbiased expert. Experts have in-depth knowledge and experience in a specific area, and an opinion about their field of interest. Even if we just want raw data, the perspective of the expert colors the information that's gathered. We wouldn't use an expert if she wouldn't tell us the right way or the best way to deal with our challenges. We want answers when we use experts, not just descriptions of our options.

Sometimes the expert's perspective makes a difference and sometimes it doesn't. The important question to ask yourself is, is this one of those times where perspective matters?

Examine the background and experience of the expert. Ask yourself:

- Is he the best fit to address this issue?
- Does her knowledge give her the background I need?
- Is his experience relevant to my challenges?

Virtually every expert will have flat sides and limitations. Ronald Reagan used his experiences as an actor and the president of the Screen Actors Guild to learn the skills of leadership and management. He was known as the Great Communicator. One commentator suggested he did fine as long as someone else handed him the lines. He drew on his acting skills to put across a message, not his depth of knowledge.

Reagan certainly didn't have the same broad understanding of government that Lyndon Johnson or George Bush had. These presidents had spent their careers in government service. Their experiences provided a basis of expertise that a newcomer to Washington couldn't hope to learn in the time he had in office.

Look at what side of the issue an expert endorses. Is it the same as or different from yours? Will that matter? The National Transportation Safety Board, the U.S. Department of Transportation, and the National Association of Tire Manufacturers can all give you information about tires and highways. Which one do you turn to? What could you learn by asking the other two? If you understand they have different views and agendas, you can filter the information they give you.

What's the hidden agenda an organization or individual might have? How open are they about their backers? How congruent are their public and private statements? If an organization called Citizens for Animals in Research takes out a full-page ad in your local newspaper urging a no vote on a pending ballot issue, how can you tell their position? Can you tell if they are vivisectionists or antivivisectionists? Does their position on this issue affect the validity of their position on the ballot issue? Go beyond names and titles to examine what they really do and what their agenda is. Why are they taking the position they do? Who is on their board of directors? Where do they get their funding? Who are their supporters?

Is your expert really the right person for your question? If you're interested in nutrition and vitamins, do you ask the clerk at the local health food store, your physician, an independent supplement dealer, or a registered dietitian?

When I was a practicing therapist, I always asked new clients where they'd heard of me and why they chose me. The answers ranged from amusing to astounding: everything from the yellow pages of the local phone book, to attending a seminar I presented, to their friend who didn't like me!

The single best suggestion for finding an expert that will be helpful to you is to invoke the *three-source rule*. Find at least three sources of information or help and investigate each one of them. Ask them about their background and experience with cases similar to yours. Ask them for references, for names of clients who've had similar needs, and permission to talk with clients. Start with a short-term contract, a trial period, so you can decide if you can work together. As the contractor, you're paying. You get to decide if the expert is right for you, not the other way around.

Doing the Research

Research isn't something just scientists or academics do. We all do it everyday. We just don't call it research. Whether we're deciding which new movie to see, which car to buy, where to invest our retirement funds, or if we'll marry the person who just asked us, we're doing research. We're collecting raw data, facts, figures, opinions, and background and then organizing it all into usable information. Research gives us the data to develop into the information you need. While we often focus on decisions and implementation, collecting data is a big job in itself.

There's so much data available. And it's increasing faster than we can keep up with. Some wits have suggested that reading *The New York Times* cover to cover can take an average reader a week. There are thousands of magazines and newspapers published in the United States today, countless more pamphlets, newsletters, special reports, and trade periodicals. Walking into the local superstore bookseller can be overwhelming. So many books—so many topics! And they all have different points of view and different answers to your questions.

It's hard to know where to start finding the data you need. Do you go to the library? The encyclopedia? The local newsstands for a magazine? Get a book from a friend? The Internet?

The most popular current answer is go to the Internet. The answer you seek is there somewhere. But where? A twelve-year-old searched on "whales" for her sixth-grade science report. She received a message that there were over ten million responses to her request, and a suggestion that she narrow her search. So she entered "whales in Alaska." Again the response came back, too many responses to process. What's a kid to do?

Using the Library to Get Started

Finding the answer you need starts with knowing the question you're asking. But how can you ask the right question if you don't know enough about a topic to know what to ask? Or when you don't know the jargon and specific terms used for that issue?

Go first to your public library. Ask the reference librarian for help. Reference librarians have special training to take a general need to know and narrow it into a question that can be understandably and helpfully answered. Librarians can also tell you about experts on your topic. They can point you to reference directories and bibliographies, and on-line or electronic catalogs to speed up and automate your research. Many libraries offer their users access to the Internet and assistance in designing effective searches. Almost all libraries have electronic card catalogs and databases of periodicals. Most of these terminals are connected to a printer and a countywide or citywide computer server. You see which books and magazines are available at which branches and when they are due back if they are checked out. You can put a book on hold or transfer a book from one branch to another, all with a few keystrokes. You can then print out all the information about a book, including the call letters, so you no longer have to make cryptic notes on tiny pieces of paper.

Gone are the racks of periodicals and the dusty, musty stacks of back issues in the basement of the library. Electronic databases for periodicals let you find the articles you need on your subject, from any magazine that's ever been published. A directory points you to the microfilm cassette or microfiche sheet that holds all the pages of all the issues of hundreds of newspapers and magazines. The microfilm reader incorporates a copy machine, letting you make your own copy of the articles you need.

All of this with a helpful reference librarian attached so you can find your way through the maze of print and electronic data. You can get the answers to questions you didn't know you had or didn't want to ask. If you feel uncomfortable asking your local reference librarian for help, go to the library in the next town or the county seat.

Using Bookstores for Research

Bookstores can also give a quick overview of what's current and popular. You'll find books with different points of view on the same subject. Usually the books you find in a bookstore will be more recent than those you find in the library. Public libraries, like most local government functions, feel the budget squeeze, too. Many of them have had to cut way back on new acquisitions of books. There are also those of us who are industrial library users going first to the new books section and checking out anything that catches our eye. We give it a quick look and take it home for a more in-depth scan.

Scan the shelves in your topic area for the latest books on your questions. How many books are available? What do the titles tell you? You're sure to find conflicting points of view and advice. *Women Who Love Men Who Hate Them* is bound to differ from *Doing What You Have to Do to Save Your Relationship. Praying Your Kids off Drugs* probably offers different advice than *Standing up to Teen Drug Users.* At least look at books that might differ from the way you usually approach problems and situations. You're here to get a fresh look at an issue you've been chewing on. If what you knew was working for you, you wouldn't be looking for more information.

Check out the book. Look at the publishing history, usually found right after the title page. Is this a new book, or a reissue of an oldie? Usually there will be a list of other books this author has written. Check out the table of contents. Are these topics that start to address your questions? Does the book have an index that can point you to the specific topics you are looking for?

Skim through two or three chapters. Don't read it word for word, but get a feel for the approach and the attitude of the author. Is there a bibliography or a suggested reading list at the back?

Look for the author's profile. What's their experience? Their exper-tise? How did they get to be an expert?

The book you're looking for needs to fit your questions. It may well be wonderful and work well for a friend, and not be right for you. When I was looking for information on retirement planning, a friend suggested a book she had found very helpful. When I checked it out, I realized immediately it wasn't for me. She'd spent her whole career in a corporate job with a company-sponsored retirement program. I've been an entrepreneur for most of my adult life, providing my own re-tirement programs. The book was addressed to women like her, not like me. What for her was a valuable tool, for me was useless.

On-Line Research

So how do you not get millions of responses to your on-line searches, but find data you can use? Consider the questions you have, your needs for the data, and how much is enough.

In responding to a request for proposals, Paula found several terms she didn't understand. She was pretty sure they were trendy terms for work she had been doing for years, but needed to verify the new language. She entered a term in the "search on" field of a major search engine on her Internet provider search page. Then she stood back.

Sure enough, she got more responses than she needed. Hun-dreds. She quickly scanned several of them. She verified she knew the concept under a different name and went on to a new search. She didn't really read any of the articles, didn't stop to check the sources, nor did she download or print any of the files. She could see every one she checked referred to a familiar concept. Her question was answered.

Paula was looking for a quick overview. She didn't need in-depth knowledge, just validation and verification. She might also use this same approach if she just needed a quick overview of a new topic. By scanning several articles or postings, checking the dates and sources much as she would have checked a book in the bookstore, she could get lots of information fast. She might download several of the articles, print them out, or mark the sites with a bookmark to come back and read in depth, if she wanted to capture more permanent references.

Finding more in-depth information on the Internet is similar to going deeper in any research. You use what you're finding to point the way to further questions and areas of inquiry. The joy with the Internet is that you can usually find the next topic or area by simply clicking your mouse pointer on the highlighted words and jumping to the linked sources. The hazard is jumping to a totally unexpected spot, or not being able to find your way back there three weeks later when you need the citation of the information you laboriously uncovered. This is where bookmarks can be invaluable.

Losing a reference on the Internet is no different from reading a magazine article or book, finding just the right piece of information, and then not finding the magazine or book again. Or making a mistake in the notes you do take. If you aren't thoughtful and organized with your research, you'll end up with a mess, or answers that have to include the phrase "I know I saw it somewhere," no matter what sources you use.

Any topic imaginable has an Internet bulletin board and/or chat room. These sources can be really helpful and really frustrating. Some forums are little more than gripe-and-whine sessions, others have esoteric agendas, and still others strive to provide accurate information, but don't honor your needs or values.

If you just want to find someone to tell you what to do, this is the place to go. Post a question and lots of people will tell you what to do, how to do it, and what they think of you for needing their advice in the first place, or what they think of you if you won't follow their advice. Lots of Internet users have strong feelings and viewpoints and aren't afraid to let you know. This is not necessarily the place to go for sensitive treatment or kid gloves. Yet most of the respondents seem to be willing and eager to be of help. They just offer their own brand of help.

E-mail

E-mailing friends and colleagues is a quick way to get information and opinions. You can ask the same question of a big group of people, or have a group of people you regularly survey. By their very nature, e-mail notes are informal, focused, and demand attention. They're often a way to get a response from people who are not calling you back or who don't respond to voice mail.

Most people who are on-line respond to e-mail requests before regular-mail requests. If you want a personal response and the phone hasn't worked, ask in an e-mail.

Final note: If the last few paragraphs have left you perspiring and frantic, if you are still afraid to turn your computer on, if you know you have to bite the bullet and get literate on your computer, ask a kid for help. Either your own or one of the neighborhood kids can jump-start your technology learning curve.

Shadow Board of Directors

Shadow boards of directors are a low-tech technique for accessing the expertise of others and increasing your confidence and options. A shadow board can be as helpful in getting a variety of perspectives, and giving you access to information, as a regular board is. Use your shadow board of directors to push you out of your rut. They can help you find other ways of doing what you've been doing or to get the expert advice. The only difference between a regular board and a shadow board is that shadow boards exist only in your own imagination.

Your shadow board is portable, light, and easy to carry, so you can have it with you all the time. It challenges you to sharpen your thinking skills and to expand your perspective. A shadow board of directors teaches you to consider the views of others, whether you agree with them or not. It also makes available experts who are living or dead, known to you or strangers, talent you could never buy.

To build your shadow board of directors, choose a variety of people for their strengths and skills. Choose them for their specific skills and talents, knowledge and gifts, no matter what their limitations might be. You'll be tapping their strengths, not their limitations. Make sure you have the people you feel you need or could profit from, no matter how outrageous anyone else might find them.

You're going to use your shadow board of directors to help you think through and make decisions that you face. You'll use them for input and advice. Some of the members will change depending on the topics or the questions; others will be your old standbys.

For example, my standard members include Einstein, because he is so smart. He thinks in ways about things that I can only hope to emulate. Liz Taylor is also on my list. She can be gorgeous no matter what her size, is very loyal to her friends, is not afraid to speak out on difficult or unpopular issues, and is one classy lady. I just wish I had her violet eyes.

Marti Burns is a composite character, a combination of two cognitive therapists: David Burns, who wrote *Feeling Good: The New Mood Therapy*, the best book on combating depression I have read and recommended, and Martin Seligman, a psychologist whose pioneering work includes *Learned Optimism* and *What You Can Change . . . and What You Can't*. Together these two men, in my embodiment of Marti Burns, help me deal with my bouts of feeling bad, and help me confront myself when I get into irrational thinking.

Jane Johnson is another composite character, taken from two friends and colleagues who are the best technical manager and human resources manager I've been privileged to work with. Their high ethical and moral stance, willingness to do the hard work, clarity in thought and action challenge me to meet their level of expertise. I ask them how they would handle the hard situations I face in corporate consulting challenges. Then I listen.

The list could go on, but you get the picture. These are people I have known personally, or through their work, or in my image of them. I match their expertise to the challenges I face.

If my question involves critical thinking and creativity, Einstein is always the chairman of the board. But I don't even think to include him for grooming or social questions. Liz gets the honors here. A quick conversation in my mind with her, and I know how to solve the problem with dispatch, class, and grace. I don't think I'd use her for my marriage consultant, though. Wedding consultant, yes; marriage consultant, never.

My shadow board of directors complements the real experts I use, the research I do with the help of my local librarian, and the time I spend browsing bookstores and searching the Internet. By going step by step, asking good questions, and thinking through the answers, I can get closer to the information I need to help me face my challenges. Looking for help from experts can quickly bring me closer to the answers I need.

Exercises for Chapter 7

TAKE YOUR FUNCTIONAL IQ

Run your own IQ test to identify your strengths and areas of expertise, not just the "book learning" that comes from a formal education. List your strengths, first of character, then of habits.

List your areas of expertise. What can you do well? Don't discount "simple" skills like baking a super lemon meringue pie or teaching a child to read. Everything counts here. These are the areas you know a lot about.

How do you keep current and up-to-date? What do you do to continue learning and growing? Some of your answers here will certainly include the reading you do: magazines, newspapers, and even novels. Include the informal classes you attend and the discussions you have with friends that stretch your mind.

What do your best friends say about you? If I were to ask them, how would they describe you? (If you aren't sure, ask them!)

HONE YOUR RESEARCH SKILLS

Start with one part of the challenge you are facing. For example, you may have just found out a loved one has a strange or frightening disease. Think about what you want to know, i.e., is it contagious, do people have a lot of pain, what resources are available? You get the idea. Then take your list of questions to the research librarian at your local library. Work with her to find not just the answers to your questions but have her help you find out how to find answers.

DEVELOP YOUR OWN SHADOW BOARD OF DIRECTORS

Use your colleagues, historical figures, authors, celebrities to build your own shadow board of directors. Focus on the strengths and areas of expertise you need to face the challenges you have. List the people you could use and the skills and strengths they bring to your board.

CHAPTER 8

TELL YOURSELF THE TRUTH

S o here we are, lazy thinkers with faulty memories being pulled by loved ones to be who they want us to be. How do we take charge of ourselves? How do we be true to ourselves? How do we move past denial to detachment? How do we uncover the shame and guilt of family secrets without unraveling the fabric of our lives? How do we confront collusion and finally figure out what's really true?

By telling ourselves the truth.

Telling ourselves the truth means that we have to move beyond the fairy-tale world of children's stories. That world doesn't exist in this age. As painful as it can be, we have to deal with the *what is* and the *what is not*, not *what should be, what could be,* and/or *what other people need to do to live up to our expectations.* Need I also say, we need to acknowledge what we're doing or not doing to live up to our own expectations?

Life isn't fair. Good people *do* have bad things happen to them. When we stay at wishful thinking or "denial" about what's happening, we're unable to deal with what is. If we don't know what's going on, we can't take care of it.

The reality is, sometimes people do rotten things. Sometimes people change. Sometimes they change their minds, and sometimes they're influenced by people or ideas that we don't like. Nothing is ever going to stay the same. Even if we couldn't predict the change, don't cause it, and don't want it, we can't avoid it.

Denial

You've heard the accusations. The smug righteousness. The trivial condensation of your pain: "You're just in denial," or even worse, "Denial isn't just another river in Egypt."

The look on your accuser's face. Their tone of voice. Their unwillingness to hear anything you say in your defense. All these signs say they're right and you're not dealing with "reality." You should just stop it, right now! Stop feeling and thinking what you feel and think. Start seeing things the way they do, the right way.

Their accusations and unwillingness to hear what you say assume denial is a conscious, intentional process: we choose not to attend to what is obviously happening. We really know what we should be doing, but choose not to do it. We're purposely avoiding taking action. And that's bad. We're bad.

But denial is neither that simple, that deliberate, nor that bad. While your accusers may know more in general than you do about the challenges or issues you're struggling with, they don't necessarily know more about you than you know yourself. And even if they're right, they have no right to be abusive toward you as you're trying to resolve challenges in your life.

None of us sees our own situations the way others see them. We really believe we're right and know what's happening. We consciously choose to do what we think is right, even if things aren't getting resolved or we don't feel better. It's hard to understand why others accuse us of being in denial. It sure feels like we're doing our best to deal with the challenges and issues we face.

So let's look more closely both at denial and at how denial operates when you're dealing with imposed changes.

First Reactions

In any crisis, most people react with "denial." You can hear them say it: "Oh, no!"

And those words of initial denial can mean any one of a number of things:

- I can't believe it. It couldn't happen.
- I don't want it to be happening.

- I want things to go back to the way they were just a few minutes ago.
- I'm sure that it's all a bad dream. (Usually this is what you think when you first wake up and for a minute you're sure everything's just fine.)

Everyone reacts this way. Everyone has these initial responses to crises, horrible accidents, or betrayal.

It's normal and expected. We don't want things to change for the worst.

We don't want what's happening to happen, so we call out, "Oh, no!"

And it's a good thing we do. This initial reaction of denial helps us deal with the shock. Denial is a defense mechanism. We use it to protect us when we've been assaulted. Our bodies need this time to take care of us.

With an accident, this initial reaction doesn't last long. The reality of the crisis demands action. We have to get help to the injured, arrange for medical care, fix or replace what has been damaged. We start to accept the reality of the crisis by dealing with the details and taking action. Initial denial helps us as we take charge. Only later do we realize the significance of what's happened.

Long-Term Denial

Long-term denial is fostered by more subtle or unbelievable changes. Long-term denial is also much more problematic for both the people caught up in disbelief and those around them.

How could anyone not know what's going on around them? How could someone continue not to recognize what's obviously happening? How can others charge you with denial when you really don't know? And how come they get so angry at you when you don't know?

One way to think about denial is with the passivity model first outlined by therapist Jackie Schiff in her work with seriously disturbed patients. This isn't the only model, but it can help us think about how we approach problems and crises.

Using this model does not imply that people who are in long-term denial are seriously disturbed. They're trying, as best they can, to cope with the crisis they're faced with.

Schiff said we operate at one of four levels when we're stuck in passivity, or in our case I'll use the word *denial*:

- Level one is no acknowledgment of a problem. Nothing happened. He didn't do it. It didn't happen. You say to yourself, "I can't understand what everyone is making such a fuss about. Of course it isn't true."
- Level two acknowledges the event. It did happen. But you trivialize or minimize the importance or the impact of what happened. It's no big thing, you say. Or it really didn't hurt anyone. It won't make any difference. This isn't so bad. Why's everyone making such a fuss?
- Level three acknowledges there is a problem, and it's important. But, you tell yourself, there's no solution. So you just have to keep on keeping on. Or as one woman said, we just have to figure out how to live with it and get on with our lives. There's nothing that can be done.
- Level four recognizes a solution exists, but someone like you couldn't implement that solution. It might be easy for other people, but you don't have the courage, the strength, the resources, or . . . fill in the blank. Other people may be able to fix things, but not you.

Long-term denial occurs when someone gets stuck at level one or level two: not acknowledging there is a problem and/or minimizing the impact or importance of the problem.

When you get caught up in this kind of denial, one of two things is happening: Either you don't have the information and education about what's happening so you can figure it out, or the person or institution who's caused the crisis is acting so out of character, so far from the assumptions and expectations you have for them, that you find it hard to believe that what's happening has actually happened. Let's look at lack of information first.

Lack of Information
Just because you don't have the information needed to make sense out of the crisis doesn't mean information isn't available. Other people may have the information. You just don't have it.

It may be that you've never come across this situation before. Or it doesn't fit what you know about these kinds of things. Or you may think you know what's right, and find out there's much more information you didn't realize you needed or could have had.

It's as if your manual on how to program your VCR was written in Japanese, not English. Then your friends and family get mad at you for not being able to program the VCR on the first try. Sure, you know about VCRs. You know most of them can either play tapes from the tape-rental place or record programs off the air.

You may have rented lots of tapes. Or even own tapes. You have no problem playing tapes.

It's trying to figure out how to record a program that's hard. Then when you turn to the manual for help, you can't make sense out of it. So you go back to renting and buying prerecorded tapes.

Soon you don't even think your machine is capable of recording. When someone asks you if you can record a program for them, you reply, "My machine doesn't record." And it doesn't. It never has and it probably never will.

You don't experience this as denial. It's an accurate representation of your experience with this machine.

Knowing how to program your VCR, or not knowing how to program your VCR, is trivial compared with resolving life crises. But there are some real similarities.

You know a lot about your life and the people in your life. You know what you expect and plan for. You may have lived with the person who's challenging you for a long time. You think you know all about what he's capable of and the things he can and will do.

But you may not know it all.

Not knowing leaves you in a vulnerable and disempowered place. You get enmeshed in other people's definitions of reality and start to doubt your own thoughts, feelings, and behavior. After all, this is a person you love.

It's easy to start feeling as if you're responsible for keeping it all together. It's easy to get lost in the dailiness of the relationship and the problems. And then you get accused of being in denial.

Denial and Deception

Significant relationships greatly impact the process of "denial." Let's say we are sitting here in a house in Massachusetts, and you point to a rattlesnake coiled on the floor between us. I look at the snake and say, "There's no snake there." That's level-one denial.

Or if I say, "Well, maybe it's a snake, but it's just a harmless garter snake, not a rattlesnake," then I'm not denying the snake, but denying by minimizing the danger of the snake: level-two denial.

But let's say we are sitting in a suburban home in Massachusetts, and you see just the tip of a tail of a rattlesnake behind my chair. I can't see it from where I'm sitting. You tell me there's a rattlesnake in the room. Then the snake slithers quietly away and hides behind the baseboard within the walls.

At the same time, people I know and trust tell me you're a liar. And I know there are few, if any, rattlesnakes in suburban Massachusetts.

So I discount what you, a perfect stranger, are saying and listen to my friends and family.

I think about what I already know about rattlesnakes and the likelihood of having one in my house here in Massachusetts.

Then my spouse, whom I believe to love me, respect me, and tell me the truth, also tells me you are lying.

Now, who would I believe?

It is easy for you to say that I am in denial. You saw the snake.

I not only didn't see it, but I didn't expect to see it, it's now not visible, and everyone whom I love, trust, and respect is telling me that it doesn't exist.

My saying the snake doesn't exist is not denial. It's how relationships work. We believe the people we know and trust rather than strangers, especially when they are telling us something hard to imagine.

I'm not in denial. I know there's no snake.

Even if the snake rattled, or if I heard something move behind my chair, it would take me a long time to realize the people who were closest to me were deceiving me and a stranger was telling me the truth.

During the time it takes to sort this out, to realize a loved one is lying and has betrayed us while strangers are telling us the truth, we're accused of being in denial, or being in a dysfunctional relationship. Or being sick, bad, or crazy.

We're none of these.

It's not dysfunction, it's life!

We base relationships on lots of assumptions, but one of the most important is that the people we love won't hurt us or betray us. Strangers may hurt us, but not the ones we love.

We don't automatically stop and question our assumptions every time something happens. We don't automatically consider our loved ones wrong and strangers right.

We can't have a relationship without these assumptions. The assumption that your loved ones will be true to you is the most important assumption for healthy relationships. That's why I said it's life, not dysfunction.

We all operate with a set of assumptions, a set of relationship rules that we believe our loved ones share and honor.

Unfortunately when it comes to imposed change, reality doesn't match our assumptions and beliefs. People who say they love us *do* hurt us. The people we love can be strangers. They're not who we thought they were. They may even purposely deceive us.

Your loved one may tell you they love you, work hard at covering up their betrayal and deceit, and even get angry and blame you if you start to question them or their behavior.

Loved ones deceive us so they can continue doing what they're doing. Whether it's a kid taking drugs or being sexually active, or a spouse hurting others or stealing our money, they want to keep doing it. They have to keep the deception intact.

Your loved one has to convince you that there's no snake, no matter what evidence exists. They become experts at deception. And you have no reason to question their lies.

To accuse you of being in denial when you have been the target of a deliberate campaign of deception is not only not helpful, but it deflects responsibility and accountability from the deceiver to the deceived.

A major crisis; a teen who is involved with drugs; intrafamily emotional, physical, or sexual abuse; unexpected job loss; betrayal by or loss of a loved one forces you to reevaluate and modify how you see the world, what life for people like you is all about.

It takes time to assimilate the changes, to understand what's happened, to realize how many things you've taken for granted are no longer true, and to get the energy to start responding, to make accommodations and get your life back on track. It can take days, weeks, months, even years to go through this process. During that time, you'll gradually pass through all the stages of denial. As you get more information, you'll see the reality of your crisis. You'll start to understand you aren't alone. Others have found solutions to problems similar to yours. You'll start to learn from their expertise to see how you can take steps to resolve your challenge and take charge of your life.

Going through this process can be very painful. You may find you've lost something. You may find long-term friends or associates no longer fit in your life. Their belief systems and/or values are no longer the same as yours. You may have a crisis of faith. God has let you down, or you may feel you've been dealt an unfair blow. Your feelings will ebb and flow: sadness, anger, frustration, or resignation.

Detachment

As we continue to tell ourselves the truth and take charge of events and people we can't control, we'll move from denial to detachment.

Detachment lets us move painful, uncomfortable, and/or unpleasant experiences away from the main focus of our lives. We acknowledge what has happened, without the emotional charge that denial holds.

Detachment's not a conscious action. We won't wake up one morning and say, "Okay, no more. I'm done with it." Rather, one day we realize we aren't continually going back, revisiting our past experiences, and reexperiencing the pain and anguish we felt then.

You detach from an experience in two ways:

- You hold the person who caused the incident accountable, not yourself.
- You acknowledge you did the best you could with who you were and what you knew at the time.

By holding the person who caused the incident accountable for what happened, you put the responsibility for bad behavior on the person who did it and get away from blaming the victim. We start to see our crisis as something that happened to us, not who we are.

But what about those things we did have some hand in? What about being deceived by a loved one? With these incidents, we detach by acknowledging we did the best we could at the time. We learned from that experience. We're not like that anymore. We're wiser, more capable, more competent than we used to be because of the experiences we've had.

We know we've detached when we stop making current decisions based on our out-of-control past event.

> *Eileen wore only long pants and long-sleeved turtleneck shirts. Both summer and winter, she never left her apartment unless she was totally covered up, no matter how hot it was outside. When friends or acquaintances commented on how she looked, she would get flustered and quickly leave. Her friends couldn't understand why even well-meaning remarks seemed to upset her so. Few, if any, of them knew that some years previously Eileen had been raped as she was coming home from the library one summer evening. At that time, she had on a sleeveless T-shirt and shorts. She was convinced her clothing was an invitation to her attacker to take advantage of her.*
>
> *Dan was a confirmed former smoker. He frequented restaurants and public events only where there was a clear nonsmoking policy. If someone violated that smoking policy while Dan was around, he became vicious. He would loudly berate the smoker, calling him names and verbally abusing him.*
>
> *Jim's thing was alcohol. Although he hadn't had anything to drink for over twenty years, he still put alcohol front and center, the major determinant in his social life. He would not go to a party where alcohol was served, would not go to a restaurant that served alcohol, and would not associate with anybody who ever drank, no matter how little.*

All three of these people are still hooked into their crises. They're still experiencing the emotional charge and haven't yet moved what happened to them to the background of their lives. It's still in the foreground. They're still making current life choices based on their past. They haven't detached.

Another detachment indicator is increasing our social and professional circles to include friends and associates from a wide variety of interests, backgrounds, and activities. People who haven't moved on get caught up in surrounding themselves with people of like mind. It's too dangerous to have a variety of people around. You might find without this issue you've got nothing.

Watch out for "You owe me." It's a predictable feeling when someone's betrayed or injured you. But it keeps us connected and implies we can't move on until somehow they've acknowledged or compensated us. If we're still expecting compensation, we can't detach.

Detachment is more of an "Oh, yeah" response in which we're no longer waiting for the person who wronged us to admit, make whole, or even acknowledge that they may have done something that wasn't quite right.

When we're detached, we stop thinking about what's happened for long periods of time. We don't think about it because it no longer controls our lives. In denial, we don't think about it because it's too painful and we're too upset. In detachment, the upset is no longer there. It's become part of our personal history, not personal present.

Detachment lets us take the lessons we need from our experiences, discard the rest, and go on. No matter how awful an experience may have been, we learn so much about life when we face a crisis. If we don't draw the lessons from our past, we just get another opportunity to learn the lesson.

Critical-Thinking Skills

Detachment is possible when we tell ourselves the truth about what happened and how not to let it happen again. Telling ourselves the truth starts developing and honing our critical-thinking skills.

Critical thinking doesn't mean negative thinking, but careful thinking. We'll use all of the thinking processes—logic, intuition, resources—to gather and analyze data so we can make good decisions and solve our problems.

Critical thinking lets us think first and then act. We suspend judgment until we consider all of the aspects of the issues we're dealing with. We examine what's happening, what we think about what's happening, and what our options are before we choose any of them.

Respond, Not React

Thinking first and then acting means that we'll respond, not react. We decide what we want to do, rather than being on automatic pilot.

Ron's temper and need to be right all the time got him into trouble for most of his work life. Although he had lots of education, many employment opportunities were closed to him. Unable to get a professional job in his field, he was working as a clerk in a store. He was fired from that position when he punched a customer whom Ron described as being "disrespectful." When he was justifying his behavior later, Ron said he had to hit the man. He couldn't help it. It wasn't his fault. Anybody would do what he did. After all, the man had been disrespectful.

Ron was caught in reaction mode, rather than respond mode. He'd had a hard time finding any job, even this one that he considered menial and beneath him. He was furious with the store for not supporting employees against "abusive" patrons and sacrificing him on the altar of "The customer's always right." He didn't understand that most people don't respond to a verbal thrust from a customer with a physical thrust of their own.

Ron reacts to crisis, rather than thinking through what would be the best thing to do. Most of us have a hard time thinking clearly and acting appropriately when we're feeling strongly. Thinking clearly is hard when we're very angry, sad, or afraid. Thinking through a crisis takes time. We need to plan what to do to respond when we find ourselves in tough spots.

- Count to ten before you open your mouth. Take several deep breaths and focus on anything in the room, until you can calm down and choose what to do next.
- Write a letter to the person you're angry with, then sleep on the letter. Read the letter again in the morning before you tear it up.
- Don't take it personally. As soon as you start thinking the other person is deliberately trying to hurt you, you put yourself into react mode. You've given them control.

Reacting is letting the other person have control of the situation and you. Take charge by deciding how you are going to respond, rather than going along with the other person's agenda.

Suspend Judgment

Suspending judgment is the second critical-thinking skill. Too often we judge automatically. Before we even realize what we've done, we've sized up a situation and made a judgment about it. Then our judgment influences what we think and do next.

We're exhorted not to judge one another; to judge not, lest ye be judged. And yet, just like making assumptions, it's almost impossible not to make judgments. We quickly and nonconsciously, throughout the day, make decisions and judgments on just about everything we come in contact with. It's automatic.

It's a good thing we do make judgments. We need our judgments to help us make decisions about what we do, what we avoid, and to make sure that we're associating with people, things, and ideas that are consistent with our underlying values.

And that's the difficulty about making judgments. As soon as we judge whether something is like us, is consistent with what we know and already believe, we tend to put more weight on that knowledge. We pay more attention to, and give a higher value to, information that is consistent with what we already believe. We pay attention to things that we agree with and don't pay attention to things we disagree with. We do this with seemingly trivial or unimportant things: what colors we choose for our clothes, what style of furnishing for our homes, or what kind of car we drive. In the greater scheme of things, as long as these items will perform the function, i.e., keep us covered, provide us with comfort, or get us where we want to go, our personal tastes and styles aren't all that important.

If our personal judgments and preferences extend to how we get news and information, what books are worth reading, what magazines are worth our time and attention, then our judgments start to color the way we see the world. If our judgments extend to people we dismiss out of hand because of the color of their skin, their sex, their sexual preference, their education, their national origin, then we start cutting out huge groups of people who can enrich the perspective by which we see our lives.

When we hear new information and data, we judge it very quickly. If we agree with the perspective, if we agree with the point of view of the new information that is coming in, we're more willing to accept it as true, regardless of whether it is true. If we disagree with the perspective or the point of view of the report, we'll usually think the information is flawed, not accurate, or poorly presented. We may even go so far as to question the motives of the organization or people who have put the new information out.

At some level, it's a good thing we're very conservative when it comes to changing our minds and gathering new information. It gives us the stability and certainty that we need to establish a predictability in our lives. Unfortunately, we miss new or important data that contradicts or is inconsistent with what we already know to be true.

> *Tina loved her nephew Jon, but found him a real challenge to talk with. His whole view of the world was totally different from hers. She was a lifelong Democrat and liberal; he was a very conservative Republican. She was a Unitarian; he was a devout Mormon. Her values were based on broad principles; his on a code of specific rules. She adopted a live-and-let-live perspective; he discounted and dismissed anyone who didn't think the way he did, the right way.*

Tina and Jon didn't have fights, but they did have long, well-thought-out arguments. While neither converted the other, both admitted their own thinking was improved by having to explain themselves to someone who didn't think the way they did. It helped them both think about what they thought, what data they used, where they got their information, and if, in fact, they really believed what they had been saying. They each had to go back and rejudge many of their thoughts and beliefs.

We can't suspend judgment unless we know what standards, outcomes, and results we're looking for. Making a decision implies judgment, but unless our judgment is based on all the available information and data, we'll find ourselves jumping to hasty conclusions or looking for where the answer is easiest.

It's like the old cartoon that shows a man searching the ground under a lit lamppost. His friend asks him what he's looking for. When he replies, his keys, the friend then asks, "Is this where you lost them? I'll help you look." And the man says, "No, I lost them over there in the dark, but it's easier to look here in the light."

We all find it easier to look in the light than to look in the dark. Unfortunately if we stay in the light, sometimes we're not going to find what we're looking for.

Examine before Accepting

When it comes to critical-thinking skills, the ability to examine data is one of the most crucial. This is the know-your-experts step. There's always somebody willing to tell you what you should do. Make sure they're credible and have your best interest at heart.

- Who says? Check out their biases and point of view.
- Why believe them? What stake do they have in what they're supporting?
- Be logical and intuitive. Do the analysis and check out your feelings and beliefs. Make sure both are a fit.

Beware of Satisficing

Satisficing means using the first solution to a problem that seems okay, rather than examining all the alternatives. When we're eager for a solution, we'll grab the first solution that looks like it might work, that will satisfy the minimal requirements for resolution of the problem. We'll grab the first solution and miss a much better one that would be evident with a little more digging. Don't automatically go with your first idea. Make sure you have at least a couple of possible solutions so you can choose what to do. Rank your solutions next to the evidence you've gathered to see which one is really the best.

Devil's Advocate

An important final step, especially when no one is disagreeing with you, is to find a devil's advocate, someone who'll try to argue you out of your position. They can be a real pain in the behind, but they can also help uncover hidden pitfalls or problems. Find someone who, even if he or she doesn't hold the other side, is skilled enough in problem solving to take the position of an opponent and challenge you to think clearly through your solution from an opposing point of view.

Confronting Your Past
without Destroying Your Future

One of the most important things to tell ourselves the truth about is our own past. Yet as we saw in chapter six, our memories are not always reliable or accurate. It's not uncommon to have two different people, with all good intentions, giving dramatically different reports of the same instance. So how can you get resolution?

Feelings from your memories and the beliefs you have about yourself coming from those memories give you the leverage to make changes. Many difficult, traumatic, or upsetting events in our past leave us with feelings of either shame or guilt. With shame, we think *who we are* is bad, that we don't measure up. It's the outward manifestation of having a conscience and making evaluations about ourselves. Our basic self-worth and who we are as a person don't measure up.

Guilt, on the other hand, is that part of our conscience that says *what we did* was bad. In essence, we're a good person, but these particular behaviors or actions were not right.

Feelings of both shame and guilt can come from prior experiences. We can remember hearing the words of our parents, nuns, teachers, or other valued adults: "You did what? You're a bad girl. You should be ashamed."

And we make the leap from *doing bad*, guilt, to *being bad*, shame.

We can also feel shame when we're one of the major characters in a family drama that results in a shameful family secret. We don't even need to be the one who is doing shameful things. Witnessing a family member doing something bad can be enough. We're told over and over, "Don't tell. Don't let other people know what happened here." We start to believe we're unlike other people. Our family doesn't measure up. We're ashamed of who we are.

When we're told not to talk about what's happened, it becomes unspeakable. A child feels ashamed even if he can't remember why.

Collusion

Conventional wisdom classifies collusion as bad, something we shouldn't do. Like judgments or assumptions, people routinely, commonly collude. For the most part, we're so unaware of doing it, we can't admit that we're doing it even when confronted with irrefutable evidence. We don't realize that what we're doing is collusion.

Collusion is the agreement to do or to be what another person wants us to be, even if some of those things are impossible, don't make sense, and/or are contradictory. We agree to do them with the understanding the other person will do something for us. For the most part, collusion works out of awareness. We don't talk about or even realize we're colluding.

When Bill and Diane were going through the possession-division phase of their divorce, he suggested he keep the china and she take the silver. He pointed out his parents had given them most of the silver, he knew she really liked it, and that if she was willing to take the bad press with his parents, he could say she took it and his parents would replace it. Bill and Diane were overt with each other. They colluded with his parents, who wanted to think Diane the bad guy in the divorce and to reward Bill for having to put up with her.

Sandy found lipstick smudges on one of Tom's shirt collars. She pulled the shirt out of the hamper and left it on top so he could surely see it. The next day, the shirt was gone, and that evening, Tom brought Sandy home a very expensive piece of jewelry. Neither ever talked about the shirt, or the quid pro quo the jewelry represented.

Collusion is a nonverbal, unstated agreement to act in certain ways. We keep the secrets and let things happen. It's almost as if Sandy said to Tom, "I won't nag you about your running around, if you buy me expensive jewelry."

Collusion becomes the ultimate quid pro quo, something for something, that can slip over into emotional or financial blackmail very quickly. Family members who have hurt others either physically, verbally, or emotionally will "pay them off" with expensive gifts, promises of an inheritance, or a lavish lifestyle.

If the collusion in a family involves early childhood abuse, then breaking the rule of silence, speaking about the unspeakable as an adult, is guaranteed to produce angry uproar. We're faced with the same situation Mary Beth faced in chapter six where she wanted to confront her brother about abusing her when she was a child, yet didn't want to destroy her own future or the future of her family relationships. It felt like a no-win situation. If she didn't confront him, she would be condoning his behavior and not honoring herself. If she did confront him, she'd honor herself at the risk of a big family blowup.

Examine your goals and motivation for the confrontation. Are you looking for revenge? Do you want someone else to hurt just as much as he hurt you? Are you looking to shame the other person, to take him down from his position in the family? Is this a payback opportunity for you? Do you want to get back at him for what he did to you?

Or are you looking more for your own self-interest in terms of generating sympathy from the world, from outsiders, and let your family of origin be hanged?

If your confrontation objective has any of these "I'll get you" tinges to it, be assured that by trying to get them, you'll hurt yourself more.

You won't get what you want from the confrontation, especially if the confrontation has to do with previous abuse, especially sexual abuse.

The primary issue here is not sexuality but power. When people who've attained positions of power are accused by someone less powerful, they'll usually crush the person who's accusing them rather than lose face or lose their position in the community.

Even if the accusations are true, can be documented, or the family initially rallies around the person who is confronting, it's not unusual to find the attitudes and atmosphere shifting from one of loving support to one of shooting the messenger. So the person who was abused and/or victimized finds herself in the uncomfortable position of now being dealt with more harshly for being hurt and talking about it than the person who hurt her.

It is also likely that the person who is being confronted now for acts done in the past either has no recollection of the incidents or has totally changed who and what he is in terms of character and personality. As we saw in the section on memory, oftentimes the perpetrators or the abusers really don't remember, or they remember and distort or discount the importance of the event. In some ways this is because of the way that we all remember our previous experiences. They don't wake up one morning and say, "I think I'm going to distort my memory so I won't have to be accountable for it." The process is much more subtle, much more insidious, and much more pervasive than that.

Or it may well be that the person who was, at one time, mean, malicious, and abusive is no longer that way. He truly has changed who and what he is. That person who attacked you, that person who was so mean to you, may bear little if any resemblance to the person he or she is today.

So where does this leave you with your need for confrontation and putting your own past to rest without destroying your future?

Preparation is essential, knowing very clearly what you want for yourself and what you're willing to do regardless of what the other person says, does, or agrees with. The confrontation is for you, not the other person. To tie his response to the success of the confrontation means you've not detached. You're still allowing the other person to control your life.

Think very carefully about how or if you'll talk to him again if he doesn't respond or reply in the way that you want him to. He won't change his mind, no matter if you tell him forty-three more times. This doesn't mean that you can't ever talk to him about it again, but it does mean saying the same things over and over may well harden his resolve to avoid, deny, and withdraw from your confrontations. He'll quickly start to label it nagging, rather than an opportunity for dialogue.

> *Rebecca's teenage son had a very serious automobile accident within six weeks of getting his driver's license. Although he wasn't badly injured, her car was totaled and one of the other kids in the car was seriously hurt. She was furious with him and yet, after the initial angry blowup, was able to put her energy into resolving the legalities, the insurance company requirements, and monitoring the recovery of the child who was so badly injured. One day, in a conference with her son and their attorney, the attorney remarked that Rebecca seemed to be over her anger about the accident. Her son quickly piped up, "I think she's still angry. She's just not talking about it."*
>
> *And at that point, Rebecca turned to him and said, "You know how angry I am?" And he said, "Yup." And she said, "Then I don't have to say it again." He said, "Yeah, I know, Mom. Thanks."*

Later, when we were talking about the accident, Rebecca reported that as she came to grips and was resolving her feelings about the accident and her son's irresponsibility and the legal case, she realized she needed to keep him current about how her feelings and thoughts were changing.

Telling ourselves the truth means we need to understand how we shade, color, and misunderstand or misrepresent what is happening. Some of our difficulties with the truth are understandable reactions to unbelievable experiences. We don't have the information we need, or what we've experienced is so out of character for people like us, or like our loved ones, we have a hard time admitting what has happened.

Some of our difficulties with telling ourselves the truth come from getting caught up in the processing necessary to assimilate our experiences. Or we get so caught up in blaming or attached to feelings of needing retribution from those who have caused us harm.

We tell ourselves the truth by clearly thinking about what has happened, our part and the part of others. We thoughtfully respond to what has happened, not react. We suspend judgment, analyzing new information against our values and beliefs, making judgments rather than jumping to hasty conclusions. We examine before accepting, checking our new information and the points of view of others. We employ both our logic and our intuition to see if there's a real fit.

We carefully decide if and how we'll confront the past so we won't destroy our future. Telling ourselves the truth means honoring ourselves while not allowing others to run our lives. We let go of what has happened to us so as not to prevent a future of joy and satisfaction.

Exercises for Chapter 8

WHERE ARE YOU ON THE DENIAL PROGRESSION?
Think through the challenge that you are experiencing. Where are you stuck?

Are you still at the nothing's-changed stage?

Or have you moved on to "things have changed, but it's no big deal"?

Or are you sure there have been major changes, important changes, but there's nothing anyone can do about it?

Or have you realized that there have been major, important changes and others can fix things like this, but not you?

What is the impact on your feelings about yourself, about the other people involved, and about your life, based on the perspective you have of the challenge you face?

DENIAL AND DECEPTION

Are you still unsure there's a snake in your living room? Who is telling you the snake exists? Who is telling you the snake doesn't exist? What would you have to shift in your relationships to "see the snake"?

CRITICAL-THINKING SKILLS

Which critical-thinking skill is the hardest for you? The easiest?

What impact does this have on resolving your challenge?

CHAPTER 9

ARGUE FROM REASON

T here's always conflict, especially if a situation or a person is out of control. When feelings run high, reason runs low. In an attempt to "take control," many people say or do things that they otherwise wouldn't say or do. They can be hurtful, unreasonable, counterintuitive. They say and do things that don't make sense.

Then you get into one of two patterns of conflict: arguing without end, or angry blowups. Arguing without end is called bickering.

Joe and Sue bicker constantly. He says he's right and she's wrong. She counters with he doesn't know what he's talking about. They came to a therapy session still fuming from a three-day-old argument about whether people should buy decorative or functional canisters for their kitchen counters. Joe knew everyone should use functional canisters. Any other kind were tacky, a waste of money, and should not even be sold. Sue asserted people should be able to buy any kind of canister they wanted. There was no way either would give in and allow the other to win.

Joe and Sue get caught up in the argument without end. Their argument isn't about canisters. It's about who's in charge. It's about who's right, who has the power.

Both Joe and Sue use reasonable, rational, logical arguments to press their points. They also appeal to the other person's sense of fair play, guilt, previous promises, or their own power. Nonetheless, tempers get frazzled and the pot keeps simmering. Neither wins, both lose.

Angry blowups don't solve anything, either. They're tension relieving, not goal achieving. But the tension relieving comes at a price. Words said in anger, accusations, and epithets can't be taken back. Hurt and bad feelings continue long after the argument is over, especially when the argument results in withdrawal and avoidance. Both parties storm off. They never resolve the issues. But eventually they start talking again, as if there had never been an argument. This just means they get to have the argument again, because nothing has been resolved.

No one wants to lose an argument. We all lose when we don't know how to argue effectively. An effective argument gets all the issues out on the table and lets us figure out where we agree and where we disagree, what needs to be done and what doesn't have to be done to resolve this problem. Whether we argue logically or emotionally, most of us don't know how to take both sides. We're much better at confronting than responding. Much better at attack than defense. So the battle consists of a heavy barrage followed by retreat.

Like most people who experience conflict in their relationships, Joe and Sue have another problem with their arguments. They confuse having an argument with making an argument. When people have an argument, each wants to win. Each wants their own way. After all, they both know who's right. Everyone else is wrong.

Making an argument focuses on problem solutions. It puts forth a point of view, a perspective, a suggestion of what might work to resolve the issues of the dispute. You make an argument when you are more interested in what's right than in who's right.

When you focus on who's right, you get arguments without end and angry blowups. When you focus on making arguments for solutions, you resolve the issues and have fewer and fewer arguments, even though you still see things differently.

To make effective arguments, we need to keep the discussion on the issues and help each other by clarifying points, not slipping into illogical or invalid arguments or escalating into personal attacks. To argue effectively, we need both logical and intuitive thinking skills.

Logical Thinking

Logic has a long history of being the best way to think through and analyze ideas and concepts. Logic is the base for reasoning—making sense of new information and then using that sense to make decisions. Logic helps us answer questions about what's true, what's valid, what information and data is helpful, and what's not. It also gives us a way of structuring our thinking and sorting out complex problems.

Knowing how logical thinking works helps you refute arguments and stand up for yourself when others are telling you what should be true for you.

Logic itself is straightforward. The rules are few and simple. The way we get into trouble with logic is by unwittingly or purposefully not following the rules. Then our arguments are illogical. Or we'll argue logically, but the starting point we use is flawed. It may be not true or not understood or not agreed to by all the parties in the argument. Then we'll get into an argument without end, and the likelihood is that one party will overpower the other.

There are two primary ways we reason logically: induction and deduction. With induction, we start with observations and then make generalizations. With deduction, we start with a generalization and then figure out if a specific case fits our generalization.

Inductive Reasoning

We use inductive thinking to predict what will happen from what has happened. We see something happen and then make a guess, or a hypothesis, about what will happen next. Most of the time, we don't even realize we're using inductive reasoning. But we use it regularly every day, for both trivial and significant events.

We use inductive reasoning when we look at the pattern of clouds in the evening sky and predict rain by morning. Or because we've had two disastrous relationships with alcoholics, we avoid any relationships because we always choose drunks.

Inductive reasoning focuses on patterns and predictions. But because they're based on generalizations, our predictions have only a probability of being true, not a certainty of truth. We still have to check out each new case for fit and truth.

Reasoning from a Special Case

A common error with inductive reasoning is to reason from a special case or from a case that is not an accurate sample of the whole universe of like cases.

When a special case is dramatic, newsworthy, or especially touching, it is easy to reason that it represents the norm and that most other cases are similar.

Because we hear of the notorious cases of children being abducted, molested, and then killed or badly hurt by strangers, it's easy to infer that our children are at most risk from stranger danger. Yet studies, law enforcement statistics, and social services statistics show just the opposite. Close to 90 percent of childhood sexual abuse is perpetrated by a family member or adults known to the family. The sample—the cases reported in the press, which we use to draw the inference—were not representative of the whole pool of cases. Our reasoning isn't valid.

How could this happen? "Stranger danger" has been the theme of child safety campaigns for years. Stranger abductions are often more graphically newsworthy and reported to the police. Abuse by family members or family friends more often goes unreported to the police and unmentioned in the media. We don't hear about it, so we don't take it into consideration when we think about this kind of abuse.

Correlation and Causation

The other difficulty common with inductive reasoning is confusing correlation and causation. We think that because one event happened before another, one causes another.

My friends tease me because everywhere I live, there's an earthquake. And it is true. Earthquakes happen where I live, even if it's a place where earthquakes don't usually happen, like Chicago, metro Boston, and metro D.C. Does that mean I make the earth move? I don't think so. In my special case, earthquakes are correlated with, or happen, where I live. I don't cause them.

Every mother's favorite faulty reasoning makes this same mistake: "Don't go out without your raincoat or you'll catch cold." There's no doubt people do catch more colds and flu during the cold, wet winter. But cold and wet don't make you sick. Colds are caused by germs. We get more colds when we're indoors more and close to others who have colds. It would make more sense for our mothers to tell us to wash our hands with soap and hot water several times a day so we wouldn't catch a cold. Now we'd be having a direct effect on how many germs we'd have.

Are there times when we got chilled and then caught a cold? Sure. And if you believe there are no coincidences, it would be easy to attribute your illness to going out in the cold. Your reason for your cold makes sense. It's easy to see and often gets supported by friends and relatives. It's just not true.

Arguing from Anecdote

With inductive reasoning, we need more than one or two cases before we can draw conclusions and make generalizations. If we don't test our conclusions, we fall into the faulty-thinking trap of arguing from anecdote.

Arguing from anecdote is the favorite tool of radio talk-show hosts and their guests. Callers tell their own personal experiences on a subject and then draw the wider conclusion that this is the way it is, always is, or should be. If the story's consistent with the host's point of view, or if it's dramatic or just told dramatically, it provides the "proof" that both caller and host are right. Their view is the way the world really works, or should work, regardless of any other evidence.

> Some years ago, a talk-show host in the Boston area decided the mandatory seat-belt law was an affront to his freedom. He wasn't going to let the government tell him what he should do while driving in his own private vehicle. His campaign was fueled by a number of callers who told stories of how they avoided being hurt in accidents because they didn't have on their seat belts. Finally they gathered enough signatures and momentum to put the measure on the ballot.
>
> Despite the research evidence to the contrary, dismissed by the radio personality and his listeners as erroneous findings of government lackey scientists, the measure passed. Seat belts were no longer required.
>
> Several months later, my son had a terrible accident. He and one of the other boys were wearing seat belts. Their injuries were minimal. The third boy wasn't buckled up. His injuries were significant. Because the law was no longer on the books, the injured boy had no liability for his injuries. I had an anecdote to argue the other side of the talk-show host's position.

There are several problems with arguing from anecdote. It is always possible to find someone who has a story to prove a point, no matter how outrageous the point or the story. The more dramatic the story, the more people are likely to put faith in it. Audiences self-select radio and television shows, as well as newspapers and magazines. People tend to watch shows or read periodicals they agree with. The shows seldom present a contrasting point of view or allow someone with a different perspective to speak. So they end up preaching to the choir. They reinforce the viewpoint the audience already has. More important, they never ask how common or how representative of the larger population this case is. Or if this ever could/would/has happened again.

Bottom line: Inductive thinking can never prove an argument. The more cases we hear, the closer we can be to being certain. But we can never be 100 percent sure this is the way it really is.

On the other hand, one case on the other side can disprove the theory, hunch, or generalization that you have developed.

What you get with inductive thinking is a generalization with a predictability of truth. Not a certainty. And even with a high probability of certainty, the likelihood of occurrence will be like our predictions of rain. Most of the time there will be rain. Sometimes not. And sometimes we'll go to bed with clear skies and wake up wet!

Deductive Reasoning

Deductive reasoning goes the other way. It starts with a given generalization and then tests a specific case. The generalization can come from your own experience, something you learned as a kid, or even cultural beliefs and values.

Deductive reasoning uses a simple form and has clear rules. But it isn't always easy.

The form usually looks like:

All A is B. (Major Premise: what we know to be true)
C is A. (Minor Premise: a specific new case)
Therefore, C is B. (Conclusion: what we now can believe is true)

Most people have trouble understanding this type of equation and find it not so helpful when they try to figure out real-life examples. So we'll use an everyday example and then the Three-Circle Test to check out if we're being logical.

Let's put some nouns in the equation first. We'll start with the family pets, a dog named Spotty and a cat called Puff.

All dogs are mammals. (What we know to be true: major premise)
Spotty is a dog. (Specific new case: minor premise)
Therefore, Spotty is a mammal. (Has to be true: conclusion)
Now let's use the Three-Circle Test.

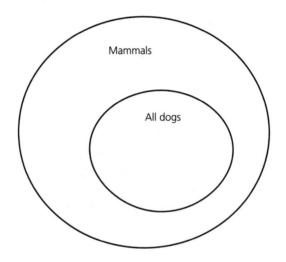

Figure 3.

The first two circles in the Three-Circle Test (figure 3) show the relationship of the major premise: All dogs are mammals. The "All dogs" circle fits inside the "Mammals" circle. Of course, there are cats, giraffes, elephants, and bears in the group of mammals, too. But let's focus on dogs.

Then our second premise, Spotty is a dog, is shown in figure 4.

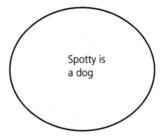

Figure 4.

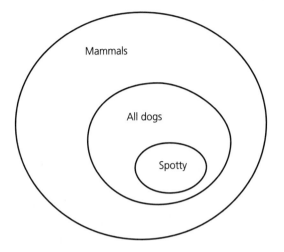

Figure 5.

Now we know where Spotty fits in the first two circles—in the circle labeled "All dogs" (figure 5).

No problem here. The conclusion holds. Our argument is both valid and true. It is valid because it kept the format. It is true because both our major premise—all dogs are mammals—and our minor premise—Spotty is a dog—are true. So our conclusion is true, also.

But let's turn it around.

All mammals are dogs. (Major premise)
Puff is a mammal. (Minor premise)
Therefore, Puff is a dog. (Conclusion)

No problem? Big problem.

The argument looks valid. It kept the form. There couldn't be any other conclusion, based on what we said (figures 6 and 7).

So the only place to put Puff is inside the mammal circle, which is inside the dog circle.

Oops . . . here's where we made our mistake. We said all mammals are dogs. They aren't. Some are giraffes, lions, bears, or ferrets.

Our major premise, the generalization we started with—all mammals are dogs—isn't true. Both premises have to be true for the con-

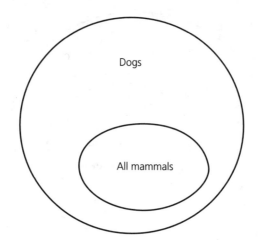

Figure 6.

Figure 7.

clusion to be true. Even with "arguing logically," there's no way Puff has to be a dog. The conclusion isn't true.

With the conclusion untrue, it doesn't matter in the everyday world that the argument is valid. The argument doesn't hold.

In some arguments, one person starts with a major premise that isn't true, like all mammals are dogs. Then he'll say Spotty is a dog. And then he'll conclude, therefore, Spotty is a mammal. Using the Three-Circle Test, the argument is shown in figure 8.

All we can say for sure is that Spotty is a dog. Because the starting point, the major premise, isn't true, we can't say we've proved Spotty is a mammal. In this case, he happens to be a mammal. We may know "Spotty is a mammal" is true. But our reasoning wasn't what made us sure it was true.

With my dog and my cat, I can quickly evaluate these logical, de-

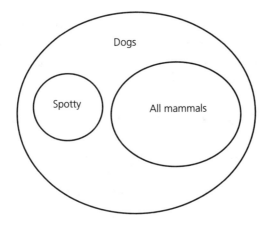

Figure 8.

ductive arguments and tell if they are both true and valid. If they aren't, I can easily explain how you're wrong when you try to use them. But in the heat of an argument, it's not so easy or so quick to evaluate arguments. Most of us have a hard time doing it in real time.

So let's look at some of the more common errors with the starting points, or premises, of arguments. We get into trouble with premises that

- are based on moral issues;
- try to express very complex issues in a simple black-and-white statement;
- we don't know enough about to evaluate;
- use the same words in very different ways; or
- use any and all disproving statements as evidence of truth.

Arguing Moral or Religious Issues

With arguments on moral or religious issues, one person will state a moral or religious belief as a given. Because they believe it, it is not only true for them, but is, or should be, true for everyone in the world. Then they use this premise to make decisions or judgments about others.

Sally had a lot of trouble with one of the women she worked with. They had different work styles, responsibilities, and priorities. Sally defined these differences as poor work habits and lack of respect for the work. She attributed these deficiencies to the fact that the woman was of another faith. Obviously, she told me, people like that had no work ethic. It was no wonder the woman did so poorly at work.

From Sally's perspective, the only people who were ethical and cared about their work were people who shared her faith. People of other faiths simply didn't have values, morals, and ethics like she did. In her commitment to her faith, she discounted that people of other faiths could feel as strongly or have moral beliefs as deep as her own.

Simplifying Complex Issues

As a graduate student, I tested children's thinking patterns to see how they worked with concepts. We showed the kids a series of pictures of cats that we slowly morphed to be dogs. We kept asking them if the animal was a cat or a dog. Eventually all the kids admitted the animal was now a dog. It had all the necessary parts to qualify as a dog. We had fun seeing how many characteristics the animal needed to be reclassified. Some kids needed the animal only to bark before changing their concept. Other kids needed the animal to have different whiskers, ears, tongue, feet, fur before they would acknowledge the animal had gone over the edge to the other category.

The problem with basing an argument on complex issues, like what makes a good spouse, a dutiful child, or a mature adult, is there is no agreed-upon line to reach to pass over from bad to okay to good to great. We fall into the trap of murky logic when we use one, or just a few, characteristics to make our case. For example, let's look at the argument:

A man who brings his check home every week is a good husband.
   (Major premise)
George brings his check home every week. (Minor premise)
Therefore, George is a good husband. (Conclusion)

Fine as far as it goes—but what if George is drunk every night, or runs around, or hits his wife and children?

Being a good husband is a complex, multidimensional concept. A single factor is not enough to prove the point. Even if a husband does one or doesn't do another of the desired behaviors, it may not be enough to prove the point.

This murky thinking can work both ways. Most of us have participated in an argument that took the form:

A good wife always does the laundry. (Major premise)
You didn't do the laundry. (Minor premise)
Therefore, you aren't a good wife. (Conclusion)

The problem with these types of arguments is that they assume there are only two choices—good spouse and not good spouse—and that the outcome is determined by a single factor—doing or not doing the laundry. The argument may be logically valid, but it is trivial and uninteresting. It doesn't reflect the full complexity of the situation.

Not Knowing Enough to Evaluate

We can also make trouble for ourselves when our starting point isn't true, or when we don't know enough about what we're talking about. This is what happened with Puff and the mammals example. Our starting point wasn't true. Most of us would agree not all mammals are dogs. We know the major premise is false. So we can quickly see the problem with the argument.

If we don't know enough to know if a major premise is really true, we can't tell if an argument holds. Someone could tell me fifty-four forty was a location in Texas and my quilt pattern was a battle cry of the Alamo, and I wouldn't know if they were right or wrong. I don't know which is longitude and latitude and what the phrase means. What I don't know can hurt or confuse me. When I don't know, others can convince me they're right, even when they aren't.

Using Words in Different Ways

We know what we mean by the words and concepts we use. It's so evident to us, surely everyone else knows what we do. We think they use the words we use to mean the same thing we mean. Yet many an argument has escalated to conflict because we don't define our terms. Logicians call this begging the question. We haven't done the foundation work for the argument. We aren't talking about the same things.

This lack of understanding was apparent in an argument I overheard about abortion. One person said:

It is always wrong to murder other human beings. (Major premise)
Abortion is murder of a baby. (Minor premise)
Therefore, abortion is murder. (Conclusion)

The other person replied:

I agree, it is always wrong to murder other human beings. (Major
    premise)
*But a fetus is not a separate human being, but part of a woman's
    body.* (Minor premise)
Therefore, abortion is not wrong. (Conclusion)

These two were going at it hot and heavy, and it looked like they were going to stay at it until they could get agreement on one side or the other. But they'd never get agreement.

It sounded like they were arguing about abortion. They weren't. They were arguing about when human life begins.

There's no way for these two to resolve their argument, because they're both taking as a given a conflicting point of view on the status of the unborn. They're both begging the question. They're each using circular reasoning: their conclusions were a restatement of the major premise, given the perspective provided by the minor premise.

This may seem like nitpicking, but for the whole abortion debate rocking this country, and indeed many personal arguments, the lack of consensus on the definitions of terms is the foundation of the disagreement, not the debates that are taking place. These arguments can never be resolved. It's like arguing about whether a pear is an apple or an orange. The way the terms are defined, the argument becomes meaningless. And they just go on and on.

In personal relationships, arguments that don't have agreement on the definition of terms can be the foundation of constant bickering and bad feelings, poisoning the opportunity for happiness and peace. People slip into an argument without end, with each party taking the position that they'd rather be right than come to any resolution. So the argument continues indefinitely, and the real differences and difficulties won't ever be resolved.

Self-Sealing Arguments

Another reasoning fallacy particularly potent in arguments of personal beliefs, ideologies, or worldviews is the self-sealing argument. Self-sealing arguments take positions that no evidence can possibly refute. While this may seem attractive, and a good way to win any argument, self-sealing arguments are both useless and, again, potentially damaging to your relationship.

One of the most common forms of self-sealing arguments is claiming the other person is not sophisticated enough or learned enough to understand the concept being argued. It is evident in the following conversation:

JOHN: All families are dysfunctional.
MIKE: My family wasn't dysfunctional. I had a good childhood.
JOHN: That just shows how dysfunctional it was. You're in denial.
MIKE: I'm not in denial. It was okay.
JOHN: You are too in denial. You're just too dysfunctional to see how dysfunctional your family was.

No matter what argument Mike offers, John will use it as "proof" of his point.

Self-sealing arguments often center on personal beliefs, attributes, or attitudes. The arguer—John, in this example—for some personal reason sets himself up as the expert, the one who knows, and Mike is relegated to the subordinate position. Nothing Mike can say will disprove John's position. Just try. John'll tell you you're wrong!

Carolyn, her mother, and two sisters appeared on a television talk show as an example of an estranged family. All four of them agreed they had been upset and angry at one another for many years.

Carolyn told of many instances when her sisters didn't treat her lovingly or fairly. She was angry at her mother for taking her sisters' side in disputes and not supporting her.

Meanwhile Carolyn's mother and sisters agreed things hadn't always gone well for Carolyn. She was difficult to be around, and they hadn't spent much time with her. Her mother kept trying to say she did love Carolyn, did want a relationship with her, but Carolyn rebuffed her advances.

Then the show host suggested that Carolyn come sit closer to her mother, rather than on the edge of the set. Carolyn jumped up and cried, "They're only doing this because we're on TV. They don't really love me. She says she does, but she doesn't."

Watching Carolyn was very painful. She not only said no one loved her, but looked like she felt unloved. She didn't want to stop being angry. She wanted to get even with her family for what they had done, not get over the past hurts they'd all experienced.

Carolyn's self-sealing logic kept her stuck. No matter what her family members said, or anyone else said, she interpreted it as "They don't love me. They don't care about me." Nothing they did or said could change her mind. Whatever they said wasn't the right thing to say, they didn't mean it, or most repeatedly, things should have been different or better many years ago, so nothing can be done today to make it better.

Carolyn was stuck on getting even rather than putting the problems behind them. She wanted her family members to hurt as much as she was hurting. She used her interpretations of their behavior to support her pain.

Logicians call personalizing an argument an ad hominem fallacy, or attacking the person, not the argument.

As a child psychologist, Leon often testifies as an expert witness in child custody cases. He is accustomed to tough examinations by attorneys who fight for their clients' rights and objectives. Sometimes those attorneys seem to attack him personally, his credentials, or his objectives for the case. After one particularly grueling court appearance, Leon's young associate asked him why he smiled when he was being so viciously attacked by one of the attorneys. "Simple," Leon replied. "When they start at-

tacking me, I know I've won. There's nothing I've said they can disagree with."

Leon had learned that when the attacks became personal, there was nothing else that could be attacked. His work was unassailable. So they had to go after him personally. Attacking the person is the fallback position of a combatant who has to win at any cost and knows he is losing.

Confronting this kind of argument is really frustrating. Nothing you can say will be accepted as evidence that you are right. Everything you say can and will be twisted to provide further proof your opponent is correct. Even carrying on a conversation with someone who is self-sealing is a real trial. No matter what you say, your words prove they're right.

One of your best responses might be to say, "If your argument holds, it should be able to predict what will or won't happen. If it can't be used for predictions, then it really doesn't say anything. Think of a specific example so we can talk about that." They will usually stomp away or claim you aren't smart enough to see it. Just smile at this point. You got 'em.

Or if you want to move out of the argument mode, just say, "I don't buy it. I don't believe all families are dysfunctional. We don't see eye to eye on this one."

Self-sealing arguments sometimes occur when one person takes an idiosyncratic view of an issue and then arbitrarily dismisses or avoids another's position because it's different. Again, no matter what you say, he or she won't agree and will say you are wrong.

What passes for conventional wisdom, or the worst of stereotypical thinking, can be self-sealing arguments. "Everyone knows Latins are great lovers," or "Women can't be counted on as leaders because they are unreliable several days a month," or "All men are just interested in one thing." When people really believe these statements to be "truth and reality, the way the world really is," no amount of evidence will change their minds.

Howard missed an important meeting and lost face with his boss. He was furious with Elaine, his admin support person.

He said she had not given him the message. She said she had. He said she was a liar. Howard didn't have the message, and Elaine couldn't produce the piece of paper with the message on it. Therefore, Elaine was lying.

When Elaine tried to explain she had sent him an e-mail message with the information, Howard replied that e-mail didn't count. Everyone knew e-mail was not real communication.

Howard and Elaine were part of a work group that was dispersed in several buildings over eighteen acres. The group had agreed to use e-mail for important scheduling messages rather than physically tracking one another down. Howard was not the only one who didn't like the change, but he was the only one who wouldn't use the new system. He'd only use "real communication"—written on paper or spoken in person.

No matter what Elaine said, Howard claimed he was right and she was to blame for his missing the appointment. His definition of notification didn't include what she had done to notify him. By dismissing e-mail as not real communication, he could say she was wrong for using it, and not have to admit he was wrong for not using it.

With self-sealing arguments, anything that happens will prove a point, so the position loses its ability to predict what can and/or will happen. Logicians call these kind of arguments vacuous, or empty. They are a form of logical fallacy, or logical error.

Self-sealing positions are difficult to refute and to argue around. They often take on the fervor of a religious or political argument and serve as sounding boards for a point of view, rather than representing any attempt to engage in discussion or dialogue. It's often more effective to declare what is happening, to confront the process of the interaction, rather than trying to change someone's position or to influence their thinking.

This becomes an example of knowing when to count your losses and stop playing the game. The only way to "win" is to stop playing.

Conflict is inevitable. We will always have differences with our loved ones, friends, and colleagues. It isn't having arguments that's the problem, but how we argue that's difficult. Arguing can bring people closer together, increase the respect they have for one another and themselves. Or it can put a wedge between people, push them farther apart, and even destroy their relationships.

When we're focused on winning at any cost, overpowering another person, it's easy to slip into logical errors, problems with defining our positions clearly, or even not using accurate data to back our positions.

By understanding the types of logical errors we can make in the heat of an argument, we can refocus on the issues, clarify our positions, and come to a better resolution of the issues that divide us.

Exercises for Chapter 9

WHAT'S YOUR ARGUMENT WITHOUT END?

How do you get caught up in your argument without end? Who needs to be right? Who needs to win? What is the "real" issue behind the "good" issue you're arguing about?

PROVING WITH ANECDOTE

Think of a situation, event, or reaction that will "prove" that your position with your challenge is the correct one.

Now think of another situation, event, or reaction that will "prove" another perspective is correct.

What does this tell you about how you are thinking and feeling about what has happened to you?

GETTING CAUGHT UP IN ILLOGICAL LOGIC

This is an especially effective exercise if you are caught up by someone who is being illogically logical. Diagram their statements using the Three-Circle Test. Start with their initial generalization. Then add the statement that "proves" you are wrong. Look carefully at the diagram. Is the initial generalization one that you accept as true, also? (Are all mammals cats?) Is it based on "fact" or "belief"? Do you (or they) know enough about the topic to evaluate the truth or validity of what is being argued? Are they trying to simplify a very complex issue into a black-and-white statement? Are they slipping into different uses of the same word? Is anything you say used as evidence that they are right and you are wrong?

With practice, we can get better and quicker at spotting logical errors, especially when the other person is trying to convince us that they are right and we are wrong. Practice! You'll be glad you did.

CHAPTER 10

OF COURSE YOU'RE ENTITLED, BUT THERE ARE NO GUARANTEES

The lead letter in *Dear Abby* this morning was from a woman who discovered her fiancé had been having an affair for a year and a half and had fathered a child with the other woman. He swore he still loved her, not the other woman, and still wanted to marry her. The writer's question: "What should I do? I love him, but will I be able to trust him? Should I marry him and live with the knowledge of his affair and love child for the rest of my life?" She signed her letter "Devastated."

Devastated's crisis confronted her very essence. She was faced with her fiancé's betrayal and his words of love and commitment. What he did and what he said didn't match. He was no longer what she thought he was.

This kind of crisis confronts not only how we think about others and our world, but who we think we are. Crisis challenges us to reconsider what we deserve, what we can expect, and what we need to be happy. Fortunately for this young woman, she was asking the right questions before she got married, not after.

It's easy to slip into feeling we deserve what we get, especially if we believe there is a direct line between what we do or think and what we get. Or as one sage said, "Show me what you have in your life, and I'll show you what you think of yourself."

We grow up getting mixed messages about what life is all about. In a perfect world, people wouldn't hurt each other. We'd get what we deserve. We'd have what we want and need. But when our life is out of control, when changes have been imposed on us, reality counters all those beliefs.

Then it becomes easy to take our lack of control personally. What is it about me that made this happen to me? How'd I get chosen for this misery? Do I think so little of myself that I want to sabotage myself, that I want to hurt myself?

Consider yourself entitled means we need to change our minds about who we think we are. We need to recapture the value of our lives and ourselves. We show we value ourselves when we trust and respect ourselves, not letting others treat us badly or take over our lives. The answers Devastated was seeking were what was right for her. Did she want to marry a man who so disrespected her that he not only was seeing someone else, but fathered a child by that woman? Did she want to marry someone who said he loved her, but showed he didn't?

We grow up knowing we have rights. Political tradition holds we have inalienable rights. Western religious tradition underscores the respect for the individual just because we exist. We don't need to earn those rights or that respect. We're entitled. Entitlement gives us permission to take charge of our lives.

But then we see stories in the papers and on TV of people who've given up their rights to others or, worse, have been treated miserably by others. They end up with a life that isn't what it's supposed to be. How could this happen?

We're caught in both an unpleasant reality and a paradox. The unpleasant reality? There are some people who think they're more entitled than anyone else. They think it's okay for them to take from or use the people around them for their own pleasure. So they do. They don't seem to care that they cause pain, suffering, and inconvenience. They do what they want to do. And the rest of us are hurt by them. Then we find *we* are the subject of the stories on TV and in the newspapers. We're entitled to our lives, to make choices for ourselves, but that doesn't necessarily mean we will get what we are entitled to.

Our political tradition promises the right to life, liberty, and the pursuit of happiness. There's the paradox. We're entitled to the *pursuit* of happiness, *not guaranteed* happiness. When we make happiness a goal, it eludes us. When we don't make it a goal but pursue other meaningful objectives, happiness comes more easily.

Believing we're entitled to happiness sets us up for thinking we can have everything we want. Just because we want something doesn't necessarily mean we need it, or have a right to it, or someone owes it to us.

Beyond the unpleasant reality and the paradox comes the hard work of entitlement and responsibility. Entitlements are straightforward, as well as subtle and elusive. Being entitled to your own life means you have the right to define your life the way you see best. You don't have to wait for someone else to tell you who you can or should be. You can stand for yourself.

Liberty is especially problematical. How much of what we do is constrained, and how much can we freely choose? What can we take charge of anyway? Who says? What about those people who do think they can do what they want with us? How do we reconcile ourselves to those who are evil? These are hard questions that don't always give us the answers we want.

Our experience of happiness depends more on how we feel about ourselves and about what we do than on what we actually do and accomplish. In other words, how happy we are depends on more sound self-esteem, positive feelings about ourselves, and feeling like we have taken charge of our lives, than what we do has an effect on what happens to us.

Both of these, self-esteem and taking charge, are affected by what we think we deserve and what we think we can do. In this chapter we'll see how self-esteem and taking charge are linked with considering ourselves entitled. In the next chapter we'll look at how they're linked with considering ourselves empowered.

Life

Being entitled to your life means you need to address both the question of who you are and the ontological question behind this: How do you know who you are? Ontology is similar to epistemology. They are the questions behind the questions. Epistemology was behind the questions: What do you know? How do you know what you know? Ontology is behind the questions: Who are you? How do you know who you are?

Knowing who you are isn't enough when you want to change. You also need to know how you came up with the understanding, belief, picture you hold of yourself. Then you'll know what needs to be changed so you can start seeing yourself differently.

Irma Jean grew up in a very poor family in a rural farming area. Everyone in her extended family had quit school by age twelve. They were needed to help farm. People like them didn't go on to high school, much less college. As an adult, and a single parent not by choice, Irma Jean lived in a large metropolitan area and worked at a large manufacturing company. Her supervisor encouraged her to participate in training, get her high school diploma, and take courses at the local community college so she could get promotions and make more money to support her family. Irma Jean had a hard time even signing up for the courses. People like her didn't go to school.

Irma Jean thought she wasn't smart enough to go to school, that school was for other people, not for people like her. After all, she hadn't even completed elementary school. It took her a while to understand she hadn't finished school because her family needed her to work, not because she wasn't smart enough or because she didn't deserve to go to school. It wasn't that she wasn't capable of finishing school. She just hadn't had the opportunity. She needed to change her mind about how smart she was.

We're forced to change our minds about ourselves when we're not in control. What we thought we knew doesn't work for us anymore. We need to look at how we know who we've been to change who we are now. We change by making conscious choices, rather than leaving who we are up to our unconscious or nonconscious thinking. Or leaving it up to other people to once more tell us who we should be, could be, or had better be.

Just as we can learn more about what has happened to us, information, and ideas, we can also learn more about who we have been and want to be. Learning more about who you are means you can make decisions that will serve you better. You can take charge of your reactions to the changes you've experienced, rather than let them run you. And you can decide to make changes in how you feel and what you do.

Your relationship with yourself, like your relationships with others, is based on both trust and respect. The more you know of yourself, the more you can trust yourself. The more you trust yourself, the more you can respect yourself. The more you respect yourself, the more you can both know and trust yourself. It's a circle that keeps getting stronger and richer.

Trust

When we trust ourselves, our lives become more predictable. We know what we think and what we'll do. We can anticipate how we'll handle challenges and situations before they come up. We can plan and be confident that we'll carry through with our plans. We can make commitments to ourselves and know we'll see them through. We can trust ourselves to act in our own best interests. We won't let others take over or make decisions for us that don't support us.

You can be the expert on you. You can know what you're thinking and feeling and can choose to express or not express those thoughts and feelings. You can learn more about yourself. It's not magic but a skill to learn. By putting the time and effort into knowing yourself, you become the expert on you.

Like the colleague who "knew" I was afraid of the redwood forest, there'll always be someone willing to tell us who we are. If we don't know who we are, and how we know it, then we'll be susceptible to their self-serving interpretations.

Knowing yourself forms the base of trust. You can't trust yourself until you know yourself. Like respect, trust is reciprocal and iterative. The more you trust yourself, the more you can trust yourself.

Respect

Entitled means honoring yourself not for what you've done but because you exist. We're human *beings*, not human *doings*. Entitlement is the affirmation of the value of who we are.

None of us is perfect. We all have both strengths and limitations. We make mistakes and errors of both commission and omission. We've done things we shouldn't have, and didn't always do what we should have. Nonetheless, we're still entitled to honor and respect.

So many of us believe that we have to do more, better, or differently to gain self-worth. We believe somehow we're not enough the way we are.

Paradoxically, when we accept who we are and honor that self, we're able to do better and more.

Respecting ourselves starts with speaking and treating ourselves kindly. If we buy into "I'm not entitled," we'll treat ourselves miserably. We'll put other people first all the time, let others tell us what to do and think, berate ourselves for being stupid or ignorant, criticize and bemoan how terrible we look, and constantly remind ourselves how awful we are. We won't expect to be paid for our contributions, but will settle for less than we're worth. We don't need other people to disrespect us. We can do a superb job all by ourselves.

But like trust, self-respect is circular. The more we respect ourselves and act like we do, the more respect we'll feel for ourselves. And like trust, self-respect isn't magic; it's a habit and a skill that we learn to do.

Entitlement and Self-Esteem

Feelings of entitlement rest on a base of sound self-esteem. And there's the rub. In all the years of being a therapist, seminar leader, speaker, and consultant, I have never encountered anyone without a self-esteem issue. Ever!

One of the exercises I often use in seminars has the participants writing a list of three things they do very well. After I give those directions, there is a moment of stunned silence in the hall, and then a lot of nervous laughter. Many of the participants have a hard time coming up with three things. They can't think of anything they do really well.

The second part of the exercise involves standing up and telling a stranger the things that are on your list. Very quickly, the noise level in the room escalates. People start talking and laughing and seem to have a great time, telling someone they don't know how great they are.

As we debrief after the exercise, we talk about the nervous laughter and the fun people seemed to be having. I ask them if there was anyone who talked to someone who was obnoxious and overbearing, someone who was just too conceited and stuck on themselves. Of course, the answer is no. Yet isn't that what we're all afraid of? If we talk about the good things we do, no one will like us; they'll think we're conceited. It will be hard to make friends. Our parents and teachers told us: Don't be so proud. Pride goeth before a fall. And so we start to hide our strengths, even from ourselves.

We have terrible problems with our self-esteem, and yet the thing we fear the most—others won't like us if we're too proud—doesn't seem to happen. It's fun being around people who are making things happen, like themselves, and are eager to accomplish even more. No one enjoys being around people who are down, don't think much of themselves, or are always very critical of themselves. They aren't fun to be with.

It is tempting to just say, Get over it, just feel better about yourself. Or if you just recognized the good things about yourself, your self-esteem would increase. While each of those tactics might help, that's too simple an answer to what is a very complex issue.

Self-esteem is a balance between expectations and perceptions. Expectations include what you think you should do and be, what others think you should be, and the rules and principles by which you live your life. Perceptions are the judgments, the evaluation of how well you are living up to your expectations. When expectations are in balance with perceptions, positive self-esteem results.

Expectations are shaped early on by parents, teachers, other children, religious instructions, and social and cultural forces like the media. Later, bosses, colleagues, coworkers, and subordinates add their expectations. Using input from others, most people pick and choose the types and levels of expectations they have for themselves. Typically expectations people have for themselves are high. So high, they may be impossible to meet.

For most people, perceptions are much lower. Whether as a result of parental injunctions against being proud and boastful, or from a fear of appearing to be conceited, most people tend to judge themselves harshly.

Increasing self-esteem means confronting early messages about self-love, conceit, and humility. There are important differences between sound self-esteem and loving yourself, and being selfish or narcissistic.

Sound self-esteem is based on loving yourself just the way you are. This doesn't mean you don't want to make some changes or to grow. It does mean you aren't waiting to feel good about yourself until you're perfect. Loving yourself means self-acceptance, recognizing both your strengths and your limitations.

When I worked in the weight-control program, we had a lot of trouble helping people understand that feeling good about themselves made it easier to take charge of their weight and their health. They wanted to wait until their weight was just right before they could feel good about themselves.

Connie Merritt, author of *Finding Love (Again!)*, has found that feeling good about yourself just where you are helps you find someone to share your life with. When you love yourself, others find you more interesting, more fun, and easier to love! People who like themselves find partners quicker!

You can raise or lower your self-esteem by changing either your perceptions or your expectations.

What you focus on increases. If you focus on the negative, how you have been wrong, done bad things, were hurt, limited, or taken advantage of, then your self-esteem decreases. This seems to be the default position. Most of us can give a long catalog list of things we did or things that were done to us that were unpleasant or wrong. That list comes easily.

But all of us are a mixture of good and bad. Sure, we have flat sides, make mistakes, and don't always do the right thing. If we concentrate our efforts on them, then we'll continue to feel bad about ourselves.

But we also have done good, were upstanding and courageous. We had fun with our parents; they helped us, made our lives easier as well as difficult. No one is totally all good or all bad. And certainly few, if any, parents ever looked at one another and said, "Let's have a child so we can really mess him up." That's just not the way life works. As parents, most of us have a far greater understanding of our own parents. We do the best we can at the time. And know that we all have days when we flunk parenting.

If we focus on what was good in the early messages we got, the strengths, skills, and abilities we developed, our self-esteem will respond more positively. By shifting the focus of the pictures and memories that we have, we can start to see ourselves differently.

Some of you are saying to yourselves right now as you read these last few lines, "Easy for you to say. You don't know what happened to me." And you're right. I don't. But then, we never know what anyone else has gone through. And for the most part, we would rather hold on to our own challenges than have to face different ones. I often work with small groups of people who have been through crisis. An exercise we always use has everyone write their "worst thing" on a piece of paper, fold the paper, and put it in a basket. Then each group member pulls a paper from the basket and talks about the experience as if it were their own worst thing. As we finish the exercise, everyone agrees they want their own back. We've all got something.

We've all got good things, too. Virgil Beasley, a therapist consultant and friend, has his clients memorialize their achievements in a "Can Do" book. Writing down what they've already done reinforces the success they've had. It also helps take the focus from the long list of things that are left to do or from just noticing the bad things that have happened. You can't hold the ledger book, matching up one good thing for every bad. It just doesn't work that way. It isn't how many or how awful one thing might be as compared to a good thing, but how we feel about each. It is the perception of each that makes the difference.

Make sure you haven't sabotaged yourself with feelings of responsibility. Insisting that you create, enable, and allow everything that happens to you, even all the bad stuff, can erode your trust in yourself. You can start to believe you hurt, not honor, yourself. It's a short step to believing that we hurt ourselves because we deserve to be hurt, because somehow we've earned the hurt we feel. Not only does this compound our pain, but it starts us down the slippery slope of feeling bad for feeling bad.

If we get on autopilot with negative feelings and self-talk, we end up feeling bad about feeling bad. Concentrating on how low our self-esteem is lowers our self-esteem. After all, what kind of a person are you if you have low self-esteem? Can't be all that good, right? You catch yourself up in a downward spiral. Einstein said it best: We can't get out of a problem with the same thinking that caused the problem in the first place.

We need to reset the level in our self-esteem gauge. We need to change our minds about early messages and defuse the power we give them. Stop letting your feelings be in charge of your actions and your self-esteem. Getting conscious about your automatic feelings and automatic thoughts is the first step in breaking the downward spiral.

Use these steps, adapted from the work of David Reynolds, the foremost American authority on Japanese Naikan and Morita therapies, known in the United States as Constructive Living. When you start feeling the familiar bad feelings:

- **Acknowledge without blame or shame** or judging the feelings you're experiencing. Say to yourself, "Here they are again.

I've been here before. Maybe I'll be here again. Here's that same old stuff." The objective is to recognize what you're feeling without feeling bad about feeling bad.

- **Do what needs to be done,** even if you don't feel like it. Pay your bills. Work on a project, take a shower, clean your house, go to the kids' soccer game. Do what needs to be done because it needs to be done, not because you feel like doing it.
- **Figure out what works for you.** What can you do that will help prevent or cut short the feelings next time? What are you doing or not doing that can make a difference? Get more activity? Develop a new routine so you don't have to remember to remember? Or make a decision and take care of a nagging situation? What can you do so you won't have to revisit the bad feelings again and figure a solution each time?
- **What doesn't help?** What are the coping, numbing methods you've been using to avoid the feelings you're feeling? Eating, drinking, watching hours of TV?

When you acknowledge without blame or shame what you are feeling and then do what needs to be done, the tough feelings start to disappear. Action, any purposeful action, is a very powerful reinforcer that you can take charge when things are tough. Then paradoxically, when you don't fight the feelings, you are in a better position to figure out what you can do in the future that will be helpful, and what to avoid or stop doing that isn't so helpful. You can get a better perspective when you aren't tied up in your feelings.

Liberty

Liberty means making decisions and choices about who you are and what you do. While there will always be limits on the choices we have, for the most part we act as if we have more limits than we really do. Certainly there are limits on what we can do and who we can influence. And we're constrained by the consequences of our earlier choices. You may say you can't do what you want to do because you have kids. You do have the responsibility for raising your children the best you can. But sacrificing your life for your children does neither you nor your kids any good at all.

Constraints are the boundaries on our choices. We can't make choices on issues or events outside those boundaries. But you can do lots with what's inside. For most people there is so much inside that if you focus on what you can do, you can build a full and satisfying life for yourself. Too often we give away the choices we rightfully have to someone else. We defer to those we are in relationships with, thinking they know better than we, or that if we don't let them take control of our lives, they'll leave and we'll be alone.

Relationship Rules

Many relationship issues and problems in working with others can be attributed to the unspoken relationship rules you subscribe to. Two of these rules are especially toxic: the belief that the other person is special, and you're not; and the fear that without another person or a relationship, you are nothing.

The belief that the other person is special, and you are not, is a cornerstone belief for people with negative self-esteem. It has far-reaching consequences. Putting the other person in the one-up position automatically puts you one down. They know more than you, are better judges of what's right or true, and can make better decisions than you. It's a short step from these beliefs to allowing the other person to make decisions for you and about you. You think they're better guides to the course of your life than you are. You put them in charge of your life.

> *Lena always let others decide for her. First her parents, then her husband. When he died, she started letting her family tell her what she should do. Her mother suggested Lena sell her home, move to the small town her mother lived in, and buy a home where the two of them could live together. Lena didn't really want to, but she was afraid to say no. She couldn't think of a good enough reason to justify saying no.*

Lena didn't stop to realize her mother wanted her to come so Mom could be taken care of. The arrangement would be great for Mom, not so great for Lena. Lena could no longer think for herself.

She let other people run her life because she felt they knew better than she what she should do.

The fear that without the other person you are nothing is a direct consequence of believing the other person is better than you or better able to run your life. The consequence of this fear is if you aren't good, she'll leave. Of course, the definition of *good* is what is pleasing to the other person. So you do everything she wants, hide things you do she wouldn't approve of, sneak around to see friends or family members she doesn't like. You've given her your life because it's too frightening to consider being all alone. You lie down in front of her so she can step on you.

To break out of this pattern means going below the surface and letting go of feelings and expectations, both for yourself and the other person. To change yourself and your perspective, you have to admit the secondary gains you get from what you're doing. Secondary gains are the hidden benefits from being in an unpleasant situation. Even the worst of circumstances holds benefits. If you get rid of the negative, you also will have to give up the positive.

Role of Evil

Having said all this about life and liberty, we have to admit there are some people who believe they're more equal than others, people with malevolent or malicious intent who have little sympathy for anyone. They'll purposely choose to use others as objects for their own pleasure and not show guilt or remorse when they're caught doing it. We can't discount that there are people who don't "play by the rules." These people disregard the humanity of others, lowering them to the level of objects rather than honoring them as fellow human beings.

Getting caught up with a person like this is extremely unsettling. Nothing you can do seems to break through to make a difference in how he treats you. That's because his behavior has nothing to do with you. Anyone who's in that spot in that time and place will get crushed. It feels random, and it is. Nothing you did brought it on.

A preferential child molester targets eight-year-old boys with brown hair and freckles. When the child turns ten, he passes them on to another molester who prefers ten-year-old brown-haired, freckle-faced boys.

A professional man beats both his first and second wives, forces clients to have sex with him, kills his ex-girlfriend after a long history of abuse, and then abandons his two-year-old child on a busy city street. Later other girlfriends and clients come forward to disclose similar stories of injury and insult.

A man has sex with every woman he knows, including all three of his daughters, both of his sisters, colleagues at work, female members of the church choir, and associates in a charitable organization. By his count, he figures he has had sex with more than a thousand women. (He is neither a celebrity nor a star athlete.)

An attractive young woman ingratiates herself with elderly, lonely widowers. She convinces them she loves them, wants to marry them, and then starts to transfer all their assets to her name. Three of her "fiancés" have died within weeks of the completion of the assets transfer.

This is a type of evil, not of Satan or organized groups, but a more trivial, banal, and daily evil. It's found in the little things, the willingness to hurt another because it feels good, the disregard or discounting of how others feel or think, or even that they do feel or think. You don't matter to people like this. You don't count. They don't see other people as human, but as objects.

If you ignore or discount that people like this exist, you won't be able to deal with them. You'll try techniques that are appropriate when working with people of goodwill. Those techniques won't work here.

There are those who will argue that evil is a mental illness and that these people need forgiveness, to be understood. I am not sure I am big enough for that job. For most of us, the best choice is to get far away. Work with your spiritual advisor and/or counselor if you find you have been caught in the snare of someone who is evil. This is not a job for one person alone.

Pursuit of Happiness

Whole schools of philosophy have been built on unraveling the necessary steps for attaining happiness. Whole colleges and universities seem driven by the mindless pursuit of fun: parties, dope, drink, sex. One parent was heard to say he paid to have his daughter major in partying. Even supposedly mature adults make decisions and judge their lives by what's fun, enjoyable, or "If I just do/get that, I'll be happy."

When we make happiness a goal, we don't find it.

David Myers, author of *The Pursuit of Happiness: Who Is Happy— and Why*, found that when we make our happiness dependent on getting or having something, we don't find happiness.

After meeting basic needs, even having more money didn't give much of an additional boost to feelings of well-being.

Neither crisis nor success had an enduring effect on happiness. The feelings associated with crisis or good fortune took center stage for several weeks, as people were caught up in the newness of the events. But neither effect lasted all that long.

Happiness is more dependent on the daily ebb and flow, how well each day goes.

Daily events, some as trivial as not feeling all that well, disappointment in missing an appointment, or not reaching a goal, can cause unhappiness. Some people, mostly men, report feeling unhappy because their team lost. Very few people in unhappy or unfulfilling relationships say their lives are happy.

Myers found the best predictor of life satisfaction is satisfaction with yourself. If you're satisfied with yourself, you're more likely to say your life is happy.

Feeling like you are in charge is the most dependable predictor of well-being. When you are in charge of your life, you feel better about yourself. When you feel better about yourself, you report feeling happier about your life.

Taking charge, even if you aren't in control, is the cornerstone of entitlement. You decide on your life. When you've decided who decides and decided how happy and satisfied you are with your life, you'll have maximized the life you are entitled to have.

Exercises for Chapter 10

EARLY-MESSAGES EXERCISE

Everyone hears from the adults in their lives what the rules are for living, the expectations for their behavior and choices. For each beginning of a sentence below, finish the sentence to make it true for you.

1. In our family, people . . .
2. You had better . . . if you know what's good for you.
3. A real man . . .
4. A real woman . . .
5. Work is . . .
6. Money is the . . .
7. Rules are made . . .
8. When you are in school, . . .
9. The older you get, . . .
10. Life is . . .

Now take a look at your answers. What do they tell you about the messages that you got from your parents and other adults when you were just a kid?

What rules are you still following? How come?

What rules do you no longer follow? How come?

What changes do you want to make about the rules you heard—or the rules you discarded or kept? How come?

Repeat this exercise several times over the next few weeks. Watch how your answers change.

I AM . . . SO WHAT?

This is an excellent exercise for figuring out who you are and how you feel about who you are. Divide a piece of paper into two columns. Label the top of the first column "I am . . ." Label the top of the second column "So what?" Then number down the page from one through ten.

Finish the first sentence "I am . . ." then pause for a moment as you ask yourself "So what?" Write the first response that comes to your mind, no matter how silly, outrageous, or profound.

Then go right on to the next "I am . . ."

Repeat the exercise several times a week. Keep your pages and review them every week.

RESULTS AND CONSEQUENCES

In every situation, no matter how difficult, there's always good news and bad news. If you aren't willing to look at both the positive results and the negative consequences of both taking action and not taking action, you can't freely make a decision to move on. Use a situation that you are currently working with to fill in the following chart. Ask yourself what you expect from taking action or not taking action.

	POSITIVE RESULTS	NEGATIVE CONSEQUENCES
Do It		
Don't Do It		

What do your answers tell you about how much you want to change?

ACKNOWLEDGE THE GOOD STUFF

Make a list of the good things you got from your family of origin and from the teachers and other influential adults of your childhood. What difference did they make in who you are? What skills and/or special knowledge did they impart? What attributes or special skills did you develop with their help? Have you told them how much you appreciate what they did for you? If not, when could you do that?

David Reynolds suggests acknowledging what you already have, even the simple tools and utensils you use daily that make your life easier, things like your pen, toothbrush, appliances, service people. How many people have worked to serve you? Express your gratitude to both the people and your possessions for making your life more comfortable and convenient.

Make a strengths list. Number one to ten twice in your notebook. List ten things you do and ten things you are that are admirable strengths. Do this daily for a month or so, then come back to this exercise periodically. You will find it easier to do the more you do it. (Most people can't list ten the first few days!)

David Myers suggests the following exercise for getting a better hold on life satisfaction. Complete the following sentence five times.

I'm glad I'm not . . .

CHAPTER 11

CONSIDER YOURSELF EMPOWERED

E ven before he crossed the finish line in first place at the 1999 Tour de France, Lance Armstrong was a winner.

In October 1996, Armstrong was diagnosed with testicular cancer that had metastasized to his lung and triggered brain tumors. He was given less than a 40 percent chance of survival and underwent two operations and twelve weeks of chemotherapy before being helped out of the hospital. While he was in the hospital, he was fired by the racing team he had been riding with.

A strong competitor before his illness, Armstrong faced his recovery with determination. After initial feelings of anger, he turned to feeling motivated and driven to get better. As he realized that he was getting better, he knew he was winning. He raced again, not just for himself and his new team, but for the whole cancer community—the patients, their caretakers, and their families. And, he admitted, he also raced for the people who didn't believe he would make it.

Like so many people who have faced such crises, Armstrong stated that the illness had made him stronger. He came back with a new perspective and a list of new priorities.

During his triumphal lap of honor through Paris after winning the Tour de France, Armstrong gave the challenge to all of us who have come through our own personal crises: "If you ever get a second chance in life—go all the way!"

Empowerment has been embraced as a management concept, almost a business practice du jour. Yet empowerment, having confidence in your competence, has an incredible impact on your ability to take charge when you aren't in control.

Everyone's caught in the middle, with both limitations and constraints on their behaviors and opportunities for taking action. Whether we face challenges in our personal relationships, health issues, dealing with the government or large impersonal corporations, we have both opportunities and limitations. Feeling empowered means we can take action on the opportunities and not be crushed by the limitations.

The essence of empowerment is living your freedom, making choices, and dealing with both positive and negative consequences of your choices. We make large and small choices every day, because we want some consequences and want to avoid others. Living your freedom means focusing on the areas of choice you do have no matter how constrained the situation. Even if that choice "only" means you can choose how you think and feel.

Empowerment lets us live our lives consciously. We admit what got us where we are and admit we can do something to get us where we want to go. Then we do it. We define our lives, rather than letting a situation or another person define them for us. Empowerment means going with what's right, rather than who's right. It's knowing when to hold 'em, when to fold 'em, and when to walk away. Knowing you can do it. And then doing it!

It is not easy work. For many people it is easier and more attractive to just drift and let the world out there shape your life. And like entitlement, there are lots of people who will be willing to tell you what to do and when to do it. We can always find someone who's willing to take the power position and run our lives for us.

Confidence in Your Competence

Empowerment starts with having confidence in your competence. Our confidence is built on owning our capabilities, being able to judge our behavior, having a realistic picture of who we are and what we can do. It's linked both to our past, what we've done, and the predictions we have of our future, knowing both what we can do and what we will do.

When Grace's husband decided he didn't want to be a husband or father any longer, she was left with the nine kids, little money, and no paid-work history. She'd spent the previous seventeen years being a wife and homemaker. With three of the kids still at home, she knew she needed to get a job to support them. But she couldn't type. So she looked in the want ads for jobs that didn't require typing, much less computer skills. She finally got a position as the receptionist in a small bank.

What Grace discounted was her ability to organize, manage, and deliver complex projects that she'd developed both as a mother of a large family and as the chair of many volunteer organizations and activities. When we looked more carefully at what she could do, she started to realize why she was so unhappy at her current job. She was more suited to managing the bank than to being the receptionist. She'd discounted her volunteer experiences as "not real work," and the organizational skills of running a large family as "it's nothing, anyone could do that."

Grace's competence was considerable. She just didn't have any confidence in herself or in being able to deliver in a paid-work setting. She knew what to do, but devalued both what she had done and her ability to produce in another environment.

Developing confidence in your competence is dependent upon a realistic view of the successes you've had. The more success we know we've had, the more likely we'll be successful in the future. The problem is, we remember more of our failures and forget, or discount, more of our successes. We remember the searing feelings that accompany our failures and burn them into our memories. Then we believe that since we failed once, we'll always fail. By focusing on our failures and limitations, we don't compromise just our feelings of deservedness, but our confidence, too.

Empowerment and Self-Esteem

Having confidence in your competence is the link between empowerment and self-esteem. How we feel about ourselves is the filter through which we see our experiences and our opportunities. Whether we think we can or can't, we're always right.

If someone has positive self-esteem and then has a setback, he reflects on the experience, murmurs to himself, "This isn't like me," evaluates what's happened, learns the lesson, and goes on.

When a person with low self-esteem has that same experience, he heads down a spiral of self-defeating behavior. He says to himself, "I've done it again. I always mess up. How could I be so stupid?" He can't see the experience as being caused by anything other than his own inability. The only lesson he sees is that he's incompetent.

When people with sound self-esteem have a positive experience, when they accomplish their objectives or make a project a success, they congratulate themselves and add it to their list of wins. They own their effort, good planning, and achievement.

People with poor self-esteem take similar successful efforts and discount their role in the success of the projects. They'll either say it wasn't a big deal, say they were lucky, or point out a blemish or shortcoming in the results.

With both the "success" and the "failure," the difference in the experience has little to do with the results achieved and lots to do with how those results were perceived.

Unrealistically High Perception of Self

Low self-esteem affects empowerment when it's rooted in either unrealistically low or unrealistically high perceptions of self. At first glance, it's understandable how low perceptions of self can interfere with our effectiveness. But unrealistically high perceptions of self, especially when they slip into narcissism, are just as self-defeating.

Narcissists, or people who are pathologically self-centered, interfere with their own effectiveness by being both shortsighted and unable to see themselves realistically.

Shortsightedness plays out in temporal issues, paying attention only to the here and now in everyday behavior and choices. The criteria for decision making is either "If it feels good do it" or "No one is going to tell me what to do." With this approach, consequences aren't considered. What counts is today, not tomorrow.

With relationship shortsightedness, there's no depth of commitment or connection. People, possessions, and jobs are seen as disposable and replaceable. The rules here are "It doesn't matter" and "There is always another if this doesn't work out." On the job, short-sightedness is expressed by choosing jobs for geographic convenience, monetary rewards, and low effort level. With the I-don't-care attitude and lack of commitment, performance is marginal at best.

Paradoxically, by going for the most, the best, or the easiest, the overall results are limited. The easy, self-centered path is limited in opportunities.

The other way narcissists limit themselves is in their inability to see themselves realistically. They're always the greatest. They're always confident, sure their view of any situation is accurate. They exaggerate their strengths and skills and minimize or deny their limitations and negative consequences. Being so sure, they're unable to get feedback from others or hear there may be another way to do what needs to be done. They're experts at insisting their way is the best way. They revel in being able to say "I told you so" when a spouse, colleague, or even a boss comes up short.

> *When Donald and Anna married, they were both in their early forties with five teenagers between the two of them. Donald insisted things had to be done "his way," whether it was how the teens dressed, how Anna vacuumed the floor, or how the kitchen cupboards were organized. Anna tried to tell him to leave the kitchen cupboards alone. She was chief cook and bottle washer and liked them the way they were. Donald just told her if she stopped being so stubborn, she'd see he was right. When she headed for the garage to organize his tools, he became enraged. No one but he knew the way it should be.*

Donald was taking a typical my-way-or-the-highway approach to his relationship with his new wife. Anna soon realized she'd never be a full partner in their marriage, but always one more incompetent lackey in Donald's kingdom. Their marriage lasted less than a year. She didn't want to put up with his constant criticism and put-downs. She knew she was much more capable and competent than Donald made her out to be. Staying married to him wasn't worth putting up with his abuse.

At work, narcissists make poor team players. They're too concerned that someone else will get the spotlight or the credit for their work. Their work tends to be splashy and perfunctory, more style than substance. With their primary commitment to themselves, their commitment to their work, group, agency, or company tends to be weak and easily broken. They'll disagree with or belittle a suggestion from someone else just because it isn't their way.

Many of the issues that older workers have with younger workers are issues of self-centeredness. With young people, self-centeredness is a developmental phase. Many young adults will be cocky and exaggerate their skills while minimizing their limitations. When this is a developmental issue, they'll begin to settle down and settle in as they learn more about their jobs and themselves. This is not the same as narcissism, which is an approach to life.

Excessive Humility

Excessive humility is the other side of the coin from narcissism. It's the unrealistically low perception of self. It takes appropriate humility to a destructive extreme. We all need some humility. It lets us see limitations and flat sides. It lets us realistically measure our strengths and talents. We know there'll be people more talented or more skilled, as well as less talented or less skilled than we are. This measure is taken without shame or blame, but as a recognition of what is.

Excessive humility is like negative narcissism. No one is worse, more wrong, less skilled, more shameful than you. Psychologists call this delusions of grandeur, except you believe you are the worst, rather than the best. It is still a delusion, though. Your assessment of self is inappropriately harsh.

> *Several months after a wonderful adventure vacation I received a holiday card from Eli with the message, "You probably don't want to send me a card, but in case you think you have to, here's my new address."*

I remembered Eli as an earnest young man, trying very hard to please, sure that other people could do anything better than he, whether it was setting up tents, cooking breakfast for the crowd, or even hauling our equipment and supplies when we made camp. He always went last in line for food and waited to take the least desirable seat when we were on the road. His excessive humility was enough to put him at the back of the bus. He didn't need anyone to tell him he couldn't take full part in the trip.

The other delusion with excessive humility is delusion of reference. This means you think you cause the ills of the world, the world is ganging up on you, or you just don't count. Either you see yourself as total persecutor, responsible for anything bad that happens, or you see yourself as total victim, responsible for nothing. It all happens to you. Either position denies your responsibility for being in charge of your life and the responsibility others have for their lives. The choices we make, and the actions we take, are ours. Our choices may affect others. We may choose to hurt or be hurt, or choose to take the responsibility or blame for another's action, but it is not automatically ours.

At work, excessive humility hinders productivity. Extremely humble people hesitate to take part in group brainstorming or problem-solving sessions, sure that their contribution won't matter or won't measure up. Even if they're encouraged by colleagues or are seen by others as having good ideas, they hold back.

When issues or problems arise, excessively humble workers jump to take the blame. Being sure they are the cause of the difficulties, they can overlook or discount other causes of problems or sources of errors. Even when coworkers can easily see what's really happened, excessively humble workers cling to total blame.

In our personal relationships, excessive humility leads us to letting the other person define who we are. We defer to someone else's judgment of us or the situation. We buy into ineffective relationship "rules" of letting the other person know us better than we know ourselves or of thinking we're nothing without someone. Both of these rules prevent us from taking charge within relationships, but let the other person take control.

Self-Esteem Habits and Empowerment

Being confident of our competence lets us focus on the task at hand. We can think things through, solve problems, ask for assistance or clarification. People with sound self-esteem aren't threatened by other people's strengths, nor do they take challenges to their ideas personally. They can see the difference between disagreeing with another person and disapproving of the person. They can disagree without being disagreeable.

Our daily habits and behaviors support or undermine our self-esteem and confidence. A lot of our automatic thoughts, responses, and actions will either help bolster our confidence in our competence or wear it down. Only by consciously choosing to realistically evaluate what we've done, accept our strengths without embarrassment, and learn from our mistakes can we use our experiences to support future success.

Practice the following self-esteem habits, which support developing confidence in your competence.

Acknowledge Your Accomplishments

Grace had a hard time seeing what she was capable of doing in a paid position because she discounted her experiences as a volunteer and at home. She didn't think she had a résumé that supported applying for anything other than an entry-level position. I encouraged her to write a functional résumé, highlighting the skills she'd developed and the projects she'd managed. Soon she saw that her volunteer work at her church and her children's schools counted as real work. She'd chaired a regional church fund-raiser, managed a volunteer crew of over three hundred people, worked with people in four states, and raised significantly more money than had ever been realized before or since. She'd been president of the three-thousand-student high school parent organization for two years as the school regrouped after having been rocked by racial and ethnic violence. She chaired a joint task force with students, parents, teachers, administrators, and community members that became a model for other schools nationwide.

Grace had the successes. And they were the result of her skills and effort. By focusing on her limitations, she'd missed what she had done.

Write your own functional résumé. Keep a list of what you have achieved. Don't wait for your manager to ask for an achievements list from your job. Make your own list of personal wins and accomplishments. Make sure you include your personal accomplishments, also. Add your hobbies, your talents, and your leisure-time activities. Reflect on how much you have done to help you get a handle on what you can do.

Accept Compliments Graciously

The appropriate response to a compliment is "Thank you." And then keep your mouth shut! So many of us have the tendency to respond to a compliment by deflecting it. "It was nothing," we say. "Anyone could have done it." Or we point out the one small part of the project that isn't perfect. Or we use humor to avoid hearing what the other person is saying. Or we immediately give back a compliment so our ledger will be even again.

"Thank you." That's all you need to say.

Use Failures for Their Lessons

Everyone fails at something. No one ever succeeds every time. Use your failures to provide the lessons that will help you succeed the next time, rather than as clubs to beat yourself up. This means you have to face your failures and admit them. No narcissism here. But it also means no excessive humility. You don't cause everything. You aren't in control of the universe, even your own small corner of it. Tell yourself the truth about your misses. What could you do differently next time? What did you do just fine this time? What do you wish you had done instead? Debrief every project, the wins and the losses.

Hold on to the lessons you learn from your failures. Let go of beating yourself up.

Choices and Constraints

Empowerment is built on choices. Every situation has both choices and constraints. If we focus on our constraints, they'll expand to take up all of our attention and energy. If we focus on our choices, we'll be amazed at what we can do, within the constraints we have.

Allen Wheelis, in his book *How People Change*, addresses both of the issues of choice and constraint. He differentiates between those things we can choose and those we have no choices about. The areas of choice he calls *freedom*. The areas of no choice he labels *necessity*.

For the most part we can correctly identify areas of freedom. We make decisions every day on what we want to do, can do, and think might be nice. Some of these decisions are trivial: what to have for dinner, which movie to go to, which friends to include in a social gathering. Some choices are more significant: who we will marry, which job to take, what career we will pursue, whether we'll have children. All these decisions, trivial and significant, reinforce our freedom. We feel more in charge of our lives, more confident and more competent.

Objective Necessity

Necessities are more problematic. Wheelis talks about two types of necessity: objective necessity and arbitrary necessity. Objective necessities, he says, are issues and factors where we really don't have choice. They are predetermined. They follow the rules of natural laws, like our genetic makeup, or the physics of natural phenomena, like earthquakes and hurricanes. Objective necessity includes physical attributes, our height, the color of our eyes, where and when we were born, gravity, the seasons, and the paths of the planets. They're impersonal. Winter follows autumn, not because we'll be inconvenienced by the cold, but because that's the way it is. Earthquakes are. They don't decide to occur or not depending on where we have built cities or left the land uninhabited.

Objective necessity is also determined by previous actions. We can't go back now and change what's happened in the past. We might take action to minimize the consequences of what happened, but we can't change the events themselves. We can't undo an automobile accident in which we were badly scarred, even though we might use plastic surgery to minimize the scars. The accident remains a part of our past. We might change how we think or feel about the past, either our personal or public experiences. We can reframe what happened to us. Or watch how historians reframe public history. Or even watch classic movies to see how current fashions influenced the telling of the story. With objective necessity, we can change how we think and feel about what happened but not that it happened. Objective necessities are the givens of our lives. We adjust to them; we don't change them.

Arbitrary Necessity

It's arbitrary necessity that gives us the trouble. With arbitrary necessity, we act as if we don't have any choice about what we do or what happens, when actually we do have choices. We just deny our choices; we deny our freedom. We act as if we have no freedom when we really do.

Arbitrary necessity, denying our choices, is rooted in doing what we think we should do. We may still be following blindly the lessons and rules we learned as children, rather than keeping current and evaluating situations for ourselves. We may be following self-styled gurus or public personalities. We may be influenced by friends or colleagues who pressure us to follow their way. For whatever reason, we don't choose what we do and think, or even see that a choice is available. And like the person who comes to believe his VCR doesn't record, by denying our choices long enough, pretty soon we don't have them. We'll have lost our freedom and not know where or when.

The payoff for buying into arbitrary necessity, for allowing yourself to lose your freedom, is avoiding responsibility. If we frame our actions as the only "choice" we have, then we don't have to be responsible for making that choice. "There's nothing else I could do," we tell ourselves. "I couldn't help it." And that gives us the relief from facing the consequences of making a bad choice.

This was the reasoning Ron used when he hit the customer in the store (chapter 8). His shoulds included not letting anyone disrespect him. If someone did act disrespectful, he had to hit the offending party. That was the way he saw the rules. He wasn't responsible. That's just the way it was. He was following the rules. It was the store's fault he was out of work and couldn't support his family. Like Donald, Ron had to be right. He had to do what he did, no matter what the consequences.

What's Right and Who's Right

By focusing on who's right, both Donald and Ron stayed at the level of blame rather than choosing to resolve the problems and issues they faced. And both of them paid the price. By focusing so much on what was in it for them, they lost an opportunity to support a family and a marriage.

When the focus shifts from being in control, insisting on your own way, and shifts to getting the job done, it not only empowers others, but releases you from having to do everything. At work or at home, people start feeling like valued members of the team. They respect and honor each other. And feel more empowered, more confident, more competent, more connected.

Choosing to Take Action

Choosing to take action is empowering, regardless of what you do. When our choices are consciously taken, when we think through the alternatives and choose, we're living our empowerment. We're taking charge, even if there are lots of other factors over which we have no choice or control.

Empowerment means making a choice between holding fast, folding, and walking away. Any of these can be empowering when our choices are made consciously and thoughtfully, rather than feeling like we've been forced into a position. Taking action on choices reinforces our feelings of confidence in our own competence.

Issues of freedom are issues of choice. These are the objectives, activities, values, and projects that call for you to make a decision and take action. There can be lots of alternatives or only a few. But there is the need to make a choice. Not to choose is to choose to lose your freedom. If you deny your freedom long enough, you'll lose it.

> *Dottie didn't marry until she was in her forties. She sold her busy travel agency and settled into her role as a homemaker, letting her husband make all the decisions. Dottie was in her late sixties when her husband died, and her sister encouraged her to come on holiday with her to Great Britain. Dottie decided she couldn't go because she didn't have a current passport and didn't have her husband to get a new one for her.*

While she ran her own business, Dottie not only helped many of her clients get passports, but also accompanied the tours to countries much less traveled to than Great Britain. But for over twenty years she had relied so heavily on her husband, she no longer believed she was capable of taking care of even the most basic of travel logistics. She was too frightened to travel, because her husband wouldn't be there to take care of her. She no longer thought of herself as capable of taking care of such complicated tasks.

Holding Fast

Every decision we make to change reinforces our feelings of empowerment, even when we decide to do nothing different from what we've been doing. The power is in the deciding, not in what we decide. If we look at our options, our desired results, and the possible negative consequences, we reinforce our power to choose.

The paradox is that even when, or especially when, what needs to be done is problematic or unpleasant, and we consciously choose not to do it, we feel less of a burden. The action doesn't change, but acknowledging our control over our decision makes it less noxious. Staying the course, holding fast is an empowering way when it's a choice, not a default.

Folding

Not every choice turns out the way we want. We may carefully analyze and consider all the alternatives and still not realize our objectives. There comes the time we may have to admit this time it's a loss. It's time to fold. More effort, or different effort, is not going to get us what we want. Time to let it go. Sometimes it's time to step back after having given it our best effort and remind ourselves life/work/relationships won't always go our way (even when we know we're right). Folding means we'll let someone else take the lead and the consequences. Then we'll keep quiet about it. We won't run an I-told-you-so game, even with ourselves. Folding is detaching, letting go.

Walking Away

Walking away is appropriate when the issue is not your j-o-b and/or you're not willing to use your energy or resources to do it. Walking away doesn't mean the job isn't important or doesn't need to be done; it's just not your job to do it. We don't have the time, energy, or resources to do everything that needs to be done. If we don't make some choices, we just get overwhelmed. Then we can't do what only we can do.

Making walking-away choices isn't capitulating or rolling over. It's making a choice.

Making choices means you see alternatives and the richness of your life. We can see lots of ways of achieving what we want and value. We see differences as differences, not making rigid judgments about what should be or what can't be. We see others do things our way, and we feel comfortable making our preferences known and choosing them for ourselves.

The important part of making a choice is choosing, not necessarily the content of the choice. When we see we've freely chosen, even if the content is the same as what someone else told us we have to do, we'll feel better about ourselves, more committed to taking action, and more likely to follow through and finish our tasks.

Consider yourself empowered means not waiting for someone else to tell you that you are special, that you're entitled to live your life the way you see best. Considering ourselves empowered means we evaluate the rules we've learned for living our lives to see if they fit for who and what we are now, not who we were when we were kids.

Considering yourself empowered means you see yourself as in charge of your life, not being buffeted by fate or other people. Considering yourself empowered means you are at the controls. You've acted on your permission to be in charge of your own life.

Exercises for Chapter 11

PRACTICE THE SELF-ESTEEM HABITS

Keep track of when you practice and the results you start to achieve. How is increasing your self-esteem affecting the way you are facing the challenges you have?

WHAT YOU CAN CHOOSE . . . AND WHAT YOU CAN'T

What do you really have no choice over? List several things that *really* fit this category.

Now look at several things that others say they don't have any choice about. How is what they think similar to or different from the ways you see these same things?

How is seeing yourself as having no choice stopping you from taking charge of the challenge you face?

CHAPTER 12

CHOOSING A GOOD LIFE: VALUES AND ETHICS

D avid Kaczynski read the published manifesto of America's most notorious serial killer with growing concern. The ideas and language were similar to what his brother Ted had expressed in the past. Then, when helping his mother move from her house, he found documents Ted had written that convinced David to meet with the FBI in their Unabomber investigation. He was afraid his brother was their man.

David's pain increased as the case unfolded and he realized he and his wife could have been unwitting accomplices in his brother's trail of bombings. They were haunted by the thought that they had purchased airline tickets that took Ted to the cities where bombings had occurred.

David's decision to turn his brother in was not an easy one. He described it as agony, wanting what was best for his brother, wanting to protect him, but afraid Ted might hurt more people. He had to put the greater good, protecting other people, in front of protecting a loved one.

David's decision addressed all the issues we face when we realize a loved one has not only hurt us, but has engaged in criminal, possibly lethal, behavior. The struggle is between knowing what is right, what is moral, and our loyalty to our loved ones. We start to question our morals and values.

When we're faced with a crisis, with a situation or person we can't control, everything we think and believe is called into question. It shakes the core of our values and ethics. We start to question what we think the world is all about, who we are and what's right. We look for the perfect moral answer to guide us through this crisis.

There is no absolute moral code. Just like there's no absolutely perfect circle. We agree to act as if there is a perfect circle, because we need a reference point for what roundness is all about. In practice, all we can do is to get closer to the approximation that is imperfect.

In the same way, we agree to act as if there is a perfect moral code so we will have a reference point for how to act in our everyday lives. We agree on this reference point so we won't have to decide every situation from scratch.

When we're faced with a crisis, we question even our imperfect moral code. We want to believe what we do is right, and the other person is wrong, not us. But what we thought—that if we did good things, we'd get rewarded—hasn't happened. We thought people were essentially good, and we found out we were wrong. We're challenged with the realization that not only what happened was awful, but our beliefs and faith have been shaken, too.

One more time, we get to reflect on what we believe life is all about. Crisis demands we rethink what we thought was certain. We don't get a choice about whether we have to rethink our beliefs. We can only choose *how*, not *if* we'll have to rethink them.

To move forward, to get on with our lives, to take charge, we need to admit there's a disconnect with what we believe, and to have a willingness to reexamine our new reality. For most of us, this means having to admit we aren't sure we know enough to know how to do this.

We've adopted our moral code from a nonconscious position. For the most part, we don't consciously and purposefully decide what's right, what's moral, or what's ethical. We adopt the morals and ethics of our parents, our teachers, religious leaders, and community. We may have a lot of experience in choosing our actions from our morals and values, but not much experience in thinking through our moral and value positions.

Like David Kaczynski, our decisions about what to do in crisis become moral issues. We have to choose between two conflicting moral positions: protecting and valuing a loved one and the greater good for all.

It's not enough to clarify our moral values and beliefs. All crises challenge us to make new judgments. We're faced with real experiences and need to decide what to do. Deciding means making judgments. We have to choose what we'll do, and what we won't. And most of the time the way isn't clear. That is what judgments and decisions are all about. We need to make a decision only when the way is not evident.

It's not politically correct to be judgmental. We equate being non-judgmental with being virtuous. But taking charge means you have to make judgments. On a national TV talk show a convicted child moles-ter yelled at me that I had no right to judge him. "Of course I have a right," I replied, "and a responsibility to judge you." Judging situations, events, and even other people is necessary if we're to live responsible lives. It is the only way we can make choices, the only way to make decisions.

But we must judge from a position of values, not righteousness.

Judging from righteousness means taking the moral high ground, seeing errors and omissions in others, but not in ourselves. Righteous-ness means only *we* have the answers, only *we* are "good," or can be "good." It's an issue of how we express our morals and values, rather than what our morals are.

Watch a group of six-year-olds. They are righteously judgmental. They know the way the world should be and what all the rules are. And they're quick to tell you how you've "done wrong." They also believe in strict, sure punishments for transgressions. No mercy here, only justice.

Most of us know adults who take this same position when they ex-press their values. They know all the rules for right and wrong, are quick to judge, and are determined to extract punishment for trans-gressions. There's no mercy or extenuating circumstances.

While liberals usually delight in pointing out how their conservative critics are judgmental, conservatives have no corner on righteousness. Righteousness is a way values are expressed, not the content of those values. Both liberals and conservatives can be dogmatic.

Elaine's ex-husband had several affairs and an illegitimate child while they were married. Now the divorced mother of two teenage girls, Elaine insists the girls should get an educa-tion and a good start on their careers before thinking of mar-riage. She counsels them to wait until they are at least thirty before getting married. She insists they give the young men in their lives time to get their wild oats sown before marriage. No men can be trusted, she tells her daughters.

Elaine's being just as judgmental as her conservative neighbors. She's sure she knows the correct rules, what's right, and what everyone else should do. She'd be the first to criticize her neighbors for telling their children to marry quickly and have lots of children. Those parents are too rigid, too old-fashioned, and just plain wrong, she'd say.

The content of our values is based on our version of that perfect moral code: what's right and what's wrong. Our values reflect both moral universals—actions or behaviors that are judged right and wrong all over the world—and moral conventions—actions each culture agrees on as right or wrong. Values give us the moral boundaries for our actions and options.

The first steps we take to rethink our morals and values are looking at where we got our morals and how they fit now. Where did our values come from? How did we develop them? Do we still believe what we used to know was true? What's new in light of our current experience? How do we express our values and beliefs? Are we still as righteous as we were when we were six? How do we resolve moral dilemmas when both sides are right? Do we still see moral dilemmas as we did when we were teens? Or when we were young adults?

We'll look at these questions from both a content and a process approach. Content addresses what's right, what we think is moral. Process is how we express our values, how we think about them, share them with others, use them to guide our decisions and our lives.

Along the way we will get a glimpse at how we have conflicts over values and the confusion between conflicts of content and conflicts of process.

What's Right

Are there universal moral values? Are there values that are shared by every culture on earth? Have there been values that are endorsed by all known religions? Have there been some values held by people since the dawn of time? Philosophers, theologians, anthropologists, and ethicists have all pondered and researched these questions. They've found two basic moral values, held for as long as they can find, for all different types of cultures, in all religions, all over the world.

The two universal values are human life and property.

These two values form the basis for religious beliefs, cultural expectations, and legal requirements. Everyone seems to agree. Don't hurt or kill other people. Don't take things that belong to someone else.

These two principles seem simple, but aren't. Each culture sees these universal values just a bit differently. What's acceptable in one society is not okay in another. Each culture derives an elaborate set of extenuating circumstances that sanction behavior that would seem to outsiders to be a break in the moral code. These extenuating circumstances not only shape the legal and moral rules of a society, but get incorporated into acceptable social behavior.

Breaks in the social code may be humorous and trivial, or not at all funny and have serious social consequences. This is particularly true when traveling in other countries, even if you are fluent in their language. Sometimes you won't even know that you are committing a serious social faux pas. Yet the locals will either laugh at you or dismiss you as uncouth.

If Jane hadn't run the length of the platform with all her luggage, she would have missed the train to the Tokyo airport. She collapsed into her assigned chair, coughing and choking from the exertion. She knew she was being rude for coughing and blowing her nose in public, both from the critical looks of her seatmates, and also from the lessons her hosts had extended during her stay. She didn't speak enough Japanese to apologize appropriately and was sure she had made one more impression of the stereotypical ugly American.

Saleem knew he was doing something wrong at work, but he couldn't figure out what he was doing that his American coworkers didn't like. He'd been working at the company for more than a year before a fellow countryman finally told him that in the United States people used ashtrays. Where he came from, everyone dropped their ashes and put out their ciga-

rettes on the floor. So he continued to drop his cigarette ashes on the floor of his office in his new job in the United States.

In both of these cases, the "locals" didn't confront the foreigner on the uncouth behavior; they just shunned him or her, made disparaging remarks, and expected the outsiders to know what they were doing wrong. The breaches of etiquette were so obvious even a local child would know what was wrong. They expected foreigners to know, too. They expected foreigners to adhere to the local customs, whatever the circumstances.

As we work and live with a more diverse population, opportunities to break the social code occur more often. Serious conflicts between immigrants and native born, or groups of immigrants, are often based in the difficulty to understand the subtle differences in acceptable behavior.

Extenuating Circumstances

Differences in the extenuating circumstances that allow for breaking moral codes can lead to even more serious misunderstandings. When we hear of someone doing something that isn't allowed in our society, we understandably judge them from our point of view. Especially when we are children.

When I was in the third or fourth grade, I was fascinated with a story of an isolated Eskimo family who put their elderly grandmother on the ice to die. A new baby was coming, there wasn't enough food for everyone, and grandma was not able to contribute anymore, so she was the one to go. The story had a happy ending when the new baby was born without teeth and no one knew what to do to feed it. They went out to retrieve grandma so she could teach them.

At some level, the truth of the story didn't matter. What was such a wonder was that there were people who were willing to let their grandma die for their child. I had never before faced the possibility of such a dilemma.

This story is similar to the moral-dilemma exercise that highlights cross-cultural moral differences. A man is rowing his mother, his wife, and his child across a river when the boat capsizes. He can save only one of them. Which one should he save? The answers to this question, and the reasoning behind them, reveal the values of the respondent. Who is more important, and why: one's mother, spouse, or child? What is telling about the answers is that each can be chosen from a valid moral viewpoint.

This is not a dilemma that challenges only children. As adults, we have to decide where to draw the line between what is okay to do and not okay to do in today's multicultural, multifaith society. How much should you take with you when you move to a culture that has different values or social norms? With issues like discarding ashes on the floor, the answer is straightforward. Conform to the social niceties so you will be accepted, seen as a team player, not passed over for promotion because you are an uncouth foreigner. Excuse yourself and take care of your coughing and blowing in private.

But larger issues—circumcising baby girls at home by excising their external genitalia, killing a goat and smearing your new house with goat's blood to insure health and prosperity, killing a young woman who has dishonored her family or hunting down the young man who has dishonored her—are not trivial issues, nor are they universally acceptable. In most cultures, they don't fit the extenuating circumstances that allow going against the universal values of not hurting or killing other people or taking other people's property.

Core Values

In cross-cultural interviews, anthropologists looked for a core set of values that would reflect the two universal values of human life and property.

They found most societies agreed on the following constructs:

- Fairness
- Freedom
- Love
- Responsibility

- Tolerance of others
- Truth

They then translated these core values into moral injunctions, or prescriptions for daily behavior. Because these values are what's important to us, this is what we agree to do and not to do.

- Do not cheat.
- Do not deceive.
- Do not deprive another of freedom or opportunity.
- Do not deprive another of pleasure.
- Do not injure.
- Do not kill.
- Do your duty.
- Keep your promises.
- Obey the laws.

Again they found a wide variety in the way these injunctions are put into play, depending on the local culture and customs. In many areas, the injunction against killing and for obeying the law are followed to such an extent that police do not carry guns. In Japan, all police officers are black-belt-level practitioners of at least three forms of martial arts, including the use of a baton. While there are no police brutality laws, as such, in Japan, and there is unlimited potential, police typically do not exercise this right at every opportunity. Conditions in Japanese prisons and jails are also very different from Western standards. Convicted prisoners often sit for long periods of time in the same position, without talking, eating, or drinking, charged to think about what they did and what they will do to make reparations. From a Western values perspective, we would judge these conditions unreasonable or inhumane. They are considered appropriate in Japan.

Understanding the cultural differences in the expression of values doesn't mean that we're suggesting situational ethics. These examples are reflective of a well-thought-out and constructed pattern of value expression. They don't change with each case. They simply reflect a culture different from our own.

It's also not an if-it-feels-good-do-it approach. We expect people to use values and morals as guides for their daily behavior. There's clear consensus on what's right and how people should behave. Transgressions are met with sure consequences that are known and expected by both the transgressor and the authorities.

Epistemology of Values

We can find the same kind of differences of expression of values within a culture. Common values and beliefs can have vastly different expressions in everyday behavior. When researchers study how moral codes are expressed, they typically find the differences are developmental. As people get older, more educated, or more sophisticated in their range of experiences, the expression of their morals becomes more complex, also.

The expression of our morals and values is dependent upon our epistemology, or the underlying logic and definition of reality we apply to what we believe. It is similar to the epistemology of thinking that we looked at in chapter five. Epistemology addresses how we think, how we believe, how we know what is true, logical, and appropriate about what we think, believe, and know. Epistemology is the process of constructing and believing our moral code and values. It answers the question: What do I believe about what I believe?

Like what we think about thinking, what we believe about our beliefs is important. We choose how to act based on our beliefs.

Moral Development

As children grow, their ability to think and reason changes. Not only do they have more information, but they can think in more complex ways about what they do know. Both the structure and the content of what they think about changes.

In a similar way, we have developmental changes and shifts in our values. We may not change what we do, but we will change our reasons for doing it. We shift from being self-centered to having a more community-centered base for our ethics and morals. We change from obeying the rules so we won't get caught to choosing the right thing to do because it's the right thing.

While different researchers have different models, most include at least four stages of moral development.

1. Personal. This stage is the me-first childlike stage, which is self-centered and rule based.
2. Interpersonal. This stage usually starts during the teen years when a young person starts to pay attention to group norms and to recognize there are several perspectives to each situation. While still putting personal beliefs first, how or if they fit into the group becomes more important.
3. Institutional. This stage marks the transition to adulthood and the realization that our community is made up of many groups with vastly different perspectives, and our team both contributes to and gets from the larger community, even if we don't all agree all the time.
4. Universal. At this stage, people see their community as part of a larger, interconnected system. We may be very different, but we are charged to treat one another with respect and honor.

How we express our morals depends on our stage of moral development. At the personal stage, we don't kill someone because it's against the rules. By the interpersonal stage, our reason shifts to not killing because we'll get caught. At the institutional stage, we don't kill others because people like us don't do things like that. At the universal stage, any killing hurts all of us. Our reasoning becomes more abstract and inclusive as we mature.

Personal Moral Reasoning

The primary factor in personal moral reasoning is following the rules. The rules are absolute, given by authority, and often have religious origins.

Small children pass through this stage as they're just beginning to understand they can't do everything their way and that they aren't the center of the universe. Fairness, kindness, obedience to the rules are all important lessons that we learn during this stage. Fairness means we share and we all have the same rules; kindness, that we don't hurt others, we help and care for others; obedience means we put aside what we want to do and follow the rules. And because we don't want to do most of these things naturally, there has to be a big person to teach us what to do, how to behave, and what's right.

Most people pass through this stage on the way to becoming an adult. But some adults still function at this stage. They're usually called fundamentalists. They unquestioningly follow the rules someone bigger, more powerful, or wiser has laid down. Because our personal moral reasoning is typically based on our religious beliefs, that older, wiser, more powerful being is usually God or God's emissary. When asked why they believe what they believe, fundamentalists typically reply, "Because God said so."

Fundamentalism is not based on a particular faith. There are fundamentalist Jews, Christians, Moslems. Fundamentalism is how faith is experienced and expressed, not what faith is followed.

In all faiths, fundamentalists are charged with believing exactly what is written in their holy scripture. Scriptures are taken on faith, not questioned. Their way is the true way; others are labeled as not "real _____" or as misguided and fallen from the fold. They'll dismiss those who choose another way, or who don't understand their way, as heretics, dangerous, or naive. Nonetheless, they'll still hold them responsible for conforming to the rules and to the consequences of their disbelief.

> At a holiday dinner, Pam was surprised to hear her new sister-in-law say she couldn't wait until Leroy, Pam's brother, became a Christian. Pam knew their parents had raised the whole family as Christians, attending the local church, making sure all the kids were confirmed. While not much of a churchgoer as an adult, Leroy still qualified as a Christian as far as Pam was concerned. Her sister-in-law corrected her. No one was truly a Christian until they had been reborn and experienced a conversion and joined her church. By these criteria, Pam didn't qualify, either.
>
> During dessert, the conversation turned particularly unpleasant for Pam. The "true Christians" at the table engaged in a vicious discussion of current events and people in the community. Their conversation included many bigoted, racist, and anti-Semitic remarks. When Pam confronted them on their "unchristian" comments, they got mad at her for getting mad at them. Who was she to judge them!

The hallmark of personal moral reasoning is to see your own way as the only way. The base of your beliefs is accepted as fact. Fundamentalists see their scriptures, whether the Hebrew Bible, the Christian Bible, or the Koran, not only as true and factual, but error free and "the literal word of God." For any of them their motto could be "God said it, the Bible (Koran) says it, I believe it."

The fundamentalists' faith is unshakable. They've accepted their beliefs because someone greater, wiser, and more knowledgeable said it was so. They choose not to analyze or evaluate their beliefs. So they aren't open to any other viewpoint. They know what's right. Those who don't follow the rules should be punished. No mercy for extenuating circumstances, only justice for transgressing.

Interpersonal Moral Reasoning

The hallmark of interpersonal moral reasoning is to see that other moral perspectives exist that may be deeply held, significant, and not the same as yours. For some people this precipitates a crisis of faith. How can there be more than one right way? Even when faced with information or data that contradicts what you have believed, there is the tendency to continue with your own beliefs. We use self-sealing logic, where any evidence is interpreted to support our chosen position, to maintain a stability and consistency in our beliefs.

At the same time, interpersonal relationships become extremely important, and many young people struggle with doing things that are against the moral code of their family of origin so they will be included in their larger social peer group. The most important questions become: Will they like me? Will I fit in? Our goal is self-preservation in the midst of change. Can I find a way that I can live with and that is acceptable to others? There's a shift from accepting the proscribed rule to seeing ourselves as responsible for understanding and formulating our own moral code.

While this is not a stage of unquestioning adherence to authoritative rules, most of our behavior is still defined for us. We'll see teens doing outrageous things, wearing carefully concocted costumes, using in-group language or slang, all designed to say no to previous rules and yes to a similarly rigid new set of rules. The rules for rebellion are just as strict as the rules for conformity.

Betty was torn about getting more ear piercings. She had had pierced ears since she was a baby, but now all her friends had added several more to at least one ear. Betty wanted to do what her friends were doing. But she knew that her father would be furious. He said girls with multiple earrings were promiscuous lowlifes. She knew her father was wrong. Her friends were good kids like she was, even though most of them wore multiple earrings. Betty was torn between staying connected to her family and connecting with her friends. She wasn't sure what was right anymore.

Adults who are at this stage of moral development will exhibit this same adherence to the group, sometimes to their own detriment. They'll allow others to do or say anything so they can be included, or so that the other person won't leave.

Institutional Moral Reasoning

As people move into young adulthood, they tend to get out in the world more. They see new ways of doing things, ways that others see as right. The moral task at this stage is both self-preservation and self-regulation. Adults are responsible for maintaining both their own stability and that of their group while making sure the system as a whole is working for everyone.

Making decisions and choosing the best way is very difficult when you need to take into account vastly different value bases.

Katy referred one of the boys in her third-grade class to the school psychologist for what looked like a serious mental illness, as well as evidence of physical abuse. She'd contacted the parents, but they were reluctant to talk about the boy's problems with her. When the school psychologist followed up, she found the boy did have serious emotional problems, and the parents were very concerned. They were sure their son had been possessed and were working with their parish priest to rid the child of his demons. The parents and the priest were beating the child with switches to drive the demons out of the boy.

Dale, also a school psychologist, was working with the teachers and students at a Native American boarding school when a boy was referred for inappropriate behavior. When

Dale saw the boy, he realized the teen was seriously mentally ill. He also knew there was little chance the boy would agree to traditional Anglo psychotherapeutic practices. So he met with the tribe's shaman to discuss the case. The shaman agreed to take on the case and several days later conducted a prayer ceremony that involved all the members of the boy's family. With their support and the powerful medicine he provided, the boy's condition improved markedly.

In both of these cases the objective was to help the child. In both cases the interventions were more typical of the child's subculture than of the school or the psychologists involved. Yet in the final analysis, it was acknowledged that both children were seriously troubled. And both the families and the children found more relief with their culturally accepted treatment than with standard mental health practices. Too often we forget to look closely at a family's culture when we are looking for solutions. We focus on our own point of view, or the dominant view of a whole culture.

The challenge in working at a system level is that you're still inside of the system. It is almost impossible to change the system except by changing the structure of the system itself. It's like lighting a fire in a fireplace to make a room warmer when you've set the thermostat to sixty-five degrees. As soon as the fire starts warming the room, the air conditioner comes on to cool it off again. You have to change the parameters of the system. You have to turn up the thermostat to warm up the room.

Lighting a fire in the fireplace is regulating the elements, like regulating yourself within a system. Turning up the thermostat is regulating the system. You've changed what the system can do. While it's easy to see how to do this with thermostats, it's very difficult to see how to change your moral and value decisions. We come with our own perspective: what we think is right. It's really hard to see a situation from another person's perspective. It's even harder to see possible solutions that don't start from our point of view.

The challenge at the institutional stage is to get out of our own narrow perspective, to understand how and why we believe what we do, and to see that there are lots of other people who are just as moral and just as committed to their beliefs as we are. When we ascribe the reason for problems to differences in how values are expressed, we get stuck in blaming and are unable to resolve the issues.

Universal Moral Reasoning

Taking a universal perspective is like seeing the poster of the universe with its billions and billions of stars spread out against the darkness, and the little arrow pointing to the Milky Way with the legend "You are here."

Universal moral reasoning forces us to get the big picture. We may see ourselves as complete, interactive, even worldly, but our own solar system, much less our community, is just a tiny speck in the universe.

Universal moral reasoning embraces the ability to suspend total loyalty to our own groups and see the need for universality of moral behavior and then act on it. It means having the courage to act toward others as we would toward one of our own, even if we see them as the enemy.

When I was traveling in South Africa many years ago, two experiences embedded themselves in my mind. One was the street market we visited in Durban, the other the women I was working with.

The smells, the sounds, and the bustle of the street market in Durban were just like what I had seen in towns and villages in Mexico. Then I realized that they were reminiscent of the agricultural markets I had seen in southern France and Italy. And at the same time, I remembered the many pictures of markets all over the world in the well-worn copies of *National Geographic* that I had grown up with. Markets are universal. Everyone has them. We're all alike. We all need to sell our goods and services and buy what we don't produce. The connectedness goes beyond the smells, noise, and products. It's the process. This is what people the world over do.

The women I worked with were amazing. I was a bit apprehensive, a white woman from the United States going halfway around the world to teach seminars to women in business. What arrogance, I told myself. But as we got to work, the same issues, feelings, and needs I had found in the United States were operative here in South Africa. Race and language started to fall away. Our gender transcended the differences. We were all concerned with the same issues: equal opportunity, equal pay for equal work, how our working affected our children, how we could be good wives and mothers while working outside the home.

Universal moral reasoning starts from that understanding of how we share the underlying values and beliefs with all people. Similarities and common values transcend differences and dissension.

Universal moral reasoning brings us back to the universal moral beliefs found around the world—don't hurt or kill people and don't take what isn't yours—and then challenges us to apply these values to everyone, no matter if they are of a different nationality, faith, race, or standard of living. Whether we like them or not, whether we agree with them or not. Even if they have totally challenged and changed your life. Only by deciding how you will believe and what you will value will you be able to take charge of your life.

Exercises for Chapter 12

VALUES: CURRENT AND PAST

Values help answer the question: Why do you do what you do? They are not so concerned with the how of your actions, but with the why. Values are deeply held beliefs about the way the world should be and is. The same value can be expressed in a variety of ways. In the exercise below, be sure to be as specific as you can, so that you can see how you express your values.

Assume a new world order in which values are very expensive and rare. Each person is allowed to claim only three values. Look over the list of values and choose which three you want.

- Achievement, a sense of accomplishment
- Creativity, being imaginative, innovative
- Fame, being famous and well known
- Family happiness
- Freedom, independence, autonomy
- Health, fitness
- Inner harmony, being at peace with oneself
- Integrity, honesty, sincerity; standing up for one's beliefs
- Loyalty, duty, respectfulness, obedience
- Personal development, use of potential; self-realization
- Power, control, authority, or influence over others
- Religion, strong religious beliefs, closeness to God

- Self-respect, sense of personal identity
- Wealth, getting rich, financial independence
- Wisdom, understanding life, discovering knowledge
- _____, a value you would like to add

For each of your three values, answer the following questions.

What does this value mean to you?

How is it similar to or different from the way your family, friends, or associates see this value?

How have your views on this value changed since you were a teen? A young adult?

How is your life different on a daily basis because you hold this value?

Is this the value you most want your children to have?

Is this value challenged in your daily life?

CHANGES IN CORE VALUES

While the expression of our core values is laid down early in our lives, a crisis can shift how we think, feel, and implement them. Consider how your views of each of these core values has shifted as you've had to deal with taking charge of a situation you couldn't control.

1. Do not cheat.
2. Do not deceive.
3. Do not deprive another of freedom or opportunity.
4. Do not deprive another of pleasure.
5. Do not injure.
6. Do not kill.
7. Do your duty.
8. Keep your promises.
9. Obey the laws.

What values have stayed the same? How come?

What values have changed? How come?

What additional changes do you want to make about the values you hold . . . or the values you've discarded or kept? How come?

CHAPTER 13

LOVE IS AN ACTION VERB . . . SO GET MOVING

Marion was happily married to her childhood sweetheart and was the mother of two little girls, when her husband disappeared one day. More than a month later, he finally resurfaced, to tell her he had been using his legal clients' escrow accounts and their family savings to support his gambling habit. Her life as she knew it disappeared as he was tried, convicted of fraud, and sentenced to prison. Once a stay-at-home mom, she went back to work to support herself and the girls while he served his sentence.

Chuck built his investment business from the contacts and relationships he made through the local Vietnam vets association. His business success provided a lavish lifestyle for Beverly, his wife of many years, and their three children. One day after Chuck left town on a business trip, Beverly received a taped message and personal mementos in the mail. On the tape, Chuck told her he was on a secret government mission, and if he didn't come back, she could assume he'd been killed. His bloodstained car was found later that week at the airport. Local authorities were suspicious of the car's condition: it looked like someone had faked the scene. It wasn't until four years later that Chuck was found, using a different name but the same scam. Once again he had married and was building an investment business using his veteran's status to find business leads.

When we hear stories of such awful behavior in people who say they love one another, we have a hard time understanding why someone would be in a relationship with someone who acted so cruelly.

When I was a marriage counselor and sex therapist, I'd hear clients and workshop participants recite long lists of stupid, silly, or tragically devastating unloving things their partners had done. Their partners had humiliated them in public, got drunk and danced on a tabletop at a company holiday party, got angry and dumped them out of the car on a lonely rural road. The lists were endless. When I'd ask why they were putting up with the obnoxious behavior or why they didn't leave, they'd say they couldn't leave, they loved their partner.

Sometimes the offensive behavior didn't seem to be all that big a deal. And yet the offended party found it unbearable and wouldn't mention it. One man was so turned off by his wife's not closing the door between the bathroom and the bedroom while she was using the toilet before bed, he didn't want to make love with her. When I asked why he didn't tell her, he said he didn't want to hurt her feelings by complaining about her personal hygiene habits. In the meantime, she had no idea why he was no longer amorous. He said he loved her, but they never made love anymore.

Another woman didn't want to tell her husband his hands were rough and hard to the touch. Instead of feeling good, his lovemaking was painful for her. She didn't want to hurt his feelings, so she just started making excuses and avoiding him. She often said she loved him. She just didn't want to make love with him.

These couples were caught up in the thrall of lust and insanity. They were confusing strong emotions with love or buying into being responsible for someone else's feelings. Somehow, we think we aren't supposed to criticize or give feedback if we love someone. It's as if it's okay to do things that are hurtful, but it's not okay to say so. Or you should put aside what you want and need, so that the other person won't be hurt or inconvenienced or asked to change. In the name of love, we avoid problems, instead of resolving them.

Is this love? I don't think so.

When asked for a definition of love, Harry Stack Sullivan, a little-known but professionally influential American psychologist, replied that when the wishes, needs, and feelings of the other are as important to you as your own, then a state of love can be said to exist.

Note, he said *as* important, *not more* important. From this perspective, love is a collaboration between two partners who share equally in the gifts and the sacrifices of their relationship. Each is called upon to give; each receives from the other. At the same time, they honor themselves. Love is based on what we do, on our actions, how we treat one another, not what we say. Love is an action verb, not a description of what we feel.

Words Are Not Enough

So many of us act as if saying "I love you" is enough. Or we are in relationships with people who continually say, "I love you," but do outrageous unloving things. Then they expect everyone will find them lovable, because they *did* say it.

> *Yetta thought her youngest son was so cute, when actually he was a darling little monster. He often broke the family rules, acted rude, or misbehaved. When she started to correct him, he'd turn on his cute face and say, "Mommy, I wuv you" in a baby voice, and Yetta would melt. "How can you stay mad at someone who is so cute?" she would ask no one in particular. Or "How can you not love him?" as if she were trying to excuse herself for succumbing to his charms. In the meantime, his big sister was not excused for her misbehavior, and the little one started baiting her into mischief so she would get punished. He, of course, would get off by being "so cute."*

Yetta couldn't understand why her extended family and friends didn't think her son was so cute. She'd get angry at them for not liking her precious child.

Then Yetta's son had serious trouble in preschool and was identified as not being ready for kindergarten. He did only what *he* wanted to do and alternately sassed or ignored his teachers. Yetta's response was to accuse the teachers of picking on him and not appreciating his special charm.

Yetta didn't hold her son responsible for his behavior or subject to the same rules his sister was. She said he was too young for those lessons.

But he wasn't too young to learn how to take over the family. He'd learned he could get away with anything he did, even things that were mean, spiteful, or infantile. All because he could pull a cute face and say "I love you."

Both kids were learning that *saying* I love you was enough. They didn't have to *act* loving. Neither child was getting the parenting they needed. But Yetta didn't see it that way. She didn't think excusing her son's bad behavior was hurting his ability to grow and mature.

Yetta didn't think through what she was teaching her son. She didn't consider the consequences of her responses to him, or even what kind of person she was helping him to become. She got caught up in the feelings of the moment: what felt good, what was more fun. She didn't consider that sometimes being loving means having to give hard feedback, set limits, and be tough. That's what love is all about. When she finally realized the harm she'd unwittingly done, she wailed she'd failed Parenting 101.

Foundations of Relationships

Yetta's children had been missing the most important lessons of life, the foundation of all relationships: It's both give and take. With family and friends, we agree to come together, to form a relationship. Each relationship we have includes choices, responsibilities, and agreements. Each relationship provides rewards and gratification. Without both giving and getting, our relationships founder.

Relationships aren't easy. They're not for wimps. They take time and effort. Typically we spend more time planning our summer vacation than we do working on our relationships. We just figure everyone thinks and feels as we do; there really isn't much to talk about.

Until something goes wrong. One of us doesn't hold up our end of the bargain. We don't fulfill our responsibilities to the others; we don't meet our agreements. Then feelings of betrayal and a sense of being out of control overwhelm us. "How could they do this?" we ask ourselves. "How could this happen to me? How could I have been so stupid? What do I do now?"

Relationship Choices

We all have choices in relationships. With friends and lovers, we can even choose if we want to be there. With parents and children, we can't choose who we get, but we can choose how we'll relate.

With our choices comes a responsibility for reciprocity. We make agreements, and each of us expects the other will fulfill those agreements. I'll do things for you and for the relationship, and so will you. We'll work together and for each other so life will be better for both of us. The success of our relationships is based on what we do, not on what we say we'll do.

> *Charlie and Robin's relationship had always been stormy. Charlie's mom was sure both kids were using drugs, or at least drinking a lot. Robin became increasingly malicious with both Charlie and his mom. She'd get angry, curse, hit, and throw things. Later that day, or the next day, Robin would tearfully say she was sorry and beg for forgiveness. Charlie always forgave her. He'd make excuses for her angry blowups. Charlie's mom finally had enough. No one was going to break windows, break down the door, curse her, and try to hit her. No matter how sorry she said she was. Saying "I'm sorry" was not enough. Robin was no longer welcome at their home.*

Charlie was caught up in the lust and insanity that characterize so many relationships. Because "he loved Robin," he put up with her abuse. Charlie's mom, being older, wiser, and needing to protect her other children, demanded Robin walk her talk. It wasn't enough to say she was sorry or that she loved Charlie. She had to start acting loving.

Saying sorry is easy; changing behavior isn't. And as we'll see in chapter fourteen, sometimes it's not enough to apologize, or to be forgiven. Sometimes the behavior has been so awful, the betrayal so basic, that it's necessary to break off a relationship.

Our choice to enter into a relationship also means we understand there are three parts to any relationship: you, me, and us. Each of us brings who we are, our strengths and limitations, our gifts and needs. And then we build a new entity by combining who we each are into a unique pattern of giving and getting. It's this combination of specific individuals and the relationship itself that makes getting together with someone so special.

The combination and the relationship is based on agreements, who does what, who gets what. We build a catalog of quid pro quos, our own list of somethings for something. The agreements we forge depend on what we've done before and on what we decide to do together. All of our relationships combine our histories and choices we make about how it will be this time.

Some agreements we talk about, others we don't. Some, like fidelity and commitment, we assume are so basic they don't need to be specified. Others, we covertly agree not to deal with. We may keep secrets or even slip into collusion. We agree on what we aren't going to do and talk about, but don't talk about our agreement not to talk.

A breakdown in any one of these areas—establishing reciprocity, honoring both the individuals and the relationship, or making agreements—can send our relationship spinning into free fall. Both people feel the relationship is out of control, and try to grab control, usually by trying to make the other person change—a futile activity. We can't change anyone else, and lots of times we can't even change ourselves.

We can't control the other person, no matter how hard we try. The only thing we can do is start taking charge of what we do, think, and say. We can get clear on what we want from the other person, how we expect to be treated, and what we'll do if our partner doesn't fulfill our expectations.

When we start taking charge of ourselves in relationships, we're more likely to get the love we want and deserve.

Reciprocity

Even little kids get it about relationships: they demand life to be fair. Proverbs tell us, What's sauce for the goose is sauce for the gander. Turnabout is fair play. We're talking about reciprocity: what applies to me applies to you. The rules apply to both of us, not just one of us.

Reciprocity in a relationship means walking the fine line between being equal—everyone getting the same things—and being fair—everyone getting what's needed. Being equal may not be the same as being fair.

Bertha's policy was to buy her ten kids the same amount of clothing and shoes in the fall before school. No one got more until the spring shopping trip. She was being fair, she told the kids. Except her kids were growing at different rates. Before time for the spring shopping trip came, two of her boys no longer had any pants that fit, and one of the girls was wearing underwear painfully too small. When these three asked for new clothes before the end of winter, she replied it wasn't necessary. The other kids didn't need any, so they shouldn't need them, either.

Jennifer and her husband seldom had health or budget problems until she had a difficult pregnancy. Bills piled up from three short hospitalizations and complications during delivery. The baby needed special care, which meant a longer hospital stay. Now two years later, Jennifer is still blaming herself for the family's tight budget and inability to afford a family vacation. She feels responsible for the family's financial woes.

Bertha wanted to treat her children fairly, without playing favorites. She confused responding to individual needs with playing favorites. Jennifer considers the hospital bills for her pregnancy her fault, rather than a family expense. Both of them have lost track of the spirit of reciprocity and have the ledger book out instead. They don't want to give special consideration for individual needs (Bertha), or they feel guilty for needing special consideration (Jennifer).

Sometimes the lack of reciprocity is reflected in a lack of respect or willingness to share family resources. There are arbitrary limits on what is mine and what is ours.

Byron was really proud to take delivery of his third airplane. But his pleasure was cut short when he heard his wife had spent seventy-five dollars to take a quilting class. He told her it was okay for him to spend money on hobbies; he was the one who made it. If she wanted to spend money foolishly, then she would have to make it herself.

Byron believed that since he was the one who made the money in the family, only he could decide how it would be spent. His wife's responsibility was to make a comfortable home for him and the three kids. He didn't want her to spend "his" money on anything he couldn't enjoy or use. Since homemaking didn't bring in money, Byron didn't count it as real work. His ledger book devalued his wife's contribution.

We'll never have a relationship that is totally equal in contributions, especially when we start equating efforts and cash. For relationships to work, each person's offerings need to be valued, as well as honoring each member's needs.

Trust

While it is easy to see lack of reciprocity with material possessions, the lack of reciprocity with feelings is more subtle and more damaging. An imbalance in trust and respect unsettles any relationship.

Trust and respect are passed back and forth from one person to the other. The more they're shared, the more there is to share. I can't trust or respect you unless you trust and respect me. And neither of us can trust or respect another person if we don't trust and respect ourselves. Our feelings for one another get stronger as we express them.

Trust in a relationship allows stability and security. Our lives can feel predictable. We don't always need to be wary of dangers around the next corner. We can relax and turn our attention to making a living, having children, caring for our extended family, participating in our community events or hobbies.

Having predictability doesn't mean we take each other for granted— just that we know what to expect. We don't think from moment to moment where our loved one is or what he/she is doing. We know they're at work, taking a class, or carpooling the kids. When we trust one another, we don't fear surprises from each other. We're dependable, we keep our word.

When trust exists, our relationships provide a refuge from the world. As Scott Peck, author of *The Road Less Traveled*, says, a trusting relationship gives you a base camp to settle into, a base that allows you to go exploring, knowing there will always be a safe place to return to.

Respect

Respecting others means valuing them. We appreciate their gifts and talents and see they enhance our lives by being a part of it. This is not to say our loved ones don't have flat sides to their otherwise well-rounded characters. They do. You do. We all do. But we've taken their measure and see there's a balance on the positive side.

Like trust, respect is built on action; words are not enough. We're kind, thoughtful, and accommodating, knowing they'll do the same for us. The way we treat our loved ones reflects not only how we feel about them, but also what we think of ourselves. It becomes a demonstration of who we are.

At a professional dinner, Bob, a man well known in his industry, treated his wife with disrespect and contempt. His comments were demeaning and uncalled for, in stark contrast to his wife's graciousness and calmness while under attack. Most of the other attendees were uncomfortable with Bob's unpleasantness. A potential client later remarked he wouldn't consider hiring him, because he couldn't respect a man who was so publicly disrespectful to someone he supposedly valued.

Bob's wife couldn't have enjoyed being treated so shabbily. And yet she decided how she'd respond to his disrespect while they were with friends and colleagues. They each behaved in a way consistent with who they were and reflected the respect they felt for themselves. She gained the respect of their friends and colleagues while he lost face.

It's too trite to dismiss Bob's disrespectful behavior by claiming he wasn't responsible for how she might feel. While it is true we can't always know or manage how others will feel in reaction to what we do and say, in a significant relationship with friends and loved ones, it's essential to distinguish between being responsible for and responsive to them.

Responsive to, Responsible For

Respecting other people means being responsive to who they are and what they think and feel. Being respectful and responsive means not going out of your way to be dishonorable and disrespectful. It doesn't mean that you kowtow to or blindly accommodate any and all demands of the other. Nor do you necessarily deny yourself in their interests.

Many couples agree to pursue individual activities, pastimes, hobbies, or community service activities on their own. He may like football games; she may like making miniatures. They make space in their relationship for individual interests. We can't always share every single facet of our lives. That's too big a charter for a relationship. We all need and can be refreshed by individual interests.

There are always going to be differences of opinions, needs, and wants in a relationship, not because men and women are different, but because people are different. What I want won't necessarily be acceptable, fun, or even make sense to everyone I want to be with.

There'll be plenty of difficult things without going out of our way to be unpleasant or intentionally hurtful. Lots of people make conscious decisions to let go of issues, activities, or feelings that aren't especially pleasing, because they don't want to take on every issue. Some things just aren't worth making a hassle over or don't matter.

And some things matter a lot. These things are so important to us, we have to go ahead and do them, even though we know our loved ones won't like it or necessarily approve. We do these things, not because we want to hurt our loved ones or challenge the relationship, but because they are a core part of who we are.

> *Deena's faith is extremely important to her. She knows her new husband isn't as religious as she, and they have come to an agreement. She'll choose the church, and he'll go to church with her at least once a month. Deena would love it if he went every Sunday. Her husband would love it if they played golf every Sunday morning. Both know it will never happen.*

For Deena, going to church was not negotiable. She goes every week, whether she goes alone or with her husband. How often he accompanied her was negotiable. Both were pleased with the agreement they made and have been able to keep it. They were responsive to the other without being responsible for them. It's a hard line to walk, but a necessary one.

When we make a commitment to be monogamous, we stop acting as though we're still single. We no longer make plans with our unattached friends to go to singles' bars. We spend time with our partners. We get upset when they hurt, and are angry at those who treat them unfairly at work. We are responsive to and accommodate their feelings and the changing expectations of our relationship.

First-time grandparents, Rebecca and her new husband were called to come quickly when the new baby developed trouble breathing. The extended family gathered, waiting for the prognosis, and then celebrated their relief when the good news came. Then the new father and grandfather started one of their ongoing arguments. Rebecca stood by, not sure what to do. The argument escalated when her stepson's mother, her husband's ex-wife, started contributing to the uproar.

Later, Rebecca berated herself for her part in the family fracas. She said she was "so codependent" she just wanted to wade into the mess, gather her husband in her arms, and comfort him. She wished she could have fixed it all.

Codependent isn't a useful concept in these kinds of situations. Rebecca loved her husband deeply. Of course it hurt to see him in so much pain. She knew how hard it had been for him as his marriage ended in divorce and all of them tried to make new lives for themselves. It was even more troublesome that the argument occurred at the same time as the uncertainty over the baby's health. She didn't want him to have to experience this pain.

That's not codependency. That's life. We don't want our loved ones to hurt. We want to help people we love when they are hurting. That's what relationships are for: doing the tough stuff.

It's not helpful when we say our relationships are addictive. There will always be struggles and challenges. Sometimes we'll do better than others. Hopefully we'll learn to be more effective as we grow together. But to label ourselves as sick, bad, or crazy, to consider ourselves as helpless, that we'll always struggle to be in control, and that we're powerless to do anything about it makes our problems worse, not better.

On the other hand, we can't stop being who we are just to make sure our partner will be pleased. Nor can we take these predictable differences personally, as a gauge of how the other person feels about us. When you give up too much for the relationship, resentments creep in, grow, and fester. Soon, you feel angry at your loved one for asking you to give up what's important to you. Even if he never asked or you offered.

What started as loving accommodation has led to a huge control issue. What *should* you do, and who is in charge of how things are done in your relationship?

It's easy to imagine people are doing things to be intentionally hurtful. But for the most part, arguments between couples are not started with malice. Each person wants what is comfortable or familiar to them. They may not even think about what impact their habits are having on others.

We can easily see how trying to control our partners doesn't work with trivial, seemingly insignificant issues: what way the toilet tissue is installed in the holder, having the bedroom window open or closed at night. We can laugh as we change the toilet tissue or compromise on the window. But the impact of more important control issues can be a major source of ongoing upset and conflict.

Whether trivial or significant, the hazard comes when change is framed as a demonstration of how much we're loved. The expectation becomes "If you really loved me, you'd do things my way, not yours."

Love has nothing to do with it. We're dealing with habitual behavior here, not loving—or malicious—choices. How we treat one another is built on unspoken, nonconscious habits and agreements we've forged.

Relationship Agreements

Agreements are the working base of relationships. They provide the ground rules for a long list of quid pro quos, or you do this for me and I'll do that for you. They determine who gives what, who gets what, who's in charge of what.

Our agreements reflect the differing roles, abilities, and needs we bring to our partnerships. Our agreements let our relationships provide for all the participants.

We make agreements on the division of labor: who does what for whom. We decide which chores which adult and which child is expected to do, how the money is made, who does the yard work or the housework. Our agreements sort out all the necessary tasks of living to make sure the bases are covered with the best person for the job, even when the job is unpleasant or hard.

Divisions-of-labor agreements are usually made consciously and overtly. We talk about what we need; we work together to make sure all the tasks are taken care of. We pay attention to how the agreements are working and acknowledge we are negotiating and strategizing together.

We make those decisions covertly when we follow the patterns we knew as we grew up. For most of us that means mom and the girls do the "inside work," and dad and the boys do the "outside work." While this type of division may have made sense there and then, check to see if it still does.

Other agreements deal with who's in charge, who has the power in the family. It's important for parents to take the lead in making these agreements and in the family. They're the adults; they're the ones who are supposed to be grown-up and more capable. Not the kids. When the parents take a leadership position in the family, they protect their children from the pressure of having to take charge before they have the skills and maturity to do so. Kids feel safer. They know who's in charge.

Leadership includes setting the standards and rules for conduct. It's the responsibility and the burden of being a parent. No matter how tired, how stressed, or how busy, it's something parents still have to do. Parenting is not part-time. It's a job for a lifetime.

By their example and chosen lessons, parents provide the learning and discipline not just for themselves, but for their children. Children learn more from what we do than from what we say.

> *Eric had stopped by his home late one afternoon to get a fresh shirt before going on an important sales call. As he was changing his shirt, he caught a few minutes of an afternoon television talk show. He listened to several mothers complain they couldn't get their children to go to school. The truant, surly teens were offering excuses like, "Why should I bother?" or "It isn't fun," or "It's too hard to get up in the morning."*
>
> *"Look at the mothers," Eric exclaimed suddenly. "They are all missing teeth. They can't even brush their own teeth. They don't have any discipline themselves. How can they expect their kids to be disciplined?" With that, he kissed his wife and toddlers good-bye and headed off to see one more customer before the end of his workday.*

As I watched Eric watch the mothers on television, and then his interaction with his wife and children, I couldn't help but admire the discipline they were both showing. Their home was clean and neat, not fancy and expensive. Their children's clothes, mostly garage-sale finds and hand-me-down outfits, were also clean and appropriate. His wife had already started dinner and was relaxing with the television as she folded the last of many loads of wash two little ones generate every day. Their discipline, their willingness to provide for themselves and one another, was evident to their children, even before the children were old enough to consciously learn the lesson. They were modeling what they wanted their children to do, not just telling them what they should do. They not only told their children the benefits of being disciplined, but were showing them how to do it.

That modeling becomes an important learning tool as we teach our children to make the shift from being "controlled" by their parents to finding internal self-control. We want our kids to make the transition from needing and wanting us to tell them what to do, to being able to do it themselves. They learn these lessons best by watching what we do and by trying and testing solutions within the safety net of parental involvement. They don't learn the lesson of self-control by being told every step of the way what they should or shouldn't be doing.

Children need to learn there are logical consequences when they do or don't fulfill their responsibilities. There's no free ride. Parents need to use a variety of lessons to help their children learn these difficult and uncomfortable truths. They're challenged to think through and design lessons and experiences for their children with the aim of shifting from the external (parental) control to an internal (self) control. Parents provide a framework for learning with the lessons and penalties, discipline and punishments they choose.

Gradually, as the children grow and mature, they stop using the reactions of others to decide what to do, and start relying more on their own assessment of the best or right choice.

When you were little, your mother told you to put a sweater on when you went outside so you wouldn't be cold. As you get older, you don't need your mother to tell you to do that. You decide when to put a sweater on. As parents, we work to make our jobs obsolete. We want our kids to outgrow relying on us, other friends, or teen idols. We want them to take over the responsibility of managing their own behavior rather than just responding to our rewards and punishments.

Children learn best both by experiencing the natural consequences of their actions and by practicing with coaching and guidance. They definitely don't learn as easily or as quickly from the "Do it my way because I'm bigger, I'm the mom, and I'm the boss" approach. They need to try out and practice setting boundaries and limits, solving problems, and realizing consequences.

Chores, homework, hobbies, after-school activities all make good laboratories for working on the concept of how much is available, what kinds of responsibilities each person has, and the consequences of not following through with those responsibilities. It gives kids practice in problem solving and bottom lines that can't be crossed and consequences if they do.

It's easier to teach these lessons if you start with your children when they're little. They quickly understand expectations for their behavior and consequences when they don't meet those expectations. Eric's children know by three and four what's okay to do and not do.

But it's also possible to run a remedial, refresher course when they're teens. Don't think that just because your kids have reached double-digit years, your opportunity is lost. It isn't.

Of course, it's appropriate to shift and change your expectations as a child grows up. Start with one problem or area of conflict, set a time to brainstorm solutions, set realistic objectives, agree to try it for a specific time, and then check to see that your solutions are working.

That doesn't mean teens will easily agree to changing their behavior and won't give you a hard time. Rebellion is predictable and preferable with teens. They're finding their own way, learning how to make a life for themselves. Their rebelliousness allows them to try out paths that aren't those their parents chose. They're trying their wings. Trying out new behaviors helps them grow stronger. When they are held too tightly, they'll be like a tree that is staked too securely. Moving in the winds lets the tree grow strong. Teens need challenges and experiences to grow strong.

Breaking Agreements

We develop agreements together with our friends and significant others. Together we modify and change those agreements as we grow, our circumstances change, and new opportunities or challenges arise. But when one of us changes, when one of us is no longer willing to uphold previous agreements, then the other feels betrayed. Trust is broken, respect is diminished. People who have broken the agreements may say the words "I love you," "I care for you," "You're important to me." But their actions speak louder than their words. Their relationships have changed. They've broken the agreement to be loving to one another.

It may well be that when they say those words, they still have loving feelings for their partner or friend. But the partner or friend doesn't feel loved. Even trivial shifts and changes can impact the agreed-upon understandings. It feels as if what one person wants is more important than the commitment they both made to each other and their relationship.

When the change is more significant—having an affair, breaking the law, injuring someone—the protests of "I still love you" are even harder to believe. Feelings of betrayal are inevitable.

It is extremely hard to rebuild a relationship after betrayal. Betrayers must acknowledge the hurt they have caused their loved ones. They need to take the responsibility for what they did. They need to be truly sorry, not just giving lip service, but sorrowful and repentant for the hurt they caused. And then, of course, make every effort not to do it again: to refrain from hurting their loved ones again in the same way.

Elliott hadn't meant to fall in love with the woman he worked with. They were such a good team, spent many hours in the office together, and even more time as they traveled from city to city to work with their clients. But he knew what pain he was causing his wife and children by having this affair. Finally, after more than a year, he decided he had to stop seeing his girlfriend. It was too selfish of him to put his affair before his family. He also knew he had to find a new job. He knew he couldn't continue to see his former girlfriend every day and still keep his commitment to his wife. Even with these changes, it took Elliott and his wife a long time to put their marriage back together. While they both say it is strong today, they both admit it is very different from what it had been before Elliot's affair.

Billy reacted differently when he fell in love with a coworker. Like Elliott, it just sort of happened. And like Elliott's wife,

Billy's wife, Della, realized he was seeing someone. When she confronted him, he said he was so sorry and swore he would never see his girlfriend again. But he continued to work with her and see her every day. Before long, they were involved again.

Again Della found out and again Billy promised he wouldn't see his girlfriend anymore. Yet when Della asked him to transfer to another part of the company or find a new job so he wouldn't be tempted, Billy angrily told Della she was just trying to control him. He promised and that should have been enough.

Reluctantly Della told Billy he had to choose. She wasn't going to stand by while he put a girlfriend before his wife and children. Saying he was sorry and promising to be different weren't enough. She was sure he meant it when he said it, but she was afraid he wouldn't keep his word. She knew trying to control him was futile, but she could put up her bottom line. Choosing to be with his girlfriend every day was choosing to let go of his wife. Della stuck with what she knew she had to do. Billy could say the words, but he wouldn't change what he was doing.

Neither Elliott nor Billy woke up one morning and decided to hurt their wives and betray their vows of commitment and fidelity. Yet they both did. What made a difference in putting their marriages back together after the betrayal was what they did, not just what they said. Both men said their wives and family were most important to them. Only Elliott translated his words into action.

Breaking agreements means we get a chance to evaluate and choose. What's right for us now? Is what the other person is now doing acceptable to me? What's my bottom line? How do I let the other person know what I feel and think about what's happening now?

These questions form the basis for our evaluation. This is the connection with entitlement and relationships. What are we entitled to have in our relationships? Are we worth a monogamous marriage? Are we worth honesty and truth from our friends and life partners? Are we worth respect and dignity? What is the level of quality we are entitled to have in our lives?

This is the values link with relationships. We have to decide what's important, how people should treat us, and make decisions and judgments about how our relationships are going. Then we have to let the other person know what's acceptable, what we feel, what we expect—and hold them to it. We can't control the other person's behavior. But we can and must think through and decide on our bottom line for being in that relationship. And how we can get and hold our bottom line. Not only must we know how to set our bottom line, but more important, we must know how to hold to it.

We literally teach people what we expect them to do and how they should treat us. They'll know from our reactions what's okay to do and what isn't. Rule number one in psychology is "Behavior that's rewarded is apt to be repeated." Our reactions to how people treat us reward what we want and disapprove of what we don't want.

Not mentioning unacceptable behavior doesn't mean it will disappear. It continues. The best reward for unwanted behavior is to do nothing. Then the unwanted behavior continues, not because the other person is mean and nasty, but because they don't know it bothers you. Or because you let them get away with it. If someone doesn't know it's a problem, they can't take steps to fix it. Marriage licenses and friendships don't come with mind-reading certificates. Tell them clearly.

> *Bernice and Claire had been friends for years. Claire was getting increasingly annoyed at Bernice's thoughtlessness. They were all little things, but Claire decided she had talk to her about it. So she thought through what she would say, practiced it, and finally sat down with her friend to tell her what was on her mind.*
>
> *At the end of the conversation, Claire commented how much better she felt having said what she did, and asked Bernice if she was upset or angry. Claire wanted to reassure her friend she still treasured their friendship even though things had been rocky.*
>
> *Bernice's response was, "What do you mean? I didn't think you were upset about anything."*

Claire was so concerned about not hurting Bernice's feelings that she didn't get her message across. You don't have to be mean or nasty yourself, but make sure your message is so clear the other person knows what you're saying, even if they don't agree with what you say.

We need to be really clear, too, on our expectations for the new behavior and what we're going to do to help them understand we mean what we say. Most people, even children, are very responsive to clear guidelines and expectations. If it's that important, let them know.

My sister Ada, a resource teacher, can teach any child how to read. Children come to her room during the day to work with her. She expects them to do "perfect work" and "perfect reading" at the level of their ability. All her students read out loud perfectly, not missing or mispronouncing any words. They even read the title page, with the author's and illustrator's names. Even the lowest of the readers in her classes are expected to turn in papers with all the words spelled correctly, and with excellent penmanship and format.

During an open house, a classroom teacher was shocked that one of her lowest students, who did very poor work in his regular classroom, was doing perfect work in Ada's class. "How did you get him to do that?" she asked. Ada said she hands out lots of erasers and won't accept a paper until it's perfect. The kids in her room learn to work to standards. In the other room they were the "not-so-smart kids" who weren't expected to do well.

People do what we expect them to do, teach them to do, and reward them for doing. When we reward people for treating us badly, they'll continue to treat us badly. It takes them a while to realize we have changed and have new standards for their behavior.

Robin was so furious that Charlie's mom wouldn't let her in the house, she threw a rock at the house and broke a big front window the next time she came over. Charlie's mom called the police, they arrested the girl, and Robin spent four days in jail, not just for the window incident, but for several other incidents that had been precipitated by her bad temper. Calling the police is a heavy-duty consequence, but it wasn't the first time Robin had damaged the house. Charlie's mom said she had to do something to get the girl's attention and help her understand the rules had changed.

A common response when spouses or life partners get involved with someone else is for them to say, "I don't mean to," "I can't help myself," or "I don't know what to do." In these cases, when someone is paralyzed into inaction in an unacceptable situation, it may be necessary to draw your bottom line and then define their inaction or unwillingness to make a decision as choosing sides. In these cases, not to decide is to decide not to go along with your bottom line.

Della couldn't make Billy stop seeing his girlfriend. But she could draw her bottom line and the consequences for his stepping over the line. She was unwilling to have a nonmonogamous marriage. Della defined her bottom line: If Billy chose to continue seeing his girlfriend, he was choosing to end the marriage.

Charlie wouldn't stop his relationship with Robin, and his mom knew she couldn't force him not to see her. And she knew if she tried to make a huge issue of it, Charlie would be rebellious and go off with Robin or get married, just to show her. But she could and did take charge of Robin's relationship and contact with herself and the rest of her younger children. She could stop Robin from coming to the house.

No one is ever going to be exactly who we want them to be. No relationship is ever going to be without problems and conflict. Taking charge with relationships means knowing what we can control and what we can't, and then making choices and changes to take charge of what we do within the relationship. Taking charge of our bottom line and holding to it can be very hard. But it's also quite satisfying, because we're honoring ourselves.

Exercises for Chapter 13

SAYING I LOVE YOU AND ACTING LOVING

In many of the seminars I teach for couples, we always do the "How Do I Love You?" exercise. Each participant makes a list of things that turn them on. We concentrate on sensuous, not sensual experiences. Each person gives five answers to the questions:

1. What tastes good?
2. What feels good?
3. What looks good?
4. What sounds good?
5. What smells good?
6. What would be fun to do?

I encourage them to post their lists on their bathroom mirrors so their partners can see what appeals to them now. Most of the time the lists shift and change during the year. A big pot of chili in front of a roaring fire may be great in November, but it isn't so great in July.

LET'S TALK

The studies that have been done on family communication indicate most couples talk less than ten minutes a day. Most spend hours in front of the television every day. Challenge yourself to turn off the TV for one program a day. Spend the time talking about yourselves, your relationship, your day. Remember the great talks you used to have, and revive them now. (You do turn off the set during dinner, right?)

TEACH THE CHILDREN WELL

During one of your talks with your partner, spend some time on what you want to teach your children. What's important to each of you? How are you teaching what you want them to learn? Are there more opportunities to focus on the lessons that are most important?

WHAT'S YOUR BOTTOM LINE?

If you are dealing with the betrayal of a loved one, be sure you have done the research to find out what you are dealing with. Think through what this means to you, the life you are entitled to have, and the competence you have to get the life you want. Decide what you want from your relationship and if you are confident that you can get it.

CHAPTER 14

FORGIVING/LETTING GO: A NECESSITY, NOT AN OPTION

For many years, I lived in the Southwest desert, surrounded by mature date palms. Palm trees grow by sending a new frond from the central core of the growing edge. The frond unfurls and gradually starts to lean over as it matures. Then it withers, turns brown, and hangs limply alongside the trunk. During the summer electrical storms in the desert, palm trees become magnets for lightning. Especially untrimmed palm trees. Those withered dead fronds explode in a ball of fire when they're hit. Untrimmed, withered fronds make the whole tree vulnerable.

Then we moved to a house with several small palm trees. They were short, but wide enough that the fronds completely blocked the path to the pool. One of my first gardening chores was trimming fronds. The trimmed trees quickly shot up several inches. As we became more consistent in trimming off withered fronds, the trees responded by growing taller and taller.

People grow like palm trees. Out of the central core of our being comes the response to new challenges, new opportunities, and new adventures. New aspects of who and what we are flourish and grow and then eventually, as that challenge becomes mastered, as the adventure becomes stale, become mature. If we hold on to old patterns, those that are no longer applicable to our new and growing edge, we find they're not only not helpful but prevent us from future growth.

Forgiving or letting go is one of the major ways we can use to move on from experiences, activities, relationships, and situations that are no longer in our best interest or that have been hurtful. Only by forgiving or letting go can we defuse the sting of these hurtful experiences, can we take charge of situations we can't control.

Uncertainty about forgiveness is a stumbling block. If we aren't sure what it is or how to do it, we find it difficult to forgive or let go.

Forgiveness/letting go is one of the hardest steps in the taking-charge process. No matter what the trauma, trial, hurt, or crisis, forgiving isn't easy. We aren't sure exactly what forgiveness means. Or we're unsure of the difference between forgiveness and letting go. Most of us aren't sure how to do either.

We know we want, or need, to forgive someone. We know we want to get free of this person or incident that's been dogging us. But just saying the words "I forgive you" doesn't seem to give us the relief we want.

Some people aren't sure what role the other person should have. We've been betrayed or harmed by someone. We want to forgive that person so we can get on with our lives, but we aren't sure what obligations or responsibilities to reasonably expect of the person who hurt us.

Maybe we're having trouble because of our own bad choices or mistakes. We've let ourselves down. We haven't done what we now wanted to have done. How can we forgive ourselves for something we did that was essentially unforgivable?

And then, a growing number of people have been struggling with the sense of trying hard to be good, knowing that they aren't perfect, but they have been working hard and living an upright, moral, and faithful life, only to find themselves betrayed or wronged by another person.

Sheri always attended church regularly, obeyed the law, paid her taxes on time, and did all she could to live a moral, upright life. She was totally surprised when she received a phone call from a woman who demanded that Sheri let her husband go so that he could marry this other woman. Sheri had no idea her husband had been having an affair. As the next few weeks progressed, she realized he'd been borrowing money by forging her signature, hadn't paid the bills, and was supporting his mistress in an apartment on the other side of town.

As the story of Sheri's husband's infidelity and irresponsibility gathered momentum, he began attending services at a new church. He became immersed in his new beliefs and professed to have a personal audience with God in which all of his previous sins were washed clean. He then confronted Sheri with a demand that she had to forgive him. Not to forgive him meant she was no longer as good a Christian as he was.

As Sheri and I talked through her situation, she said she felt like the prodigal son's brother. It was hard not to feel righteous and judgmental. She wasn't receiving much comfort from her faith, but questioning it. She said she knew she wasn't perfect, but she also knew she was trying to do the right things. Her husband had purposely hurt her and their children by intentionally doing the wrong things, and yet he was holding himself out to be more spiritual than she. He said her righteousness made her as much a sinner as his infidelity and fraud.

The Prodigal Son's Brother

The parable of the prodigal son is taught in virtually every Sunday school class. Children are told of the man who had two sons. His younger son had asked for his share of the father's property, which he quickly converted to money to finance a trip to a distant land. There, he squandered his cash on reckless living and eventually was penniless.

At his lowest point, the young man realized his father's servants had a better life than he did. He decided to return home to serve his father as a servant. As he approached the house, his father saw his son and joyfully ran to him. The older man told his servants to fetch a robe, put a ring on his son's finger, and kill the fatted calf for a feast of celebration. As children, what we hear is how grateful his father was to have his son back and how quickly he forgave him. The message is one of forgiveness: Forgive someone who has wronged you.

Children don't spend much time on the part of the story that is about the other brother. Adults do. The prodigal son's brother was not so happy with the feasting and celebration. When his father asked him to come into the party, he replied with a version of "It's not fair." He was the good son. He'd worked for his father all these years, never disobeyed, and was never given so much as a kid to provide a feast for his friends.

But when his wayward brother showed up, his father killed the fatted calf for him. The father tried to console his righteous son by explaining that he was always with him and everything he had was his. The father then went on to ask how they could help but rejoice. His brother was dead and now he lived. He was lost and now he was found.

Oh, that we could all forgive as easily as the prodigal son's father forgave. Most of us who have been betrayed find ourselves favoring the prodigal son's brother, not his father.

It's really hard to forgive someone who's purposely chosen to hurt us. It's especially hard when they demand we forgive them. Or when they put us down and say we're worse than they are because we don't forgive them. It starts to feel like they've "gotten away with it" by simply coming round and asking for forgiveness or giving a simple promise not to do it again.

Here we are, trying to be good, to live an upright life, then we're branded righteous and labeled as worse than our betrayers. It's hard not to get caught up in the belief that somehow good works aren't rewarded but evil ways will prevail.

It starts to feel as if the transgressor is "getting away with" doing bad and is facing no consequences. It's so important not to excuse, pardon, or absolve people of the consequences of their behavior even though you "forgive" them. They "get away with" what they have done when we don't hold them accountable. Even though we may forgive what they did, it doesn't mean they don't have to face the consequences. Apologizing isn't enough.

Understandably Sheri was feeling pressured. Her husband wanted to control her. He needed her forgiveness to feel better about himself. Once again, he was thinking only of himself, not caring how she felt or how he was still hurting her.

Who was more spiritual was not the issue here. He was still trying to control her. To get out of the trap her husband was laying, Sheri had to stop letting him decide who she was and what she should do. She needed to hold him accountable for his illegal behavior. She needed to resist his demands for forgiveness. He was still hurting her. Forgiveness is one of the last steps, not the first. Sheri needed to take charge of her life and avoid his continuing to hurt her. Forgiveness would come later.

Forgiving or Letting Go?

Forgiveness is personal. We can forgive only people—others or ourselves. There has to be someone to hold accountable for the wrongs that were committed.

It is inappropriate and difficult to imagine how you can forgive when there is no one to be accountable. Numbers of people are injured, or even killed, every year by acts of nature. Hurricanes, floods, fires, and earthquakes can be devastating to people who have been caught up in them. Yet how do you forgive an earthquake? There's nothing, nobody, no person there to forgive.

Likewise it's a little difficult to talk about forgiveness when the perpetrator has been a large, impersonal corporation, the government, or the military. You don't forgive an organization; you forgive people.

In situations with acts of nature or large organizations or agencies, it's more appropriate to talk about letting go, rather than forgiving. Letting go and forgiving are similar in that both of them move you from a position of expecting retribution and compensation to no longer allowing whatever has hurt you to have a center point in your life. You no longer expect to get anything from the person, organization, or event that caused you damage.

The third situation to let go of rather than forgive is with our own personal regrets. Forgiveness doesn't work with the regrets we have for what we could or couldn't, should or shouldn't have done. However, if we don't let go of our regrets, we'll find they'll eventually poison any opportunity for current life satisfaction and pleasure.

The fourth thing to let go of instead of forgive are those transgressions, those mistakes, that are not ours to forgive. We can forgive only what a person has done specifically to us. Forgiving somebody for hurting another is not ours to do. It's theirs.

As we'll see, we will also use letting go when it is beyond our ability to forgive an unforgivable act. Sometimes we can't bring ourselves to forgive someone for the hurt they've caused us. But we can get to a point of letting go of the hurt, to stop letting the pain of the past run our lives.

What Forgiveness Isn't

First we need to get clear on what forgiveness can and can't do, what's appropriate to include in the forgiveness process, and what's appropriate to leave aside.

Forgiveness is not excusing bad behavior. Forgiveness, as we'll see, is appropriate only when grievous harm has been committed. We've been hurt. Someone hurt us. There's no excuse for purposely injuring someone. Our injurers are accountable for what happened. They may tell us there was a good reason, that it made perfect sense for them to do what they did. They're responsible for their behavior even when we were inadvertently hurt in the process. Excusing is not forgiving.

Forgiving is not forgetting. In fact, when we forget as well as forgive, we run the hazard of being hurt again. This is especially true if the person who has hurt us has not repented and has not promised not to do it again. Or if someone has hurt us repeatedly and always promises never to do it again. Even if they want to believe they won't hurt us again, we need to remember they don't keep their promises. Not remembering means we'll set ourselves up to be hurt once more.

Forgiving is not pardoning. When we forgive somebody, we do it in spite of the wrong that they have done. When we pardon somebody, we no longer hold them accountable for what they've done. We can't forgive someone unless we do hold them accountable. The forgiveness comes because they have done something wrong, and then we say, "Even though that happened, I'm not expecting any more from you. I forgive you."

Forgiveness is not avoiding or discounting the conflict or the difficulties that may occur because of the hurt that has been done. Oftentimes we'll hear people say, "Well, just forget about it. Just let it go. Don't bother with it." As if not dealing with the hurt and anger will somehow magically make it go away. If we don't deal with it, if we don't deal with the conflict, then for sure we'll have an opportunity to repeat the situation in the future. Forgiving is acknowledging that hurt has occurred and that the person is being held accountable for having hurt another one. Letting go is not the same as not dealing with a situation. Letting go is a purposeful choice to detach from a hurt, to stop letting it run your life. Letting go takes as much, if not more, work than forgiveness.

Neither is forgiveness wiping the slate clean, acting as if the event didn't occur. Forgiveness doesn't provide absolution nor does it condone the behavior of the person who has done the hurt. And in fact, it won't change the facts of what's occurred. It also doesn't mean you have to tolerate the behavior of the person who was doing you wrong. In fact, in many cases the expression of "rendering unto Caesar" and "rendering unto God" means that people must both spiritually and civilly make restitution for the wrongs they've committed. Just because you've forgiven someone doesn't mean he no longer needs to face the courts or the civil and/or criminal charges he incurred.

We can be angry and hurt with what they've done without hating the person who did it. You can get the restitution you deserve without making the other person out to be a monster or the target of your rage and maliciousness.

Cataloging Injuries

One of the problems that we have with forgiveness is understanding what types of injuries are open to forgiveness and which aren't. We can be injured by the regrets of actions that we took or didn't take in the past, by mistakes that we've made, transgressions that we have committed, and evil that has been visited upon us.

Regrets

Regrets are those negative feelings, typically about ourselves, that reflect our dissatisfaction with either things we've done or haven't done, or things that didn't turn out the way that we wanted them to. We may regret we didn't go into the Peace Corps when we were young adults. Or we could have told our parents before they died that we loved them, but didn't. We may have tried for a special assignment or job that would have opened up a field of new opportunities, but we didn't get it.

Our regrets may involve other people. We can be sad and regretful that someone we know or love turns out to be less than or different from what we thought they were.

Everyone has regrets. It's a part of the human condition. By dwelling on our regrets, we keep ourselves stuck in the past. We're unable to live as full and satisfying a life today because we're holding on to the pain of the past.

Mistakes

Mistakes are errors in judgment, attention, or behavior. While some people seem to make many more mistakes than others, what characterizes all mistakes is a lack of intention to do badly or to hurt someone else. Nonetheless, people get hurt by mistakes.

Some mistakes are trivial: We push the wrong switch on the computer and lose the file we've been working on; we run into someone in the supermarket, and they drop their basket, making a huge mess of broken bottles and squished food.

Some mistakes are significant: We fall asleep at the wheel, slip off into a deep ditch, and break an axle on our car; we spill a large glass of fruit smoothie into a friend's computer and ruin it.

Whether trivial or significant, the appropriate response for a mistake is to apologize for what you've done, make restitution if necessary, and then be more careful in the future.

Transgressions

Mistakes and regrets don't involve moral commitments and agreements. Transgressions do. With a transgression, we act immorally and someone's hurt. We may not intend to hurt someone, but they get hurt because we aren't doing what we should. We know we're doing wrong; we just think we won't get caught or it won't matter this time.

So we choose to have an affair, take money from friends and family members, lie to our loved ones. We justify what we're doing, and don't think about who we're hurting. We break the stated or unstated moral agreements we have as a part of our relationships.

Transgressions are the major hurts in our lives. They are the injuries that demand forgiveness because they are essentially unforgivable. There's no excuse for what we've done. We can't deny we did what we did. There's no way to pardon or absolve people from being responsible for purposely doing something they know will hurt others. Not to hold people responsible, not to hold them accountable for their transgressions, is to diminish both of you.

Evil Behavior

Evil behavior goes beyond transgressions. With transgressions, we know something is morally unacceptable but do it anyway. Evil behavior isn't personal. It isn't directed at you but disregards you. Evil is the ultimate in discounting the humanity of another person, acting as if other people are objects, with no intrinsic human value. All of us are capable of doing evil, being caught up in the passions of our minds and bodies, and disregarding others. The sin is expected. The difference between sin and evil is, a person not only does something sinful but revels in the delight of doing it. He feels no remorse for what he does.

Forgiveness Starts with Hurt

Forgiveness starts with anger, hurt, frustration, and a sense of loss. We've been hurt. It's understandable we feel angry, betrayed, upset, furious. You know the feelings. If we don't feel bad about being hurt, we aren't paying attention. Feeling bad is how we feel when we've been hurt. I get worried when people who've been hurt don't feel bad.

Our anger and hurt reflect the seriousness and significance of the injury that needs to be forgiven.

Forgiveness isn't for trivial activities. Forgiveness isn't for being bumped in the supermarket or cut off in traffic. Forgiveness is designed to heal the major hurts. We use apologies to deal with trivialities. Our anger and bad feelings acknowledge that a serious injury has occurred. In the upset and uproar of crisis, the first feelings we have may not be anger. It may take some time to realize the extent of our injuries or understand how we've been wronged. It may take a long time to realize we've been hurt in a way that needs to be forgiven, and an even longer time to be able to forgive.

Feeling Betrayed

After hurt and anger comes betrayal or hatred for the person who's wronged you. He's broken the moral agreements the two of you had, maybe even breaking the moral agreements of society. Our feelings of betrayal come from our growing awareness that the way we thought the world would work, the rules and expectations we had for our own behavior and that of others, no longer hold. The injury we experienced shattered the way we thought our world would be. We can no longer predict what loved ones will do. We're no longer safe from random acts of perversion or violence. We can't control what's happened to us.

The hatred we feel is the opposite of the love a short time before. We can hate only the ones we've loved. With hatred, there's an emotional connection with the person we're hating. It's almost impossible to hate strangers. We don't know them well enough to feel connected to them. We may feel violent rage, or fury, but not hatred. Rage is impersonal; hatred, personal.

Reframing the Injury

The third step in forgiveness is reframing the situation. Reframing takes a situation out of one mental framework and places it into another. The new frame fits the situation equally well or, often, better. We don't change the facts of what's happened, just the perspective from which we view the facts. With this different view, it's possible to see new resolutions and change the outcome.

> *Allan's brother Sam lived on the edge. There were lots of rumors about what he was doing, despicable things really, but when Allan confronted him, Sam denied he was involved. Then Sam was arrested, and in the trial all the seamy details were uncovered. Not only did Sam do what Allan had feared, but more. More devastating for Allan were Sam's lies.*
>
> *It took a long time for Allan to get past what Sam had done. Finally he realized it was up to the people Sam had hurt to forgive him, if they could, for what he had done to them.*
>
> *Allan finally realized his job was to forgive Sam for lying to him.*

Allan said forgiving Sam's lies was hard. It finally started to get a bit easier when he realized in his heart of hearts that there had been some situations in which he had been less than forthcoming, less than truthful with Sam. The hardest part was to not judge the quality of his falsehoods against his brother's. It was hard to get past the feeling that being less than honest about the price of a new car was in the same category as being less than honest about being maliciously abusive to other people.

We all want to judge. We all want to make sure that we are coming out ahead when we look at ourselves and our less-than-wonderful behavior. We don't want to be as bad as the people who've hurt us.

We also have to reframe our view of the world as it is now, rather than what we want it to be, what it could have been, or what it should have been. When someone who's been very close to us—a spouse, a child, a parent—no longer follows the rules or keeps his commitments, we have to reframe what we know about relationships.

When someone's abusive or disappoints us with a lack of sensitivity, when a loved one does something illegal or immoral, we have to move ourselves out of the category of people who don't get hurt and into the category of people who do get hurt. We're no longer in the safe part of the world. We've lost the safety of our world. Bad things happen to people like us. And in fact, many otherwise good people do horrible things.

Considering the Injurer

Only after acknowledging we were painfully, awfully hurt, that we've been betrayed by someone we trusted, loved, or counted on to not hurt us, and realized that we've been hurtful, too, can we start to consider the possibility of extending forgiveness to the person who has hurt us.

All of the work up until this point has happened inside of us. We haven't looked to the other person for any kind of acknowledgment or admission that he was in any way wrong. If we make forgiveness contingent upon the other person changing, we stay caught up in having him decide how we think and feel and what we're going to do about our beliefs and feelings.

By forgiving, we can escape from letting the other person run our lives. All of our obsessive thoughts about being wronged, our fantasies of revenge, and our long late-night telephone calls with friends about what a skunk the other person was start to drop away as we no longer allow that other person or the event to be the front and center focus of our lives. We would release ourselves so we can go on. And in fact, if we don't release ourselves, it's almost impossible to form new relationships and to develop a satisfying and full, rich life for ourselves.

Forgiving another has some very "selfish" payoffs for us.

Consider Forgiving

We finish the process of forgiving by seeing the other person as needy and fallible. Or as Iyanla Vanzant, a favorite television relationship expert, puts it, see the other person as a perfect child of God, masquerading as a total jerk. He hurt us from his own limitations, from his own weaknesses, not because we deserved to be hurt. When we can stop expecting other people to be more than or different from what they are, we can see them more clearly.

I know what you're thinking: If I lower my expectations for the people who hurt me, I'm allowing them to be less than what they could or should be or what I actually want in a relationship.

Could bes, should bes, and wants aren't the operative issues here. We need to see other people for who they are, not who we want them to be or who we think they could be. Seeing other people for who they are takes us back into telling ourselves the truth. If we don't face the truth about who our injurer is, we can't be free of him.

The other way we get stuck is by waiting for the people who hurt us to acknowledge what they've done. We want them to admit they've hurt us deeply and to extend some effort toward repentance. We may wait a long time. We may not get what we want.

Our injurers may deny, ignore, or discount the pain we've been feeling. Or they may give lip service to their repentance by talking the talk rather than walking the walk. They still may go ahead and continue to do the very things they're apologizing for and asking forgiveness for. Where's the justice here? we ask. They keep doing the same awful, ugly things, and then demand that we apologize and forgive them.

> *Mary Anna's abusive ex-husband, Norman, continued to demand that she forgive him for the abuse that occurred in their marriage. Norman kept pointing out to her that if the pope could forgive the man who shot him, then surely she could forgive Norman for the much lesser assaults he'd visited upon her.*

Few of us have the spiritual awareness and depth of faith that the pope does. We're just fallible human beings who have our own feelings, needs, and flat sides that may contribute to our difficulty forgiving people who continue to exhibit the wronging behavior.

Easy Forgiveness, Empty Repentance

If we continue to confuse forgiveness with excusing the behavior, wiping the slate clean, absolving or condoning what has happened, then we will continue to get hooked into easy forgiveness and empty repentance.

Easy forgiveness occurs when we say the words of forgiveness, but our feelings aren't engaged. There's no acknowledgment of our deep pain or expectation for change. Easy forgiveness happens very soon after a hurtful event and becomes "just words" rather than the painful, difficult action verb that it is. When forgiveness is perfunctory or when it's demanded, there's no resolution. Forgiveness needs to be heartfelt, sincere, and freely given. All of these take time and a tremendous amount of work as we go through the stages of hurt and betrayal and are finally able to forgive.

Empty repentance is a partner to easy forgiveness. Some people apologize quickly and promise anything to avoid the pain of having to admit that what they've done is wrong. None of us want to see ourselves as deeply hurting someone we supposedly love. We can no more demand repentance than we can demand forgiveness. If they aren't freely given, they aren't worth the words used to offer them up. If you've been the one who's looking to repent and the other person won't forgive you, the pain is as exquisite as if you are looking to forgive and the other person won't repent.

How do we offer repentance? First and foremost, admit what you have done was mean, unfair, insufferable, awful to the person you hurt. This means you have to admit that you've done wrong. Big-time done wrong.

As you understand the major pain you've caused someone you care for, you have to admit his or her pain is justified. You hurt him. It was you that did it, not he. You've dramatically changed his life. By acknowledging the hurt and the bad feelings he surely has toward you, you start to accept the responsibility for your role in causing that pain. This isn't easy. Most of us don't see ourselves as somebody who, intentionally or unintentionally, brings this level of pain into someone's life, particularly someone we care for.

But it's not enough to just admit our responsibility to ourselves. We also have to go to the person we hurt and freely tell her we know how badly we've hurt her, how we understand her pain, and that, in fact, it was we who were doing it. This step of confession brings the situation out in the open and validates, for the other person, our role in the pain in her life.

No repentance can be honest and true without having a promise to stop hurting the other person. Don't be surprised if when you promise to stop or not to do it again, the other person doesn't believe you. He's been badly hurt, and rebuilding trust and respect in a relationship is hard to do. If what you've done to hurt the other person has been re-petitive, he'll wait and watch to make sure you don't slip, backslide, and do it again. This isn't necessarily because he doesn't believe your promises. He needs to be wary for his own self-preservation and needs to watch the pattern of your hurtful behavior. He knows that too often, as much as we don't want to repeat our bad behavior, we will. We con-tinue to hurt people we've already hurt.

It'll take a long time to be forgiven. Her heart may have hardened.

You can't demand forgiveness of another person. You can't force yourself on her to forgive you. You just have to wait until she is ready.

Forgiving Yourself

In every situation we can't control, there is a sense of betrayal, anger, and frustration with the other person, as well as a sense of betrayal, anger, and frustration with yourself. You'll not only need to forgive the other person but to forgive yourself, as well.

Sometimes you need to forgive yourself for being fooled when you should have known better. Or you may have put up with a difficult, nasty, ugly situation far too long, and now you realize your inaction has put you and your family or other loved ones in a serious compromising position.

Whatever the issue, forgiving yourself is appropriate to let go of your pain and anguish so you can take charge of the situation and get on with your life.

As in forgiving another person, forgiving yourself involves appreci-ating and acknowledging how angry you are at yourself, recognizing that you have hurt yourself or other loved ones by your behavior. You also have to acknowledge that this is one of the biggies, one of the big events, rather than a trivial and/or unimportant action on your part.

Forgiving yourself means having to face the fact that you were not who you thought you were or you weren't who you wanted to be. You're left with a sense of betrayal. You haven't acted in your own best interests. Who you are hasn't measured up to who you thought you could or should be. For many people, this is the toughest part of the self-forgiveness process. They literally have to redefine themselves in light of the evidence that this acknowledgment of their bad behavior has given them.

This is the time you say to yourself things like, "How could I have done something so stupid? What was the matter with me? I'll never be able to trust myself again. What kind of judgment must I have had to have been fooled by somebody like him?"

The whole process goes on and on, and while you're hating yourself, while you're so frustrated with yourself, it's impossible to focus on what you can do and to go on with your life. You can't take charge until and unless you forgive or let go of the other person and what he did, as well as forgiving yourself for getting caught up with it in the first place. This is as true if you have been raped as it is if you have been in an earthquake. You have to let go of and forgive yourself for being in a situation even if in your rational mind you know for sure that you didn't cause it; somebody else did.

Reframing

Reframing is a most helpful tool in forgiving yourself. With reframing, you look at the experience and help yourself understand you did the best you could with where you were at the time that it occurred.

Eileen, who was raped on a summer evening while wearing shorts and a tank top (chapter eight), had a very difficult time reframing her responsibility for the rape. When we looked around the area in the college town that she lived in, she finally, begrudgingly, admitted that most of the women in the summertime, on campus and off, wore shorts and T-shirts. She didn't invite the rape by her choice of clothes. There was no real difference between her clothes and the clothes of any other woman who was walking on that sidewalk on that evening.

This was one small step in reframing her trauma. She was getting another perspective, starting to consider what had happened to her from a slightly different point of view. Now, several years later, she recognized that she had allowed the rape to be front and center in her life for far too long and that, for her own sanity and well-being, it was essential that she reclaim her life and not let that be the most important thing that had ever happened to her. She even laughed when she realized that she had punished herself for years for something that she didn't cause.

This is not to discount the intensity of the pain that she went through or the terror that she felt at the time, but she said, "That man had my body for less than ten minutes. He's had my life for almost seven years. I think I've paid my debt. I don't need to punish myself any longer."

Whenever you forgive yourself, combine repentance and forgiveness so you commit to personal change. Promise yourself you're not going to get in that situation again, that you're not going to do that behavior again, and then take active steps to keep your promise. You may need to learn new skills. You may need to arm yourself with more protection. You may need to educate yourself about other options. Whatever techniques you use, your commitment to personal change is a commitment to yourself that you are not the person that you were when you did the awful thing that you did.

After having a really tough experience, you become more realistic about yourself and other people. You use the information from that experience to learn more about who you are and what the world is, and then you make accommodations to your new learning. You don't assume this is never going to happen again. You use your experiences as a tool to do better for yourself.

Reconciliation

The final forgiveness/letting-go step involves reconciliation.

Many theologians, therapists, and everyday philosophers suggest that there can be no true forgiveness unless you reconcile with the person who's wronged you. Others suggest that forgiveness or letting go can as easily involve moving on, and not require a reconciliation.

Reconciliation holds out the hope that things will be back to the same way they were before the difficulties. We look forward to reconciliation with the hope that the warm feelings, closeness, and caring will be there again. We seldom get what we hope for.

Charlotte got pregnant when she was only sixteen. She begged her parents to let her marry Otto, the baby's father. They refused, saying she was too young. Instead, they sent her to a home for unwed mothers in another state, where the baby was adopted shortly after he was born. When Charlotte came back home, she again got pregnant by Otto. This time her parents allowed them to marry, even though they were still very young.

Charlotte often said not a day went by that she didn't think of her firstborn, even though they were blessed with four other children.

Finally, when her son was twenty-five years old, Charlotte found him. She and Otto asked to meet him, and he agreed. But shortly after their first meeting, he said he didn't want to see them again. Eventually he moved to another state.

Charlotte and Otto didn't get the joyous reconciliation they had hoped for. But she says she feels better having seen him and knowing he has turned into a fine young man. She has been able to let go of her pain and shame and forgive herself for her youthful indiscretion.

In many instances, people who've hurt one another badly move on in anger. They aren't willing to reconcile or even speak with one another again. Sometimes people will move on and not have an opportunity to come back together into the relationship that they had before. Other times the person who was so hurtful may have subsequently died, moved away, or become unavailable, so reconciliation is not possible. In a perfect world, it may well be that reconciliation is the goal. However, it is not always achievable.

Sometimes we have to make the hard decision that what happened was so awful, so threatening, or dangerous, that even though the other person wants a reconciliation, it isn't in our best interests to come back together.

This was Beverly's decision (chapter thirteen) when Chuck wanted to get back together. He said he missed her and the kids, but then she realized he was having her followed and her phone calls were being monitored. She decided if he could fake his own death and not contact her for years, she could no longer trust what he said, but had to trust her experience of him as the truth. She was afraid of him. She didn't want to put herself or her children in a position where he could hurt them again.

Adele had a major falling out with Brenda, her lifelong friend. The two women had been very close, but their disagreement highlighted serious values and ethics differences. Adele decided that although she could forgive her friend for the disagreement, she didn't want to continue the friendship. The differences in their values, what they wanted from life, and how they wanted to live their lives were just too divisive. She wanted another path for her life.

Adele and Brenda had been growing apart for quite some time before the disagreement. It took the falling out for Adele to realize how different they had become. She now says it is sad that she doesn't have the friendship in her life, but the price was too high. She forgave her and moved on.

Forgiving/letting go is essential if we are to move on and make a new life after challenge. We forgive our wrongdoers not for them, but for us. It allows us to let go of our past and start to forge a future that will allow joy and satisfaction into our lives.

Exercises for Chapter 14

CATALOG YOUR CHALLENGE
Getting ready to forgive, or let go, starts with telling yourself the truth about the injury you've experienced.

REGRETS
What part of your challenge includes regrets you have about what you did or didn't do?

MISTAKES
What errors in judgment, attention, or behavior were made?
   Who needs to apologize, and to whom? (Don't forget yourself!)

TRANSGRESSIONS

What moral commitments and agreements were broken? Who broke them?

How were you affected?

Who needs to be forgiven, and for what?

EVIL

Is there an element of evil involved in your situation? What will you do about it?

FOLLOW THE FIVE-STEP FORGIVENESS PROCESS

Go to your notebook one more time and start thinking through the forgiveness process. This is not easy and will probably take more than one time through before you are clear and able to take action. Be kind to yourself. Give yourself the time and the consideration you need.

1. Acknowledge the hurt and anger of the injury. Understand how significant it was.
2. Acknowledge your feelings of hatred and betrayal.
3. Reframe the situation. What's your part in what happened?
4. Consider forgiving the other. See him or her as needy and fallible, too.
5. Decide what you're going to do about the relationship. Do you think you can reconcile, or do you need to let go and move on?

CHAPTER 15

SO DON'T JUST
SIT THERE, DO IT!

Polly lives in a wonderful small town on the Sonoma-Mendocino coast of northern California. Her house is nestled under a grove of redwood trees, with a sunny meadow out her back door. While she'll get the rains of a northern California winter, she enjoys months of sunshine, a long growing season for her garden, and never worries about snow and ice. She makes a comfortable living working from her home, often traveling to large cities around the country, but more often working with people by phone and through the Internet.

When she sees colleagues at professional meetings, they often exclaim how lucky Polly is to be living in such a wonderful place. They wistfully say how they wish they could do what she is doing.

Polly's reply is always the same: "Luck had nothing to do with it. I was tired of the rat race of living in a big city, where snow and ice were constant winter visitors." Her work had meant a ninety-minute commute twice a day, to and from a job that was no longer challenging or fulfilling.

Polly didn't wait to get lucky. She made a lifestyle choice and then implemented plans to make her choice become a reality.

"Just do it" is a phrase made popular by Nike shoe ads, but I heard it over and over again when I was a girl. I grew up in a large family that was the combination of two families. In five short years my family changed dramatically. Both my grandparents and my mother died. Then my father remarried a widow. Between them they had seven children. Within a year, a baby brother completed the new family.

With eight kids, the house really rocked. Mom kept her cool with superhuman powers of organization and delegation. All of us had chores, and each of the big kids had to look out for a little kid. There was little opportunity to whine and moan and groan that we didn't want to do what we were supposed to do. With that many kids around, you did what you had to do. When we asked for dispensation from chores, or special consideration for cutting back on the work that we had to do, her reply was "Just do it."

Just do it. Just do it. I must have heard the phrase a million times as a teen. And I have to admit, it wasn't what I wanted to hear. I wanted to get away with slacking off. I couldn't understand why my mom was so resolute. It wasn't until many years later that I finally discovered where her strength and determination came from.

My mom's first husband was a young physician. They married just as they were finishing their professional training in the midst of World War II. Congenital health problems not only made him ineligible for military service but also made life insurance unavailable. They settled in a small town, to start a medical practice and a family. Their third child was just a few months old when her husband suddenly died.

My mom was left with three children under five and no life insurance, then she discovered a fourth child was on the way. Pictures of her taken at that time show a beautiful young woman, with deep circles under her eyes, so thin the bones in her face were etched in sharp relief. She was twenty-seven years old.

When I first saw the picture and heard her story, I was older than she was when the picture was taken. I was struck by what she must have had to do to make a life and a living to support her young family. When I asked how she kept going, she replied she just did it. She just did what needed to be done, whether she wanted to or not, whether she felt like it or not, whether it was fun or not. She just did it.

Then I knew where the words of my teen years came from. It was what had made it possible for her to get through her crisis, to take charge of a situation she couldn't control.

Just doing it, just doing what needs to be done is the final step in taking charge of situations we can't control. But it isn't a quick step.

First we need to know what our *it* is. We have to know what we want out of life. Knowing what we want is sometimes called having a purpose, the big picture. Our purpose and mission in life lets us put our wants into gear. Knowing what we want means we can start setting goals and working toward them. We can deal with the blocks and challenges that are inevitable as you start taking charge, and then evaluate what we've accomplished, what we need to change, and what next steps to take or opportunities to seize.

Taking action is usually what we mean when we talk about taking charge. But if we haven't done the internal work, if we don't take the time to make the changes in how we feel about ourselves and what we can do, if we don't build confidence in our competence and let go of the need to make the person who betrayed us pay for what he or she did, then all the action we can think of to take won't be accomplished. As Einstein said, we can't solve our problems with the same level of thinking that brought them on. We have to change our perspective about ourselves, our problems, and our options before our action plans can be successful.

Finding Your Purpose

Action planning starts with the big picture. When our lives have been out of control, when we've been challenged, is the perfect time to call a halt to what we've been doing, and start looking at what we want for ourselves. For Polly that challenge came when she faced major changes in three parts of her life. A long-term relationship ended when he found someone new. A number of her friends moved from the area. And she realized she wouldn't get promoted to her boss's position, even though she had been filling in for him for almost a year while he was out sick. She had done his job, and her own, with no more pay and little recognition, and no hope she'd permanently take his place. Polly figured there had to be a bigger message here. It was time for her to decide what, and where, she wanted the next chapter of her life to be.

When we take charge, we can decide what we want out of our

own lives. And, of course, do what it takes to get us there, even if we don't want to do the work, don't feel like it, or it isn't fun. If our purpose is compelling and a fit for our lives, it propels us into action.

We don't get what we want when we drift. When we drift, we're pulled by what makes sense in the moment, what other people want or want us to do and be. We go along because we don't have other plans, haven't thought through what we want, or don't have the confidence that we can figure it out for ourselves.

We tend to drift when we're in survival mode. In survival mode, we just get through a day. Waking up breathing counts as a successful day.

If you've been dealing with legal logistics, a financial mess, or been in survival mode, one day at a time may have been your mantra or prayer. It works in survival. But continuing with one day at a time as a life plan is only a way to exist, not a way to take charge and thrive.

One day at a time is the antithesis of being in charge, getting what you want, and living a life of joy and fulfillment. There comes the time to move beyond survival to rebuilding. There comes the time to start taking care of what we need to do and accomplish today to take care of tomorrow.

Finding our purpose, our mission, a direction for our lives, keeps us going when tough times come. Charles Garfield, who's done so much work with peak performers, claims having a purpose in life, knowing what's significant and important for us, provides the why that inspires every how.

Defining our purpose reconnects us with our values. It puts into practice what's really important. Purpose grabs our passion, what really counts. Knowing our purpose allows us to break through the lethargy that so often comes after crisis, the lack of motivation that so many of us feel, and brings new energy into our lives.

Knowing our purpose means we can plan for tomorrow by what we do today. We can take care of ourselves in the present and plan for the future. Our purpose provides a direction by which we can live our lives.

Every life has purpose and meaning. But sometimes it is elusive. It may be difficult to state the meaning or realize how it's been shaped by the choices and experiences we've had. It's tempting to want to start fresh and decide on your life purpose. But it doesn't work that way. Purpose is discovered by reflecting on your behavior, values, and choices. It's acknowledged, not invented.

Life meaning has many labels: the cornerstone, the center of influence, core values, the principled center. Whatever the label, it represents a combination of values, beliefs, and interests. It's what makes us and our lives different from any others. It brings the spark of life, of specialness, to who and what we are.

Finding the unique meaning in our lives is our own task. Others can't tell us what to do, or what the best meaning is for our lives.

There's no one right plan. But it's important to have a plan. Unless you have a plan, you don't know if you're playing football or soccer! It is possible to have a full, satisfying, and exciting life playing either game. We just need to know which one we're playing.

Finding purpose is a balancing act. Purpose is a balance between specific and general, inspiring and attainable. It both fits the world we live in and transforms our world to something new. Purpose is lived in the details of daily behavior, as well as providing structure for the overall plan of our life. Stating our purpose helps keep us focused and flexible at the same time, reflecting the changes we experience as we grow, as well as the changes other people and circumstances bring into our lives.

Defining the meaning in your life is an activity that will take some time. Don't try to hurry the process. You'll be discovering and uncovering your purpose and meaning, rather than inventing it. The best place to look for clues is in what you have already been doing and feeling.

Projects on Purpose

As you define your purpose, a list of achievements and activities that embody that purpose is almost self-evident (Figure 9). As you get excited about what is most important in your life, you will start to see what you want to do and can do. Your purpose points to many projects.

If you're like most people, there'll be far too many things to do

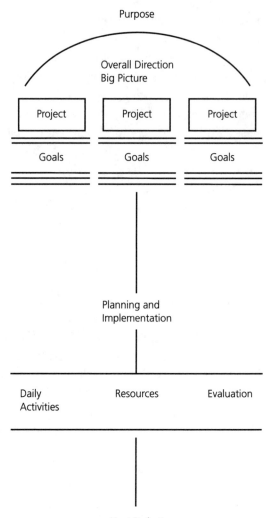

Figure 9.

with the time and resources you have. You will need to prioritize and organize your activities so you can optimize your achievements. You'll need to select one project to work on.

Ask yourself what to do first. What's the most important? What is the base for other activities? What do you need to learn how to do? What new skills do you need? What information? What network of supports to build? What other resources will be helpful?

You can't do everything at once. You need to stop and make a plan for every project. Your plan needs to address not only what to do, but who will do it and when it needs to be done.

If you are looking at a life plan, you're looking long term. A life plan is not a one-year project. It will be developmental, incorporating changes that take place as you and your loved ones grow, change, mature, and find new facets of your lives. You'll need to put off some activities and rearrange others. If you're in a family with young children, you'll spend lots of time with children's activities and responsibilities. That's what you do when you have kids. Later you'll have lots of time that isn't kid centered; they will be off making lives of their own, forgetting they have parents for a while.

Planning means choosing which projects to work on, setting goals to accomplish those projects, and then implementing your goals. Taking action on goals means dealing with challenges and feedback, resetting your course, evaluating your progress, and starting a new project.

With a clear life purpose, you'll be able to develop many projects that are linked to one another through your purpose. As you grow and change, as your life circumstances shift, and as you discover new opportunities and interests, you can add new projects to reflect your ongoing purpose.

Setting Effective Goals

Deciding which project to work on points to what goals to set. By looking at the overall project and the objectives you want to achieve, you'll see the specific goals that need to be met. Setting specific goals lets you break down the project into manageable chunks.

Effective goals set purpose into action. They transform your wishes into results, while bridging planning and results.

Being effective with goal setting means knowing what goals to set, as well as how to set them. No matter how well the goal is crafted, if it's the wrong goal, it's a waste of time.

Determining how long long-term and short-term goals should be depends on the project and what else is going on in your life. Long-term goals can cover three to five years up to fifteen or twenty years. Long-term goals need to serve a purpose exciting enough to sustain activity, interest, and passion for a long time.

Short-term goals are found in smaller projects or as part of larger, longer-term projects. They need just as much care and planning to achieve the desired results as do goals that are a part of a longer project. The effectiveness of the goals doesn't depend on the size of the project, but on how well the goal is stated. Well-stated goals lead to successful implementation and desired results.

Writing Your Goal Statement

The same process is used for setting long- and short-term goals. The effectiveness of the goals doesn't depend on the size of the project, but on how well the goal is stated. Effective goals focus on results, fit with purpose, and are action oriented. Goal statements are specific, measurable, and target dates and allocate resources. They answer the five questions: **Who? Will do? What? By when? At what cost?**

Who? is one resource question. Ask yourself: Who do you now have? Who else do you need? Do the people you have, have the skills and resources they need? What name will you put on this goal statement?

Will do? is the action-verb question. This is what separates "being" and "doing" goal statements. What activity will they do? What will they accomplish? If you were a fly on the wall, what would you see people doing?

What? is the results-desired question. Be sure that it is measurable, specific, and objective. Again, this question addresses the being and doing results issue. Can you touch the results? How many? How much? Can everyone else see that the results are achieved? Is there any question on what is a result and what isn't?

By when? is both a results and a resources question. Time and resources questions address the reasonableness issue. Is this a stretch but not overwhelming for the people who will be doing the work? How much time do you have? What happens if the deadline is missed? Do you have enough people to do the job in the time allotted?

At what cost? is also a resource question. Few people have an unlimited budget, and any money allocated to one project will not be available for other opportunities. Any project is a trade-off. This question can also tell you when to cut your losses and abandon a project that is spiraling out of control without obtaining the results you want. When do you say enough? Do you have enough money to do the job? Enough equipment? Contacts? Skill? Will you lose other opportunities? What happens if you don't have the money for a full budget?

Where can you take cuts? How much can you cut and still accomplish the activity goal?

To be motivating, a goal needs to be a stretch but not impossible. If a goal is too hard, we have a tendency to give up. You know you're going to fail, so why try. If a goal is too easy, you may not even start. There's no challenge, so why bother. Anytime you wanted you could do it, so you don't bother to do it. But as Csikszentmihalyi, the University of Chicago psychologist, found in his study of flow, when you hit the balance between the challenge of the activity and the skills and abilities you bring to the challenge, goals themselves become highly motivating. You want to see if you can be successful and will work your hardest to succeed.

Scheduling for Results

It's typical to overestimate what you can accomplish in a day, and then underestimate what you can accomplish in a year. To be effective in scheduling and planning, you need to know how long a task takes. It's impossible to know precisely how long something takes if you've never done it. So start with a guesstimate. But then keep track of how long the work takes so you can plan more effectively in the future.

Organize your list of necessary projects and goals, noting which are dependent on others for their completion, which can be done at the same time, and which can be done at any time. Line them up so they flow into a sequence, noting how long each step will take.

Now, start scheduling backward from your deadline, being sure to give yourself wiggle room for unforeseen circumstances. If you know the last step will take only three days, give it another day or so. Build in reporting dates and benchmarks. Where do you need to be thirty days out from deadline to be on track? Where do you need to be sixty days out? Continue working backward, including the parallel projects and the anytime projects, until the schedule is filled in.

Now it's time to panic. You'll realize you should have started three months ago last Tuesday to finish by your deadline. Welcome to the world of too many plans, too little time. The hard question now is, what can go? At this point, most consultants advise: *You can have it cheap, you can have it right, you can have it fast. Choose two.*

For the most part, when we are talking about life planning, time is the usual choice to slip. Taking a little more time is usually of no real consequence, and the results will be better for it.

Linking Purpose to
Daily Behavior

How do you know what's the best use of your time right now? Link your daily behavior to your purpose. It helps you make choices and see the value in seemingly insignificant or trivial tasks. It keeps you on line in your willingness to do what needs to be done to get what you say you want. It is one thing to say what you want, to choose projects that will get you what you want, and set goals that will achieve those projects. But you still have to do the work. You still have to pay the price by just doing it.

Linking your purpose to your daily behaviors underlines the responsibility and the discipline you need to bring to your projects. When you have an overall objective and know you can reach it by doing what needs to be done, then doing it gets priority. You can make your choices about what you are doing consciously, knowing that every little bit helps.

For example, one of your projects in support of your purpose of an independent self-sustaining life may be getting a newer, more reliable car. Choosing not to spend eight dollars for lunch every day is obviously the right choice. By doing the math, you quickly see you're spending about two hundred dollars a month on lunch. Putting that money aside gets you to your goal of a new car that much faster.

It's the little things done consistently and persistently that make the huge difference in achieving our projects. Whatever our projects are. Even with exercise and fitness. New medical research has shown shorter periods of exercise done more often are more effective than longer periods of exercise done less frequently. Even if the longer exercise sessions add up to more overall time, they still aren't as effective.

A second technique to use in linking daily behaviors to long-term projects is to build in momentum sustainers. If you're like most people, you start out a new project great, and then lose track of it in the bustle of all your other obligations. By building in appointments with people to check in with and appointments with yourself for review, you force yourself to be accountable. You might want to set up weekly goals for yourself or make an agreement to accomplish specific tasks by your next check-in date.

Additional techniques for linking daily behavior and long-term projects include:

- Paying attention to your goals and to your everyday behavior. Remind yourself that what you are doing is building on your purpose. Put up reminder notes around your house to keep your purpose front and center.
- Figuring out how long specific tasks take so you won't skip out by telling yourself it takes too long or you don't have the energy. At one point I decided I would get more serious about housework, especially doing the dishes. I had told myself it was too big a hassle to fiddle with before I went to bed. I was embarrassed to discover cleaning up the dishes actually took five to seven minutes.
- Using lost, or fiddle, time to punch a hole in a bigger project. I no longer leave dishes in the living room, at my desk, or next to the bed. I take them into the kitchen when I am going, rather than waiting to make it a task to be done.
- Building in an artificial deadline and put yourself on a schedule. Play a game with yourself, and even reward yourself, for being a good kid when you've done one of those necessary but not fun little jobs.
- Giving yourself credit for what you have done and the hassle and work it was to accomplish it. I live in a wonderful town. When I tell people where I live, their reaction is usually "You're so lucky to get to live there." Like Polly, I tell them luck had nothing to do with it. It is part of a project I have in giving myself the lifestyle I want.

Relapses and Collapses

When I was a therapist, I'd work hard to help people finish their therapy and live their lives without need for constant therapy visits. Inevitably, as the time came for termination, most of my clients would fuss and fume. What would they do if things got bad again? I tried to assure them that they now had the tools to take charge and do much better than they had done in the past. It wasn't enough. I finally started encouraging them to come in for what I called a thirty-thousand-mile checkup. I figured if it was good enough for our cars, it was good enough for us.

The reality is, there is no change program without relapses, slips, and a need for midcourse corrections and checkups. We can't know everything we need to know going in. And we can't accurately predict what will happen.

Building in checkups lets us catch our problems before they get out of hand. I'd tell my clients to come in for a checkup if they had questions about whether things were still going okay, rather than waiting until things were a real mess.

When you're working by yourself, do an audit. Ask yourself if your change program is working: Is it getting you what you want? Are you on track? What's doing great? What do you need to bring back in line? What's missing?

Ask yourself what help you might need. And who can help? What else do you need to do and can you do? What do you know or can you do that you're not using for yourself right now? What would it take to add that to your project efforts?

When I am working a project intensely, I build in checkup points both monthly and weekly. I need to know how what I am doing is working or not working, and what needs to be added.

I also need to know when I am finishing a project. And then make a clear decision if I'll start the next one right away or take some time off to smell the roses.

Taking the time to enjoy what you have designed for yourself is an important part of building your life around purpose. It's no good to say what you believe in for yourself and then not do it. It's no good to design a life for yourself and be so busy building that life you have no time to enjoy it.

Getting Stuck and Unstuck

Stephen Covey, author of *First Things First*, says the way we see what's happening leads us to what we do, and what we do leads us to the results we get. Years ago in a training class, I heard another student recite:

I can reveal
   The way that I feel
   By the things I say and do.
By changing what
   I say and do,
   I can change my feelings, too.

It works both ways. It often takes longer for our minds and self-concept to catch up with our new behaviors and actions. So we experience blocks, an uncomfortable feeling that can stop us from doing what needs to be done to accomplish our goals and projects.

We overcome blocks by choosing what we do based on what we think, rather than on how we feel. Don't let your feelings decide for you.

As much as you work to feel more entitled, more empowered, to let go and move on, you won't get there until you start acting differently from the way you were. Act your way into new feelings; don't feel your way into new actions.

"It Feels Funny . . . Not Like Me"

New behaviors feel funny. They're unfamiliar. You haven't done them very often. It takes lots of repetitions for new actions to feel comfortable and no longer clumsy. Your discomfort is both physical and psychological. Physically, our bodies aren't used to moving in this new way. Psychologically, we're not used to this new way of seeing ourselves, what we can do and should do.

Habits are both mental and physical. Our habitual actions are learned by our bodies, as well as our minds. Some habits are mostly physical, like what leg we put into our pants first, or the patterns we follow as we brush our teeth or fold our arms in front of our chests. Other habits are mostly mental: how we approach problem solving, patterns of speech, decision-making strategies.

Most habits are both mental and physical. We choose or discover patterns of action that make sense to us, that get the results we want, and then strengthen those habits by repetition. And our bodies and minds get used to moving in well-known and practiced patterns each time we approach a situation.

The same way a dirt path or road we use over and over becomes worn and more defined with each use, our behavior wears patterns in our nerves and muscles, too. And like slipping into the well-worn ruts in a road, it's easy to slip into the ruts of habitual behavior.

Changing our habits means we have to pay attention to what we are doing, to watch carefully that we don't slip into the rut of least resistance. We have to keep up our resolve to do a new action, even though the old one feels more comfortable, more like us. When it comes to changing our behavior, we have to put up with the discomfort of doing something unnatural, not like us.

When it comes to choosing new thoughts or mental activities, the same resolve is needed. Our thoughts, just like our actions, can easily slip into the same old ruts. Without realizing what's happened, we can get drawn back into old thought content and process. The challenge then is to catch ourselves, to say out loud, or just in our heads, *Stop, I'm choosing to think differently now!*

"I'm Just Not Motivated"

All behavior is motivated. While we usually think of people who are energetic as motivated, and those who are more lethargic as unmotivated, both are motivated. They're just motivated to do things very differently. We can talk about not being motivated to do a specific thing, but not not motivated at all. Our lethargic friends are motivated to take it easy. Not to hurry and scurry.

You may say you aren't feeling motivated when you're feeling overwhelmed, not in charge, and out of control. It's common to feel stuck when we can't see what to do, or feel that anything we do won't get us the results we're looking for.

It's also typical to feel as though we lack motivation when we're depressed or physically or psychologically run-down. Taking care of yourself, getting help with your depression, getting more sleep, eating more healthily will help you start to feel better, and as you feel better, you'll feel more energized.

The other common block to motivation is having nothing that matters in your life. If you are living without purpose, have no goals, no projects, and no control, you'll feel unmotivated. The root word for *motivation* in Latin is the word for push, energy, shove, drive. Motivation is the energy or drive behind your behavior. If there's nothing you care about, or if you don't care about a specific project, then of course you won't be motivated to do that project. There's no meaning, no pay-off for doing it or not doing it.

Procrastination

The unfortunate truth is that it takes more energy to avoid doing something than to do it. Procrastination seems to be fueled by the magic belief that, if you just put off your task, it'll get easier—and clearer—and your ability to deal with it will get better. In the meantime, the pain of procrastination starts to set in.

Soon it is impossible to think of anything else but what we're putting off. We might start to shuffle papers around, pretending to get something done; but in the end, paper shuffling is tension relieving, not goal achieving. As the deadline comes closer, we may get something done, but typically less than or of lower quality than if we gave ourselves more time. The scenario ends with a promise, never kept, of starting earlier next time.

If you find yourself in the procrastination cycle, stop and take stock of what you are doing.

- **Acknowledge** that you are procrastinating again. Not from a position of blame and shame, but of interest and involvement. If you don't acknowledge you do it, you can't change it.
- **Assess** the situation. What is the worst thing that could happen? When have you done this before? What do you know about your procrastination pattern?
- **Act** now. Not, what do you need to think about, or how do you need to feel, but what can you do now to get started? Act yourself into thinking, don't think your way into acting.
- **Accept** that you decided to procrastinate, but that you didn't follow through with that pattern this time. Procrastinating is not like you anymore. Start to see yourself as someone who gets things done.

If procrastination continues to be an issue with you, go back and reread the chapters on entitlement and empowerment. Typically procrastination is tied up with your feelings about yourself, what people like you should do and can do, and the confidence you have in your own competence.

Emotional blocks are difficult and frustrating, because it's very hard to see how we are stepping on our own shoelaces. We can keep falling down and not realize that we are our own worst enemies. Underlying many emotional blocks is the belief that if we just could think it through and understand our behavior, we could think our way into acting. Actually the better rule is to act our way into thinking. We can change our thinking patterns and feelings about ourselves by taking action; again, whether we feel like it or not, whether we like it or not, and whether we want to or not.

For the most part, breaking through blocks means we won't feel like doing what we need to do. It will feel funny doing it, not like you, and you won't be able to do it well, much less perfectly. That is why it is called breaking through a block.

Exercises for Chapter 15

WHAT ARE YOU WAITING FOR?

Many people stop themselves from taking the first step because they aren't ready, things aren't settled, and so on and so on. You name it, they'll tell you why they can't start yet. Taking charge of your life is not starting a genetic research project. You can start wherever you are. Check yourself for the following common blocks:

- I'm waiting until . . .
- I need more . . .
- If only they . . .
- Now is not a good time because . . .
- My mother would . . .

(That last was just to see if you were paying attention . . . or was it?)

DEFINING LIFE MISSION

Starting to define your life meaning, purpose, mission can be an overwhelming task. Use the following exercise to get you started. Like any exercise, it won't give you the secret answer. It will help you to discover that the secret is: There is no secret!

Make a list of what you want to have, what you want to do, and what you want to be during your lifetime. Spend some time brainstorming all the fun, serious, outrageous, and polite things that you can think of. Then put the list away for several hours, or days, go about your daily life, and come back to the list. Review your initial list. List additional items you have remembered, just thought of, or your spouse or friends suggested.

At the top of three clean sheets of paper, write "Most important," "Less important," and "Am I kidding myself?"

Transfer each item on your original list onto one of the three sheets. Don't discount any items yet. For each of the items, even the seemingly trivial or outrageous ones, look at the meanings and the feelings it has for you. Even seemingly outrageous or trivial items can be important sources of information.

One woman put "Queen of Sheba" on her original list of things she wanted to be. It ended up on her "Am I kidding myself?" list. But when she looked at her feelings and the meaning of this wish, she realized it spoke to her desire to make things happen for her "subjects" without hassle and interference. It resonated for her long-held desire to help the homeless children in her community. She wanted to make things happen for them, without dealing with what she called bureaucratic nonsense and red tape.

Let your lists alone for several hours or several days. When you go back to your lists, look for items that are in direct conflict—choose which one is more important. Mark the items that have similar feelings or meaning to you.

Add any new ideas, or items, that you may have thought about.

Finally rewrite your list onto one piece of paper. Choose the most important item first, then the next, and on until you have ten items on your list. Put your list away again. When you come back to it this time, read over the list as if someone else had written it.

What does this list reveal about the person who wrote it?

What values are visible in this list?

What dreams does this person have?

What is the reason for living for this person?

How are you expressing these values, dreams, and purpose in your current situation?

What do you need to do about what you've learned about yourself?

A LIFETIME LIST

One of the major reasons that people don't accomplish what they want with their lives is that they haven't written it all down.

Start a list of lifetime accomplishments: What you want to do before it is all over.

This is a list of projects and/or experiences, not lifestyles and/or career directions.

For example, taking a helicopter ride, going to all fifty states, and crossing the International Date Line have all been on my list.

List as many things as you can think of and then keep the list handy so you can keep track of your progress. Many people report just putting an item on the list helps make it happen.

WRITING EFFECTIVE GOAL STATEMENTS

PART I: CHOOSE A GOAL

To practice writing goal statements, choose a project that you have been working on or one that you'd like to start.

Write the title and the nature of your project.

Writing effective goal statements assumes that you have chosen an appropriate activity, one that will get you the results that you want and will support rather than detract from the accomplishments of the project.

Describe the activity that you want to work on.

Ask yourself, how does success with this activity support my project?

How will success help me get the big results I want?

How can I insure I'll succeed?

How will not succeeding with this activity affect the project?

The purpose of this part of the exercise is to make sure you are working on the right activity and know what impact both success and failure will have on your desired results.

Practice writing a goal statement for your project. Make sure it is both an appropriate activity that will support your project, and one that is well written.

Who?

Will do?

What?

By when?

At what cost?

PART II: FIRST AID FOR GOALS

What happens if we can't think of what goals to do, or what goals are next for a project we're working on?

A software engineer friend suggested using the software-writing model for goals. Start with a big statement, and then get more and more specific with each pass.

We'll use going to the grocery store for food for dinner as an example.

Your first statement of what we need to do might be:

Get in the car and go to the store.

The second round might be:

Get my keys and my coat. Go out to the car. Get in. Drive to the store. Park the car. Buy the food. Get back in the car. Drive home. Park the car. Bring the groceries into the kitchen.

Each time we write what we need to do, we get more detailed:

Find my keys, put them in my pants pocket. Take my coat from the closet and put it on. Open the front door. Walk out of the house. Close the door.

Do I need to go on? We probably wouldn't do this with an everyday project, but with a new project, it can be really helpful in figuring out what we need to do and when.

"SO WHAT'S THE WORST THING?" EXERCISE

One way to stop ourselves when faced with tough times is to catastrophize, frighten ourselves with our worst fears.

Use the following exercise to confront those fears. Ask yourself:

What's the worst thing that could happen?

Why would it be so bad? What would happen? What would you do?

How likely is it that the worst thing that could happen will happen?

What could you do to avoid, prevent, or lessen the impact of this worst thing, even if it does happen?

CHAPTER 16

WE ALL GET SOMETHING

How often our lives change with one phone call.

I'd been working out of town and had gotten home late the night before. My husband mentioned he had an early meeting downtown, and I threatened him not to wake me up. I was going to sleep in.

I wasn't sure who was calling. It was a man, but I didn't recognize his voice because he was crying. Then I realized it was my husband. He was trying to say he was in jail. He had been arrested. For child molesting.

I couldn't believe it. Not him. It just didn't make sense. He was a child psychologist, was just finishing a term as the president of the county psychological association. We shared a therapy practice, and he also worked as the clinical director of a residential program for emotionally disturbed teenage boys. He was on the board of directors for the local YMCA, sang in the church choir, and was on the board for Big Brothers.

I didn't even ask him if he was guilty. I knew he wasn't.

Later that afternoon, our attorney told us we would be in for a hundred days of hell. As it turned out, those hundred days stretched into a thousand before all the suits and legalities were finished.

Even though he was the one who had been arrested, my life was never again going to be the same. It was the first time I was aware of getting caught up in someone else's crisis. I didn't call it Imposed

Change then, but I started to see how situations we couldn't predict, didn't cause, didn't want, and couldn't avoid could take over a life.

I had no choice. I had to take charge of a situation I couldn't control.

There was no question what was in control. I wasn't, nor was my husband. Our lives were being controlled by the legal system, the decisions that were being made by his employers and clients, and the children who said he had victimized them.

For a long time, I believed him. He kept assuring me he hadn't done what he had been accused of doing. Given the choice between believing someone I loved and believing strangers, like most people, I believed my loved one.

Then a neighbor told me about her son. And I knew the accusations were true. I couldn't discount the accusations as coming from "crazy kids with a vengeance." This was a child I had watched grow from toddler to teen. This was a family who had lived next to us for years. This was too clear not to be true.

Nonetheless, my husband continued to deny he had done anything wrong. He was never formally charged with any crimes; the grand jury had found insufficient evidence to indict. Other than that one day, he never spent time in jail.

But I knew he wasn't telling the truth. More and more victims came forward. I had my own child to protect. I made the hard decision, filed for divorce, and made plans to take my child away from the only home he had known.

I wish I could say that was the end of the hassle and pain. It wasn't. I kept trying to fix things, kept trying to make sure everyone else was taken care of, that my ex-husband would see the error of his ways and accept responsibility for what he had done, so I could get on with my life.

Finally, after one more hassle with the logistics of bicoastal parenting, trying to arrange a holiday visit for my son with his father, I got it. He had been his old denying self, complaining about people still picking on him, and saying that he hadn't done anything wrong. I got it. I finally understood he would never change. He would never take responsibility for what he'd done. He seemed to be doing just fine, and I was making myself miserable over what he'd done, blaming myself, trying to figure out how to change what had already happened.

I was letting him ruin my life. He wasn't ruining his. I was letting him ruin mine. I was feeling guilty and ashamed, but it was he who had been doing wrong. He was the guilty one, not me. He had brought these changes into my life, not me.

With the revelation of what I had let him do, I finally faced the truth. He would have to deal with his actions. I was finished with him and what he had done. It was empowering to realize that although I couldn't control what had happened, I could take charge of what I was going to do about me and my life.

I sat right down and made myself a treatment plan. I decided to use myself as my own therapist. It was time for me to start taking care of myself. It was time for me to start taking charge.

Taking charge means doing what you can do, rather than waiting for the situation to change, the other person to act, or a white knight to come and rescue you. Doing what you can do means finding the options that are available, and then making choices about those options.

Taking charge when you're not in control, taking charge of Imposed Change, means telling yourself the truth about what's happened. We need to find out about what has happened to us, who else has had this trouble, how we are like them, and not like them. We need to find out what other people do in similar circumstances, what the experts say. And of course, how our particular case is different from any others.

Taking charge means assuring ourselves we aren't dysfunctional, sick, bad, or crazy just because something's happened to us. Taking charge means reassuring ourselves that we are smart enough to think clearly about what has happened, to trust ourselves, and to make decisions that will take us where we want to go.

Taking charge means valuing our lives, seeing we're entitled to live the lives we choose, rather than being coerced by well-meaning friends, family members, and loved ones to be who they think we should be. Taking charge means holding our own as others try to make the argument for us to do what they think we should do.

Taking charge means letting go, forgiving, and moving on. Not waiting for those who have hurt us to apologize, make restitution, or just admit they were the ones who hurt us. We can't wait for them to change to start to change ourselves. We can't wait for them in order to heal ourselves.

Taking charge means taking action: finding our purpose in life, setting our goals, and implementing our plans.

Taking charge means changing our minds and changing our behavior.

Taking charge means giving ourselves our own lives.

This is the gift of Imposed Change. As we successfully pass through the despair and grief, the anger and shock to rebuild our lives, we become more of who we are. We grow and become stronger with the challenges we face. We learn more about ourselves, our lives, our relationships, and our potentialities. Our lives may never be the same, but they don't have to be ruined. It is up to us.

ABOUT THE AUTHOR

PATRICIA WIKLUND, PH.D., is a nationally known psychotherapist and the author of the highly acclaimed *Sleeping with a Stranger.* In addition to hosting her own cable television show, *Let's Talk About,* for two years, Dr. Wiklund has made appearances on *20/20, Oprah, Leeza, Maury Povich*, and *Phil Donahue*, among other key shows. A consultant to national companies as well as not-for-profit organizations and government agencies, Dr. Wiklund makes her home in Sonoma, California. She can be reached on the Web at www.TakeChargeNot Control.com.